ENGLANDS

Propheticall Merline,

Foretelling to all Nations of *Europe* untill 1663. the Actions depending upon the influence of the *Conjunction* of *Saturn* and *Jupiter*, 1642/3.

The Progresse and motion of the Comet 1618. *under whose effects we in* England, *and most Regions of* Europe *now suffer.*

What kingdomes must yet partake of the remainder of the influence, viz. of War, Plague, Famine, &c.

When the English *Common-wealth may expect Peace, and the City of* London *better times*

The beginning, and end of the Watry Trygon: *An entrance of the fiery Triplicity,* 1603.

The Nativities of some English Kings, and some horary Questions inserted: performed

BY

WILLIAM LILLY, Student in *Astrologie.*

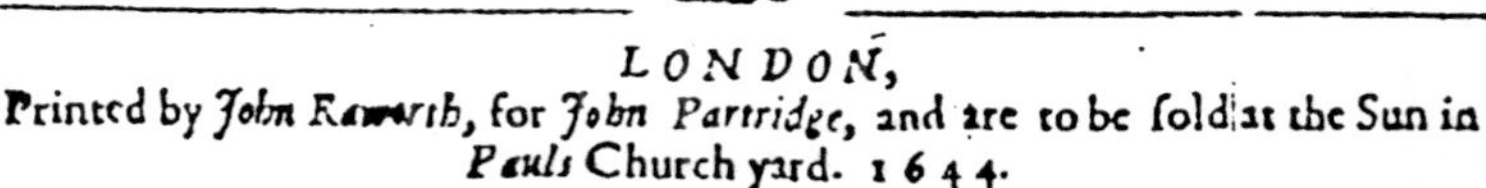

LONDON,
Printed by *John Raworth*, for *John Partridge*, and are to be sold at the Sun in *Pauls* Church yard. 1644.

Printing Statement:

Due to the very old age and scarcity of this book, many of the pages may be hard to read due to the blurring of the original text, possible missing pages, missing text and other issues beyond our control.

Because this is such an important and rare work, we believe it is best to reproduce this book regardless of its original condition.

Thank you for your understanding.

TO

The Honourable and truely Magnanimous, Sr WILLIAM WITTYPOLL *Knight*, increase of health and all Worldly Felicity.

Worthy Sir,

BE pleased to receive this my maiden Dedication (of the ensuing discourse) as a thankfull Testimony of those due respects I really owe unto you; for those manifold favours I have received from you, since, by means of the vertuous *Robert Tolmach* Esquire, I had first acquaintance with you.

Some, I know, may, and will wonder at this presumption of mine; let them so do: the integrity of my own heart howsoever, empty of all sordid or by-respects, will not suffer me to mistrust your charitable Construction, or favourable entertainment of these my loving intentions towards you: be your selfe pleased; let the censorious vulgar frown, or act their silly parts, and I care not.

The Subject matter is of an Art (not so contemptible, as either the illiterate Divine, or sturdy Mechanick, do fancy) or is it altogether unknown to your self; for your frequent conversation with the learned in forraign parts, and your own judgement, guided by your reading, do inform you, that *Astrologie* is no vaine or triviall learning, if rightly understood, and handled by an able hand. For honour of the *English* Nation, I wish the work had been more absolute and compleat; such as it is, I present it, with my Cordiall love to your generous self, and hope in aftertimes it shall be no dishonour, that you were the loving Patron, and very friend,

Sir, Of your much Advanced Servant,

WILLIAM LILLY.

TO THE IMPARTIALL AND UNDERSTANDING READER.

IF the times now present, and those I see approaching, make me the dolefull messenger of more misfortunes, the indifferent Reader will, I hope, excuse mee: For truth is truth, and a spade is a spade, if I might freely so call it. No profit hath induced me to put ink in penne, or penne to paper: no private revenge: no desire of fame, by publishing a work of this nature, of it self so contrary to the stream of these times: Sixteen years I happily lived under the government of Charles *our King; I was in no particular in that space of time oppressed; I felt no pressures, either of Ship-money, Billeting of Soul-*

diers,

diers, or the like; no High-Commission had influence on me; no Star-Chamber; no Court of Honour: Like an Hermit fourteen miles from London *I lived neere* Oatlands: *But, the heavens appearing cloudy, and foretelling mee a storme was comming, I left my Countrey habitation* 1640. *and came to* London, *where now I am, and in which place I dayly hear the noyse of warre, and sound of trumpet, neither of which affright me; and yet I well know the ancient and moderne Prophecies of this City; some predicting one thing, some another. Safety is in* London; *It will bee;* Usque dum? *We want unity to make us perfectly happy. By Gods blessing, from, and in this City had I my subsistence in fortune: With this City, and its fortunes, and the most honourable Citizens thereof, will I adventure, purse, person, and what may, if any thing can be, more deare; Holding it more honour to be buried in the ashes of the Citys ruines, then to survive a Monarch after such a Catastrophe.*

But Grave, and ever gallant-minded Citizens, your fame and zeal to Religion, and the Publique good shall flourish, when nothing but the Treasons, and cowardly backslidings of your Enemies shall be recorded: Those who are your enemies, the Parliaments, Religions; God himself will memorize to all Ages, to the perpetuall infamy of those untrusty families, that undertook their Countries Protection, and have dishonourably, in a time of sad distresse, not onely deserted, but fomented, and augmented their Countries ruines, with their persons in Arms, their purses open, their Associats countenanced; and to what end? but to enslave themselves in the first place, and the whole Kingdom, after their unlamented deaths.

Can either God overlook these perfidious men? or posterity

rity be unmindfull of their generation in time to come?

Many will despise this Work for my meannesse, and want of education, being my self no Collegian of either University: Its not set forth with Eloquence, our Art denying us that lustre; but truth is eloquence, and eloquence is truth: No mortall mans envy do I care for; I have hitherto outlived envy, and beheld the confusion of mine enemies, or in a fair way for it:

The Work had been more compleat, had I not been as much, during its writing, oppressed with taxes, and weekly assessements, as ever Bellantius *was fearfull of the approach of his enemies, while he wrote against* Mirandula: *Let us bee equally pardoned. Its true, it hath cost me more hours, then at first I intended, yet I do not repent it, my knowledge was thereby the more increased. Some things I have purposely omitted; I love Monarchy, and would not easily displease my* Soveraigne: *To none living but himself, if ever, will I communicate my private* Reserves.

The generall good do I aim at, and that men foreknowing the evills to come, might more patiently abide them, and with lesse trouble of minde receive them: Our Summer and Harvest are past; our Winter is not ended; and why? there remains a kinde of men,

Omne nefas proni patrare, pudoris inanes,
Crudeles, violenti, importunique tyranni,
Mendaces, falsi, perversi, perfidiosi,
Fœdifragi, falsis verbis infanda loquentes.

but notwithstanding all their dissembling; Violenta fraude peribut. *And so let them, and all thine enemies, Oh misera-ble* England.

I could wish no man would carp at the Subject I write of:

But

But knowing its of Astrologie, exploded in vulgar conceptions, it will procure me many enemies; but why it should, I know not. If they are both Christian and Protestant, so am I: Would they reform Church and Church-Government? so would I: Do these honour their King? I do: Do they adhere to the Parliament of England *sitting at* Westminster? *My living in the Strand, and willingnesse to Conformity, subscribes my consent. Why shall the difference of Opinion, in point of Learning, put us at oddes? And let none mistake my meaning, when I write, This Planet, or that Constellation did, or doth such a thing; I mean, The influence of that Planet is such, it enclines (God permitting) to such or such acts,* &c. *Let man live meerly as a Naturall man, without sparks of Grace, the influences then predominate; but where Grace rules, the Stars obey. This I mean in mens qualities,* &c. Calvin, *I know, is enemy to Astrologie.* Melancthon, *as grave a Divine, and more learned, as most hold, was friend to, and Student in it; witnesse his version of the two last Books of* Ptolomie *out of Greek into Latine, and his many Epistles in commendation thereof.* Perkins *was so peevish and bitter, if that* Posthumus *Tract be his, not an Almanack must be framed; if made, not bought, though the price were but two pence. Let that be that good mans errour. Yet I never knew any Divine of so tender a conscience, but, if five pounds were given him to preach a Funerall-Sermon, would be so hard hearted as to refuse it: Such Baits are smilingly swallowed; and that party much extolled after his decease, that in his life-time never knew what it was to have a good word:* Tot homines, tot Sententiæ. *One* Chambers *wrote against us; but had such a Lesson returned by the learned Sir* Christopher Heydon, *in answer of his folly, that very grief killed*

killed the old worme-eaten Cannon of Windsor, nor to this day hath any adventured to answer that learned Knight : Since his time one Melton *and* Vicars *have railed but wrote nothing to purpose, one pretends every Astrologer makes a speech of an houre long to the querent, its ill time so spent, if that were true, one can returne very few answers in a day :* Henry E. *of Northhampton, of a noble family, writes against Judiciary Astrology, and Comets, the Book was yet never thought worthy of answer, the Gentleman was learned but he never made it lesse appeare then in that discourse, intending to confute that subject of which he knew very little, if any thing at all ; It were a great madnesse in me to write of Physick, or to treate of the common or civill Law in which I have no judgement : All the Antagonists I meet with, mistake the ground of Art, and father* Spurious *bastards upon us in stead of legitimate issue ; they seeme to infer, that we believe fatall necessity, or that things contingent must necessarily come to passe according to our predictions ; and they do urge the darke sentences of Oracles against us, they yoake us with Sorcerers, Negromancers, Magitians (though I hold it an honour to be Magus in that sense King* JAMES *tooke the word in Demonolagia) they call us figure flingers, Stargazers, Wisemen, and what not ? but what have we to doe with Oracles ? do we raise the dead, or require responsion from the deceased : do we invocate Spirits ? or consult with them ? doe we use more then nature ? have not we our principall Bookes publickly sold, and licensed by every Common-Wealth ? I will insert some horary questions into the end of this Booke, and a Nativity, that posterity may see how innocent wee are of the many false imputations fathered upon us. And although many have no conceipt of questions, thinking* Ptolomey *did not approve them ; admit he did not : yet if the Centiloquium be his, the question is ended, for therein many of the Aphorismes belong to questions. But if he did not, if Art since his time have found out more then he knew, shall we reject that knowledge because he spoke nothing of that? the most learned of these times maintaine the Earths motion, he the contrary, and so the noble* Tycho *: was all learning buried with* Aristotle, *or Astrology with* Ptolomy *? How great is the differenee betwixt those Phisitions that follow* Galen, *and those that adhere to* Paracelsus *? to despise the one or other were starke madnesse. In matter of question I have given satisfaction, as many well know. I*

 have

have also erred, but it was in not heedfully observing my Rules; or when the question was not radicall: I hold a Radicall question like a perfect instrument in the hands of a workeman, with which instrument if good worke be not made, he is no workeman but a botcher: yet sometimes men propound such questions, as put the poore Artist to his trumpes; amongst the rest, one propounds, if he shall enjoy such a woman for his wife, his own wife, the quesitees husband being all alive, its impossible to resolve this, for I see not how the lives of so many can be included in one question, two at least not consenting to the Quere; but, (Stultus interrogator facit sapientem deviare) We ty not men to believe we can doe this or that as Perkins unjustly taxeth us, and as many ignorant people do imagine; our manner of dealing is thus: One looseth a spoone a peece of Plate or any thing else? every man would willingly have his own, or know which way, or by whom its stollen or convayed: he commeth to us, and askes our advice, if we can helpe him unto it againe, this I confesse is the ordinary question and manner of proposall: I think no man ever warranted the goods againe; that cannot be done; only thus much we doe, we erect our figure, and give answer whether man or women did the fact, their quality and shape, domesticall or not, to what part of heaven the things are carried, the probability of being obtained againe or not. Who can be angry at this judgement? we cannot name any man or woman; but yet by our description many come to know the thief, and to have their goods, and to discover a knave or slut they little mistrusted: is any man prejudiced in this, &c. I have many times described a man or woman so exactly as might be, yet the parties durst not challenge them for any such manner of people; though they much mistrusted them, but time did after find them out, and they have miraculously bin discovered guilty; I confesse theft especially in London is a difficult question, for here is variety of men, women, and children A man is exceedingly in love, he desires to know if he shall have the party desired; I set my scheame, describe the party, tell him I conceive she is not allotted for him, and where and what kind of people, or thing impedit his suit: he leaves off, is this prejudiciall? doth he not herby prevent abundance of sorrow which would follow if he proceeded farther?

A man is sick, he inquires, if his disease be mortall, the better to dispose of his affaires, admit I say he is like to die, and name the day or neare the time; the querent upon this makes his peace with God, sets all in order; yet

lives

lives, and then I lye: this happens not once in one hundered figures; is this prejudice to the querent? as men we may erre, for I never speak positively in such a question: life and death are of God. One inquires for perferment, if he shall obtaine it, if we put him either in the way whereby he is advanced; or give contradiction not to prosecute upon radicall grounds, what impeachment to Art or to the querent is this?

A Merchant intends to set out a ship to such a Coast, or part of heaven, he comes to be advised, do we injure him if we admonish to adventure to that part of heaven which may be most advantagious for a happy return; many I am sure are undone for lack of advice, few hurt that ever I knew: only if men make our art a God, and rely on it as upon an Oracle, without having relation to the Al-seeing providence of God, it converts truth in to falshood, and causeth God to obfuscate our judgement; I ever abhorred to meddle with any that superstitiously ran a whoring after the Art, or that would believe it must inevitably come to passe because I had said that I conceive inquisition for things lost, or stray, or the like questions are ancient, as we find by Saul *and his fathers servant, and the phrase of speech they used, I find not that either* Saul *or his servant were reprehended for it. Many are as ill satisfied about nativities, as questions, the Art being reproved by many, understood by few; I will indeavour plainly to satisfy all of our manner in the judicatory part. One brings me the time of his birth, viz. the yeer, moneth, day, and houre of the day, or neere it according to estimation; and some accidents, as sicknesse, casualty, perferment, marriage, or the like, and this reduceth the estimative time to certainty: what do I now? I judge upon the generall good or ill may befall that party in a naturall course of life during his days, as also of his temperament, constitution, qualities, person, &c. Then I direct the advantagious yeeres, and discommodious either for health, losse of estate, perferment, &c, Now if I say in such a yeere of his Age, by reason that one of the five Hylegiacalls, which is the significator comes to the □ or ☍, or ☌ of a malefical Promittor and that this intimates a sicknesse proceeding from the depravation of this or that humor, & name it especially that is vitiated, and say, in time consult with the Phistion and prevent the disease, and be sure to evacuate that predominating humour principally, what hurt is in this manner of direction; wherby* (longe ante) *he is delivered of the peccant humour before it could radicate, and from a pestilent fever or a long lasting quartan*

 tan

tan Ague, so that when the significator and Promittor meete, the native is crazy two or three dayes, and no more, scarce that, whereas otherwayes his life might have bin indangered and be a long time sick: In these our now troubles and before they came in whose nativities I found ill directions, I advised to moderation in their actions according to the nature of the direction, by which meanes and other private advise, even in these times they live and enjoy as their own what others have totally lost. Its not the least part of my quiet of mind, that I have done many offices of friendship in this nature, nor know I any that repine in following my advise, some that did not, have, and will perpetually rue it. The grand question is betwixt King and Parliament, I have for the most part declined my resolution concerning any such demand: How happy had many bin, if having advised, they had obeyed the rules of Art: If I tell any one that about such a yeer he shall be in danger of drowning, having well considered his nativity; ought not this man more then formerly avoyd going to Sea, passage over dangerous waters, &c. and so by Gods blessing avoyding the occasion he perceiveth not the effects, or very little, slipping perhaps with his foote where otherwise the whole body might be indangered. What Gentleman is there living, but if he be wise and have foreknowledge that in such a yeere he shall find his tenants inclinable to take new leases, or renew lives, and that they will be more inclinable then, than at other times, and it will be more profitable, &c. who is he that will refuse this opportunity? Mens dispositions are not allwayes alike, I say, Sir, upon such a direction you will in this yeer exhaust your stock, & from or by such manner of men receive detriment, he that is judicious will avoyd suretiship that yeer, and profuse expence in his living, Cards, and Dice, &c. I have known my directions observed by some, from whom I have afterwards received thanks and acknowledgment of the verity of Art. Seasons are not all alike, the Sun shines now, it rains to morrow: ther's not a man upon the face of the earth whose temperament is alike at all times: is not the meekest man we know, angry sometimes, and inclined to passion? Let me come nearer home to the subject I was speaking of, Had it bin lawfull, and His Majesty commanded, if any Artist had long since acquainted him, that about such a yeere he should have some scuffling with his subjects and mentioned the quarter of Heaven from whence; had the prediction proved false, His Majesty received no dammage thereby, but when he had seene part of the prediction

verified,

verified, & the remainder approaching it might have moved him somwhat to consider of the events which might further ensue, if the cause were not taken away. But sith our lawes give us not that liberty, or any I know is weary of his life, that taske is yet unperformed. Augustus Cæsar loved Nigidius Figulus. So did Vespasian Seleucus the Astrologian, and had many directions from him, although derided by Cornelius Tacitus for it. These were not the worst of men or Emperours, &c. But let those things passe, some may and I know will challenge me, because I stile my booke Merlinus Anglicus, or Propheticus: its easily answered; may not any father name his own child; how many are called Alexander, Cæsar, Charles &c. and yet Kings take no exception thereat. Some will say Merline was a Prophet, time will make it appeare I am no lier. If I should acquaint the world how Merlin made his predictions: fire and figot: though for those prophecies of his that have come to my hands, I truely acknowledge them no more then Astrologically set down so that without excellent judgement therein no mystery of his can be unlocked; he appeares an excellent Naturalist, and joyns both Art and Nature in one. All I aime at, is to let the World know, I know nothing: Many of my judgements are obscure, part whereof shall not be fulfilled during this generation; a time will come, and he will appeare, that will publish more then the world yet knoweth, or shall know of me, and will thank our age for what I have done, and will hereafter (God permitting) doe; These times suffer not all truth to be unmasked, I adventure into the world amidst the most troublesome times England ever did see, or hereafter shall see; from these sad daies have I gathered experience, but no profit or wealth: Omnia mea mecum porto: Long live those honourable Oaken friends I have, and I feare not: Had I no support of private fortune, hard were my hap, if I could not sustaine my life; let the Sunne shine upon me, I care for no more, it was the desire of Diogenes: but I am content, having reduced my mind to my fortune, &c. Upon the subject I write, viz. the conjunction, I have perused no mans notes, nor assistance in judgment have I had from any; yet let me with much thankefulnesse acknowledge, that my ancient learned friend Mr. Nicholas Fiske hath freely lent me either his Manuscripts or any bookes in his Liberary treating of this subject, with much love and willingnesse, from whom since my happy acquaintance with him I have received plentifull enlargment of my judgment.

ment.

ment, and the whole Art of direction in Nativities; who were he not English would be more esteemed; nor am I more beholding to the father then the sonne Mr. Matthew Fiske, who at all times gave me the exact places of the Planets, and calculated for me the severall Scheames of the conjunction of ♃ and ♄ 1603. 164$\frac{2}{3}$. and 1663. of whom I may say without offence, that few of his yeeres (if any) in Europe can parallell his excellent gifts and endowments in all the learning of the Mathematiques, he is to his further honour as religious as learned; such are the parts he now hath in his tender yeeres; what may or might they come unto, if some Alfonsus or Rudolphus would take notice of them, &c. The matter I handle is Astrologie, and what conjunction in 164$\frac{2}{3}$. but had I not looked backe to the Comet in 1618, I had been mired and gravelled. Authors speake in generals of these conjunctions, no one Author giving any great satisfaction, or teaching to handle one in particular the more I laboured the more I perceived the key to unlock these conjunctionall influences. I could have enlarged the booke to a volume but its needlesse, such as it is, or as I durst let it be, receive; and let not the title or matter trouble thee. I intend God willing, (the Sunne and Saturne 1647 not impediting) to enlarge Dariot, and fit him with examples of all kinds, and to make some peeces of Ptolomey speake English. Onely we, of all Nations, make least use of this Art; whether the defect be in the Nation or in us, because few of us attaine to any great perfection (if any at all) in this Art, I know not. I confesse our weaknesse is great, yet let me speake experimentally what I have seen in my time. I have had much acquaintance and society with Schollers of other Nations reputed learned in Astrology in their owne Countreys, but I really affirm, that none of them were comparable either to that grave, reverend, and profoundly learned Doctor Napier, or to his surviving kinsman Sir Richard Napier Knight, excellently judicious in Astrology, Physicke, and Philosophy; or to Mr. Thomas Allen of Glocester-hall, or to Mr. Bredon a rigid Ptolomician, or to Mr. Nicholas Fiske curious in the art of directions, and exquisite in all the parts of Astrologie. Let them shew me a man hath given better proofe of his judgement in Astrologie, then my friend Mr. Booker in his Annuall prognosticks. I intend to write of the famous Eclips in 1654, and of the next conjunction of ♄ and ♃ 1663, at what time Italy will be purged, and we cured of our madnesse, without Mission to Anticyras. Lord God how many

changes

changes shal this poore Island suffer; & most part of Europe before 1666 *then remember the hand-writing in* Daniel,*chap.*5.*v.*25. Mene, mene, tekel, upharsim: numeravit, numeravit, appendit; dividuntque. *Not far from that time shall that of* Merlin, *if not long before, be fulfilled:* Currus Lunæ turbabit Zodiacum, & in fletum prorumpent Pleiades. *In the meane time,* Oh quot regnorum mutationes, oh quot lugubres & flebiles infortuniorum casus! quot timenda periculorum discrimina, perturbationes, quot immensa flagitia, oh quot turbidas & perniciosas seditiones! quot inopinata seu insperata mortis exitia, oh quot malorum & improborum exaltationes, cælorum conturbata acies, inudanter emittendo eructabunt? oh quot pauperes & egeni extollentur ditabunturque! Divites vero oppressi depauperabuntur, quot subditi dominabunt, & domini obedient, Principes principatibus exuti erunt: oh quot homines vino temulenti, luxuriosi qui se gulæ adhibebunt, quot spintriæ, mastrubatores, gulosi, semibelluæ, Carnifices, crudeles, deceptores, & sine ratione proditores latrones, viros prudentia, scientia ac sapientia ornatos deridebunt, lacerabunt, dilaniabuntque & conquassando interficient, sed tunc animis opus, sapientia firmis. *This age immediately shall see all this and more performed, if God work not a miracle. Shorten, oh God our English and Scottish sorrows, and quickly discover that people that ruine us invisibly, and would destroy Religion. Our sufferings are great, they may be more. Let England patiently endure this charge, the white harvest once past, the English shall branch into many families. Oh the black Character that the next age will stigmatize those families that unluckily deserted their Country, & whom the next generation will spue out into froth. We expect a full settlement in Religion now, things divine are not subject to the Stars, or Constellations, yet heare me & REMEMBER, Religion in its full purity will hardly flourish untill about* 1670. *I conjecture, but determine not. Should I deliver what I know, or rationally could deduce from the heavens, Kings and Princes would be angry, but amend nothing. Monarchy I extreamely love, so long as like a gentle river it keepeth within its banks, but when like an extreame flood it over-flowes our medows and pastures, it wants then repression & repercussion into its limited bounds. Nobility and Gentry I honour, yet they would storm and call me to account if I should utter* tantum quantum.

How

To the Reader:

*How many things would I more deliver, were not my tongue silenced? they were happy that left their judgment to posterity, and concealed them during their lives, they had by this meanes liberty to speake whole truths, we but by peecemeale and fragments, and yet in some danger for that. Its my comfort, some will finde my key, (*sparsim & divisim.*) *Rex *is not alwaies a King, nor* homo *a man, words have severall explications &c.*

Let my willingnesse to serve my Countrey bury my failings. I write cordially, Deo, patriæ, tibi, Anglo, Scoto & Hiberno; *we were one, though now divided by treachery of the most horrible plots of a Iesuiticall party. England and Scotland will long unite, Ireland wil in time come in, when the blood of the massacred English Protestants is restored, which it will* usque, usque, *untill the Irish name be almost extinct. Halfe this Century shall not passe till the English shall know they are both beloved and feared. We shall not be alwaies slighted, Scotland & England shall in full measure of time ruine the greatest enemies Protestantisme ever had, and set their feet upon the Lyons inheritance, where now the crawling Crab stands, but then shall the Crabs mistris creepe into----When Mars forsakes the Lyon, and enters Virgo; this I say,*

And God who dwelleth in the Heavens, shall then,
Save the remainder of the sonnes of men:
Then peace and knowledge of the truth shall flourish
The earth her plenteous fruits shall likewise cherish.
It shall not be divided as before,
Nor to the plough be subject any more.

England and Scotland in the interim hath unthankefull neighbours. Let that people know, after my daies, nay perhaps before, nay what will ye say if suddenly, An eye for an eye, a tooth for a tooth. We have formerly been thought to turn the ballance of Europe, our condition is now very low: one time and two faire gales of Wind make us sit and steere the ship, but welcome, welcome to that man that concludes our miseries and loves the English besides. Let us pray for peace.

Cauda Scorpionis procurabit fulgura, & Cancer cum Sole litigabit.
Ascendet Virgo dorsum Sagitarii & flores Virgineos obfuscabit.

The first line is fulfilled and fulfilling.

The Acts of the second draw neere, and will approach: motu violento.

London, April. 17. 1644.

William Lilly.

Merlinus Anglicus Astrologicus,

OR,

A Mathematicall Discourse of the Effects which may succeed that Conjunction of *Saturn* and *Jupiter*, which was 1643. *Feb.* 15. what Regions of *Europe* shall most suffer by it; in what nature the events shall be, and when they may determine.

Of some things considerable before judgement.

ASTROLOGERS divide the *Zodiack* into twelve Signes, so called and charactered, *Aries*, ♈ *Taurus* ♉, *Gemini* ♊, *Cancer* ♋, *Leo* ♌, *Virgo* ♍, *Libra* ♎, *Scorpio* ♏, *Sagitarius* ♐, *Capricornus* ♑, *Aquarius* ♒, *Pisces* ♓: Every Sign likewise is divided into 30. degrees.

There are also seven Planets; *Saturn* ♄, *Jupiter* ♃, *Mars* ♂ *Sol* ☉, *Venus* ♀, *Mercury* ☿, *Luna* ☽; There is also the head of the *Dragon*, and tail; the head is thus charactered ☊, the tail ☋ thus; these are no Planets, but Nodes, &c.

The Planets have their severall natures, and so have the twelve Signs.

Every Planet hath two signs allotted for his House, (the *Sunne* and *Moon* excepted, who have but one apiece.)

Saturn hath for his Houses, *Capricornus*, and *Aquarius*.
Jupiter hath *Sagittarius*, and *Pisces*.
Mars hath *Aries*, and *Scorpio*.
Sol hath *Leo*.
Venus hath *Taurus*, and *Libra*.
Mercury hath *Gemini* and *Virgo*.
Luna hath *Cancer*.

Besides this, every Planet hath exaltation in one or other of the signs: As *Saturn* is exalted in *Libra*, *Jupiter* in *Cancer*, *Mars* in *Taurus*, *Sol* in *Aries*, *Venus* in *Pisces*, *Mercury* in *Virgo*, *Luna* in *Taurus*, &c. being in any Signe where they are exalted, they are powerfull in their influence.

The Signs have also another division, As

Aries, *Leo*, *Sagittarius*, are cholerike and fiery, and so make up the fiery Triplicity.

Taurus, *Virgo*, *Capricornus*, are earthly, and so make the earthly Triplicity.

Gemini, *Libra*, *Aquarius*, are aiery, and make the aiery Trygon.

Cancer, *Scorpio*, and *Pisces*, constitute the watry Triplicity.

The fiery triplicity is governed by *Sol* and *Jupiter*.

The earthly triplicity by *Venus*, and the *Moon*.

The aiery by *Saturn*, and *Mercury*.

The watry by *Mars* alone, according to the best Authors.

Triplicity, Trygon, and Triangularity, are all of one signification, and signifie in effect thus much, *viz.* That three Signs of one nature, make a triplicity, trygon, &c. As *Aries*, *Leo*, *Sagittarius*, make the fiery triplicity, and so of the rest.

Through the twelve Signs the Planets continually move, and in their direct motion, they move out of *Aries* into *Taurus*; but when they are Retrograde, they move backward, *viz.* out of *Taurus* into *Aries*; but the *Sun* and *Moon* are ever direct, and so consequently never Retrograde.

The Planets besides have severall aspects each to other; which are either good, indifferently good, or very ill.

A Sextile aspect consisteth of 60 degrees of the *Zodiack*; As, when *Saturn* is in 15. degrees of *Aries*, and *Jupiter* in 15. degrees of *Gemini*, there is then a sextile betwixt them, or they behold each other with a sextile. This aspect is indifferent good.

A Quadrate aspect, or a quadrature containeth 90. degrees of the *Zodiack*, as if *Saturnus* be in 15. degrees of *Aries*, and *Jupiter* in 15. degrees of *Cancer*; here is a quadrate aspect betwixt them, or they behold each other with a quadrate, or square aspect, for all is one; And this is ill, but not very ill.

A Trine aspect is, when there is 120. degrees difference, or distance betwixt two Planets, *viz.* If *Saturn* be in 15. of *Aries*, and *Jupiter* in 15. of *Leo*, there is a trine aspect betwixt them; and this is a very good and promising.

Opposi-

Opposition is, when Planets are distant 180. degrees from each other, *viz.* *Saturn* in 15. degrees of *Aries*, and *Jupiter* in 15. degrees of *Libra*, they are in perfect opposition to each other; and this opposition is an aspect of hate and continuall enmity.

Conjunction is, when two Planets are in one and the self-same Sign, degree, and minute, as now *Saturn* and *Jupiter* are in 25. & 26. minutes of *Pisces*: The characters of these aspects are Sextile ✶, Quadrate □, Trine △, Opposition ☍, Conjunction ☌. There are also many other aspects of the Planets, which are mentioned in *Keplers* Introduction to his *Ephemerides*: But in regard I have hitherto found no great matter in them, I forbear to speak of them: Nor is it my purpose to make an Accidence, but to explicate some words of Art.

A further Introduction to the Work, and of the nine Conjunctions preceding in the watry Triplicity.

MY onely intention was to have treated of the present Conjunction, but seeing I have opportunity offered mee, and that it will be very pleasant to the Reader, to consider of times preceding this Age; I have adventured to begin my labour something further of, and am contented in an Historicall manner, to set down all those nine Conjunctions which fore-went this I now am to write of. The Reader is to understand, that the Conjunction I write of, is of *Saturn* and *Jupiter*, and of their first meeting the seventh time in the watry Triplicity.

About the year of the World, 519. these two Planets had their first conjunction in *Cancer*, the first sign of the watry triplicity; and this was the first conjunction they ever had in the watry Trygon. 1.

In *Anno Mundi* 1333. they returned again into the same Trygon, and made their first convention in *Pisces*, the last sign of the same triangularity, and this was their second return. 2.

In *Anno* 2144. these heavenly bodies came to a conjunction in *Scorpio*, the second sign of the watry Trygon. 3.

In *Anno* 2492. by Cœlestiall ordinance, they again entred the watry Trygon, their first meeting being in *Scorpio*, the second sign of this Triplicity. 4.

Anno mundi 3756. *Saturn* and *Jupiter* the fifth time began their meetings, in the Aquaticall Trygon, and sign of *Cancer*. 5.

About the year after Christ 590. the sixth time *Saturn* and *Jupiter* 6.

Jupiter made their revolution, and began again to make their conjunction in *Cancer*, the first sign of this Trygon.

If we may beleeve *John Ganivetus*, otherwise called *Amicus medicorum*; he tells us, That *Saturn* and *Jupiter* made their seventh return into the watry Triplicity, about the year of our Lord God, 1425. the thirtieth day of *August*, 17. hours and 45. minuts past noon, the position of the heavens fitted for the Elevation of the Meridian of *London*, being as followeth:

Beginning of the watry Trygon, 1425. or, the Sabbaticall return of the two superiour Planets into the watry Trygon.

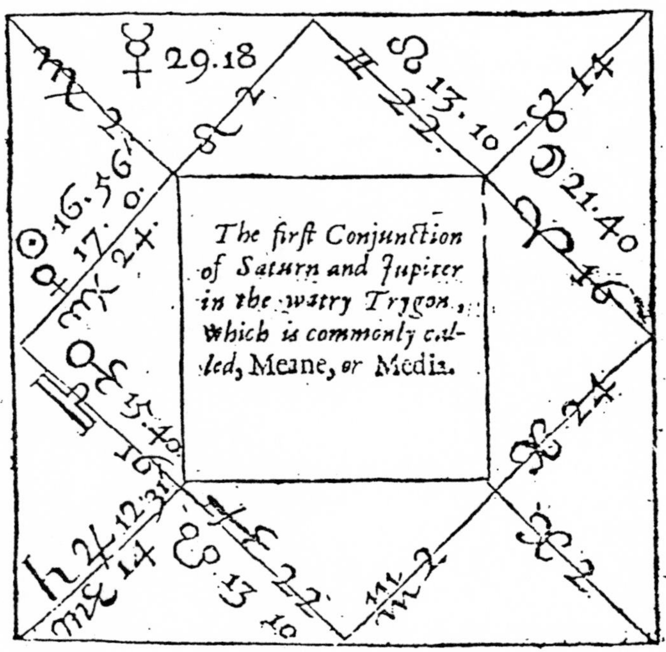

The judgement of *Ganivetus*, fol. 141. different 2ª. was thus; *Innuitur igitur propter elevationem Saturni super Jovem, quod potestas Ecclesiastica in multis partibus opprimetur, a temporali potestate, maxime in substantiis Ecclesiasticis, & effectus illius conjunctionis non videtur per integram evacuari ante quinquaginta annos, quia fuit mutatio de triplicitate ad triplicitatem, & longo tempore fraudes, & bella debent habere locum*: That is, Because *Saturne* is

elevated

elevated above *Jupiter*, Ecclesiasticall jurisdiction in many places shall be oppressed by the Temporall powers, chiefly in Church-livings or dignities: It seems, the effects shall not fully determine in fifty years, because it is the mutation of one triplicity into another, and deceit and warres are to be permanent a long time.

He speaketh also something more of the effects of the same conjunction *fol.* 213. *differentia* 3ª. *Quia conjunctio fuit in signo aquatico, judicandæ sunt pluviæ multæ, quas consequitur corporum humanorum humectatio excessiva, quæ est causa putrefactionum humorum, quam consequitur febris, & ratione excessus nimii, consequitur perniciosior febrium species, quæ est pestilentialis, &c.* Because the conjunction was in an aquaticall signe, we are to judge much rain to ensue; after which followeth the humectation of humane bodies in excesse, which is the cause of depravation of humours, upon which ensue feavers; and by reason of too much excesse, there ariseth a more pernitious kinde of feavers, and more pestilentiall: Thus far he.

The Signe wherein they now began their return was *Scorpio*, a sign of the watry Triplicity, the house of *Mars*, a very treacherous and false sign, fixed and malitious: *Conjunctiones in signis aqueis quia est trigonus Martis, significant multa bella & inventiones operum mechanicorum propter Martem, & hæreses graves & magnas, dogma Mahumeti & aliorum lex & religio sub eo trigono initium habuit:* Conjunctions in aquaticall signs, which is the triplicity of *Mars*, denoteth many wars; and strange inventions of Mechanicall instruments, as also grievous and very great heresies: the opinion of *Mahomet*, and the Law and Religion of other heretiques began under this Trygon. They that are conversant in Histories, may do well to see, if these predictions did not jump right with the times succeeding this conjunction.

This Conjunction found us in *England* engaged in a war with *France*, and much division and faction amongst our Nobility, under an innocent King, *Henry* the sixth, being then about five or six years of age, neither capable to give or take counsell. Of the affairs of other Nations let their own *Annals* report. *France* was no lesse inraged then *England*; *Spain* had much division about succession; and after some stirs, *John*, sonne of *Ferdinand* of *Arragon* succeedeth in right of *Blanch* his wife. The year preceding this Conjunction, *Constantinople* was besieged by *Amurath* the second, but not taken; And also the valiant *Zisca* died of the plague, a

stout

ſtout defender of the *Bohemians* for their Religion. 1431. the Councell of *Baſill* began, and *Henry* the ſixth was crowned at *Paris*; and in the year 1444. Printing was invented at *Straſburg*, by *John Guttenburg*.

But I am to examine, Whether any ſuch actions might be predicted by Aſtrologie.

Wee are to conſider the Conjunction was in *Scorpio*, and *Mars* the diſpoſer of it in *Libra* his detriment; doth not *Mars* amongſt the Planets, govern *Aries*, the aſcendant of *England* and *France*? and did not theſe two Nations, for many years, continue in bloudy wars, &c?

The Religious are ſignified by *Jupiter*, very unfortunate in the figure, and alſo by *Venus*, Lady of the ninth Houſe, which together with the third ſignifieth Religion, is not ſhe combuſt, and in the twelfth Houſe, as alſo in her fall? This being the firſt conjunction in the triplicity, hath principall and double ſignification of the moſt generall actions that ſhall happen in Chriſtendom, during the continuance of their meetings, either in *Cancer, Scorpio*, or *Piſces*.

As the Conjunction is in the third Houſe (which judgeth of kindred) it portended much ſlaughter, bloudſhed, and perfideouſneſſe, ſhould be committed by men of one conſanguinity and blood: And was not this exactly verified, in the Uncles and Kindred of *Henry* the ſixth, who never left perſecuting each other, untill a Kinſman, *viz.* the Duke of *York*, father to *Edward* the fourth, had almoſt thruſt *Henry* the ſixth out of his Throne, which yet he did not, but left it to his ſonne, who perfected that work, and cut off whole families of the Royall Houſe, to all which hee was more or leſſe allied.

The tenth Houſe repreſenteth Kings; Is not *Mercury* Lord thereof in the tearms of the infortunes; But taking the *Sun*, who generally is the Significator of Kings and Princes, is he not in the twelfth Houſe of the figure, and oppreſſed by the ſextill of *Saturnus*, in ſigns of long aſcentions; though I could not have ſaid, *Henry* our then King, ſhould have been depoſed by any Aſtrologicall judgement, yet I could have foretold him, By that poſiture of heaven, that both *England* ſhould ſmart, and the King of *England* be in great perill, by his kindred and ſubjects: and that the Conjunction did portend infinite affliction unto him, &c. I could infinitly inlarge this point, but our own Hiſtories ſpeak ſo feelingly of thoſe

times,

times, I forbear further discourse, and come to the next *conjunction* succeeding this, as I have it in a *manuscript* wrote by *John Escuidus Anglus*, of *Merton* Colledge in *Oxford*.

The second Conjunction of Saturn *and* Jupiter, *or, The first little Conjunction in* 12. Cancer. 21. *July* 1444. *In the watry Triplicity.*

In this year it was that *Julian* that unlucky Cardinall, perswaded and also effected the breach of league with the *Turks*, whereupon followed the battell at *Varna*, in which *Ladislaus* was slain, the Christian Army defeated, to the great prejudice of all Christendom: also *Henry* the sixth married unfortunately with *Margaret* a *French* Lady; immediately after, our *English* Nobility began to be divided into faction, and so continued their malice, that by their own folly they brought upon them a Civill war, which scarce ended untill most of the ancient Gentry were either destroyed, or strangly impoverished, & their poor King captived. About the time of this Conjunction, the *Venetians* by an inundation lost as many goods as were valued to be worth a Million of gold. We say *Cancer* is ascendant of *Venice*.

Let any indifferent reader peruse those histories, that do treat of the affaires of *Europe* from the year of our Lord God, 1444. to the year 1464.

Did not the *English* lose in *France*, what had been fortunately conquered by *Henry* the fifth.

Mahomet took the most noble City of *Constantinople*, whose ascendant is *Cancer*, the sign of the Conjunction.

Scotland hath *Cancer* its ascendant, nor was it, during these times, lesse ingaged in domestique broyles than *England*.

Nor can *France* rejoyce in any felicity she enjoyed, the most parts whereof were afflicted with the sword, &c.

A Conjunction of Saturn *and* Jupiter, *or, The second little Conjunction in the watry Triplicity.* 8 *April.* 1464. *in grad.* 6. Pisces.

This Conjunction in *England* beginneth with the imprisonment of *Henry* the sixth, and the Revolt of the valiant Earl of

Warwick from *Edward* the fourth, as daring as any English King.

During some yeares after this *conjunction*, here was nothing but quarrelling in *England*; the truth is, we enjoyed no great happinesse under this King *Edward* the fourth: as he entred with blood, so did he continue, and when he dyed, nothing lamented was he of his people, who love no tyrannicall government.

This King his posterity were requited with as much curtesie, as himself bestowed on the house of *Lancaster*.

I onely observe, that the meeting of the two superiours in the watry Triplicity, hath been obvious and disasterous to the Kings of *England*, their Nobility, and Commonalty. And the reason thereof I conceive to be, because most, or all of these Princes had Nativities discordant from that Triplicity under which the *Norman* Monarchy began, which was the earthly; and therefore there needed more circumspection in the mannaging of their affaires; and indeed as some have judged, our Kings were *Bellipotentes*, but not *Sapientipotentes*.

If the transit of *Saturnus* without the assistance or strength of other malignant Promittors doth afflict any Hylegiacall place or places, he aspecteth either with Quadrature or Opposition in the Genitures of private persons. Why shall he not then afford matter of trouble to the Kings of *England*, as often as he is in Conjunction with *Jupiter* in that sign, which is opposite to the ascendant of their Monarchy, *viz. Pisces*? Let any Chronologer see the successe we have, when a *conjunction* is in *Pisces*.

The third little Conjunction of Saturn *and* Jupiter, *in* 24. Scorpio. 1484. 25. *Novemb.*

One year before this *conjunction*, *Martin Luther* was born, whose Nativity I have inserted, that posterity may see how it concurreth with this *conjunction* in regard of the great mutation which ensued in Religion by his meanes.

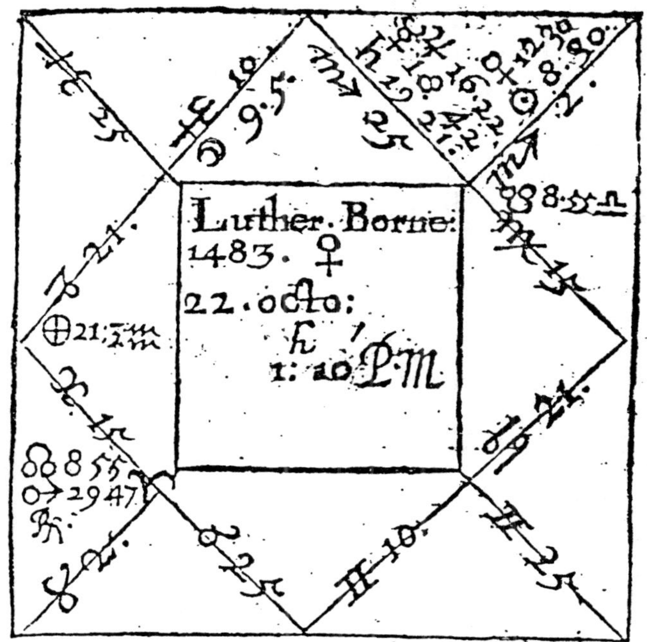

You see the place of the *Conjunction* is *Luthers Medium Cœli*: here are five planets in his ninth house; the *Conjunction* of so many Planets in the house of Religion, incited him to be more stirring and active, and to do wonders therein, being the instrumentall means by Gods permission of that Reformation which hath since succeeded: nor do I believe *Gauricus*, that sends his soul to hell after his death.

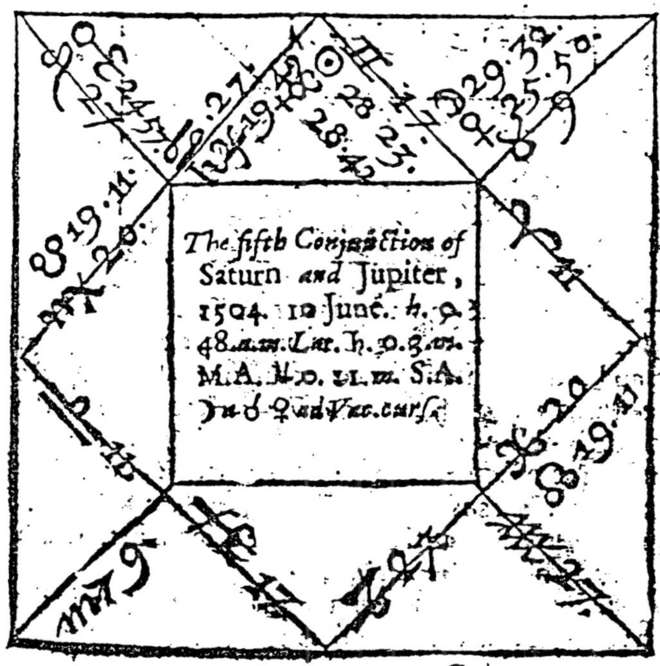

The fourth little Conjunction of Saturn *and* Jupiter.

This

This very year the *Moors* of *Granada* were inforced to become Christians; and *Henry* the seventh the most politique and covetous of all the *English* Kings, employed *Empson* and *Dudley* about penall Statutes, which begot great affliction to the *English* Nation, who love freedome and to be Masters of their own goods: but he not long after left all to *Henry* the 8. who knew how to spend more money than his Father could lay up: whose Nativity, *Cardanus* writes, is thus.

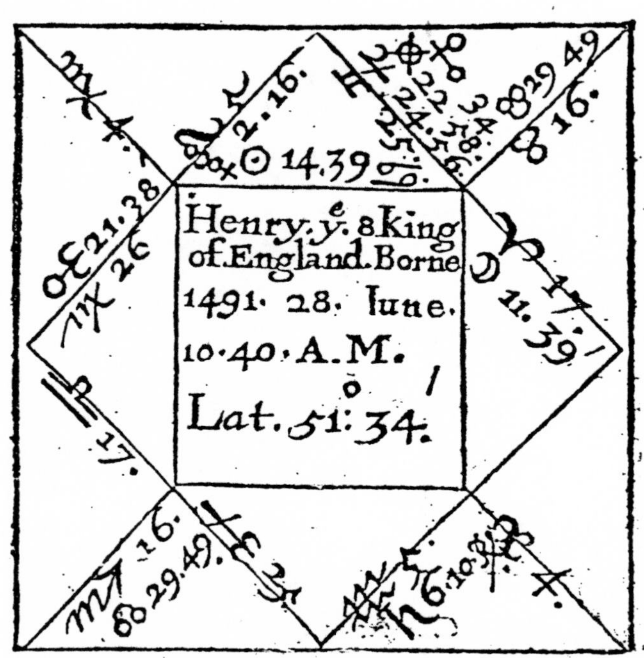

A judicious eye may see the Sympathy that this Princes Nativity hath with the posture of the preceding Conjunction, a consideration very remarkable, and much assistant for better discovery of the effects which shall succeed after any of these *Conjunctions*. Here is almost the same degree ascending both in the Nativity of the King and *Conjunction*; a good sign that the effects should not harm that Prince. The Conjunction of the superiours is in the 10th house of heaven, the Luminary of the time, *viz.* the Sun at the birth of the King, is in the tenth house and neer the degree of the *Conjunction*,

The place of *Jupiter* in the birth is neer the place of the Sun in the *Conjunction*, his cruelty (for he was cruell) is represented by the position

sition of *Mars* so neer the degree ascending: and his dis-affection to his wives, appeareth to me so be signified by the unluckie quadrature of *Jupiter*, lord of the seventh, and of *Mars*; as also by the squar of *Luna* to the *Sun* in Cardinall signes and Angles of heaven. For the number of his wives; the *Moon* her application to the *Sun*, to *Jupiter* and her being in *Sextile* to *Saturn*, and in *Trine* to *Mercury*, and in *Quadrate* to *Venus*; might induce an Astrologer to judge he should have many wives, and wenches, but not from hence define the certaine number.

The *English* had never any Prince of that largenesse of heart, nor any that did so great matters, if we consider the strength of an Ecclesiasticall party he had to encounter with, whom notwithstanding he foiled at their own weapon.

None was more valiant than he, or more vicious; No affront during his raign was offered to the *English* Nation, which he did not retaliate in one kind or other; but he is dead, and his actions give cause of wonder, if they be rightly considered; if he was subject to imperfections, he was a man; yet we have cause to account him a brave man, that durst in those times oppose a proud insulting Clergie. In some measure we must acknowledge him to be the first that permitted the Gospell to be preached, though not in its purity, yet after a more pure manner then formerly: he was blessed with a on and a daughter, who after him established the true Religion as to this present 1643 it continueth, and long may it continue without any addition in ceremony or doctrine.

But I return to the *Conjunction* in 1504. in the Scheam of whose true Position, you find four plannets either in house or exaltation all in good houses, the *Sun*, *Mercury*, *Saturn*, and *Jupiter* in the Royall house of heaven, and *Venus* and the *Moon* both in the ninth house (*viz.* of Religion) and where they are essentially strong; an evident signe matters more than ordinary were ensuing. And you have also a Comet shewed it self this year 1504. It is not recorded in what sign or part of heaven it appeared; but the effects of that no doubt did co-operate with the *Conjunction*; we finde during these 20. years, *viz.* from 1504. to 1524. That *Martin Luther* first published his Propositions against indulgences, *viz.* 1517. the first step to his greater quarrell with the Pope: *Zuinglius* Preached the Gospell at *Zurick*; *Eccius* and *Cajetan* dispute; the Pope Excommunicateth *Luther*, his Books are burned; *Luther* burneth the Popes Bull at *Wittenburg*. I finde that all *Conjunctions* of *Saturn* and *Jupiter* in *Cancer* are

 ominous

ominous to *Rome*, this *Conjunction* being the fift of this Triplicity, it seemes matter now grew fit, to put in Action what was intended by the first according as *Ganivetus* had predicted. God now stirring up active men to performe his Decrees.

The sixth little Conjunction of Saturn *and* Jupiter.

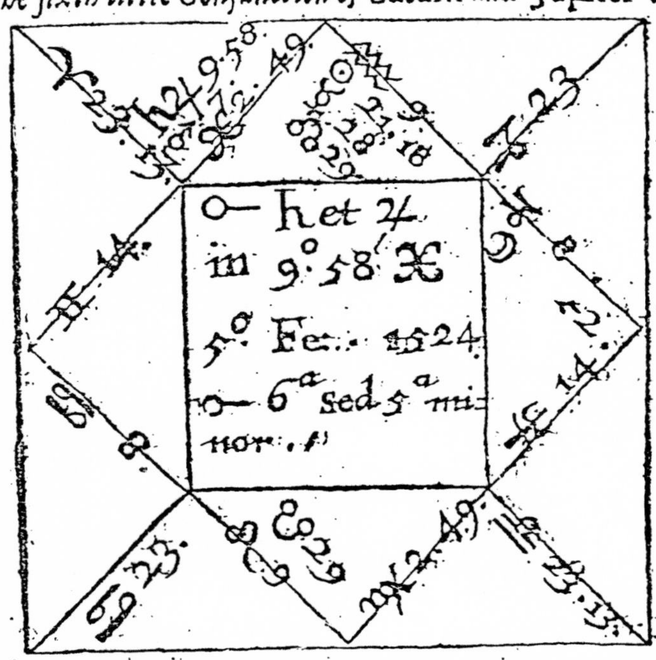

Now let us consider if *Saturn* being Lord of the ninth, and in the sign of *Pisces*, if he do not stir up some broyles for Religion, and some stormes to the *English* Kings.

The very year of this *Conjunction*, there was a Reformation of the Clergie at *Ratisbone*, and the same year of Religion at *Wittenberg*. The King of *France* is taken prisoner by the Imperials at the siege of *Pavy*, and the next year enlarged by meanes of our *Henry* King of *England*.

1525. The Duke of *Laneburg* and *Governour* of *Sweden*, become *Lutherans*.

1526. The *Landgrave* of *Hessen* goeth about to reform his Churches, and the meeting at *Spire* for Reformation.

1527. The heresie of the Anabaptists beginneth to spread it selfe, and *Luther* and *Zuinglius*, as also *Oecolampadius* contend each against other about the Sacrament of the Lords Supper.

This

This year was the sweating sicknesse in London: and the Duke of *Burbon* and Imperials besiege and take *Rome*, and sack it to purpose: and now begins the dislike of *Henry* the 8. to his Queen *Katherine* a most vertuous Lady.

1528. At *Bern* the Masse was abolished: and Images and Altars cast down, so were they at *Basil*.

1529. The name of Protestants began upon the protesting of the *Elector* and *Lantgrave* against a Popish Edict. In that year *Saturn* by Transit passed through the signe of *Taurus*, and *Jupiter* of *Leo* both fixed signes, Popery will never prevaile totally against it.

Forraigne Universities pronounce the marriage of *Henry* the eight unlawfull. *Wolsey* the *English* Cardinall groweth in disgrace, the first leading Case to the downfall of Popery in *England*; which the year 1530. followed to some purpose; the Clergie in *England* being condemned in a *Præmunire*, and pay a round sum, *viz.* one hundred thousand pounds to the King.

The same year the *Augustan* confession was exhibited to the Emperour, being composed by *Melancton*; and the *Smalcaldian* league betwixt divers Princes of *Germany* for defence of the Protestant Religion.

1532. King *Henry* was divorced from his Queen, and married the Lady *Anne Bullen*, by whom in the succeeding year he had *Elizabeth* afterwards Queen of *England*, a Mother to the *English* Nation.

Anno 1534. The Popes power was abrogated in *England*, but I think it not fit to accept of that year for the first year of allowing Protestanisme in *England*; perhaps it was done for respective ends in the Prince, &c.

Anno 1535. *Geneva* expelleth the Bishop, and alter Religion. In the same year the most active order of the Jesuits began, instituted by *Ignatius Loiola*, confirmed after in the year 1540. Whether the Comet that appeared in 1533. *Ensiformis*, did point out that learned people I know not; but immediately after, there was in all parts of Christendome much alteration in Religion, and many novell Sects amongst the learned. And as if the heavens did take notice of the times, which immediately succeeded, and of the plentifull matter there would be to work on, there appeared from the year 1530. to 1541. no lesse than eight Comets or blazing stars, they came after the *Conjunction* in *Piscibus*, and did co-operate in the effects which were designed by that *Conjunction*, &c.

1538. The Bible was commanded to be read in the *English* tongue and this year began the *Antinomian* Sect, which denied the Law to be taught; and do they not now 1642, 1643. again under a *Conjunction* of *Saturn and Jupiter* in the signe of *Pisces*, trouble the *English* Synod?

I conceive *Protestanisme* had now its first erection and allowance in *England*; for the permittance of the *English* Bible, certainly gave us the first light and fruits of the Gospel.

1539. Reformation was made in *Misnia* and *Brandenburge*, 1541. The act for supremacy was made, and here in this year it was that the six bloody Articles were made; so that in effect we professed our selves Protestants, and yet executed men for holding Protestant tenents: Its hardly to be discerned what Religion it was that was most in force some years. But as I said formerly, there hath not been any *Conjunction* of the two superiours in the signe of *Pisces*, but it hath in one kind or other been obnoxious to the *English* Kings, Nobility and Commonalty of *England*.

The years 1540. 1541, and 1542. were full of action not onely in *England*, but in all or most parts of *Europe*: the Scottish Nation suffered much by the distraction of the Nobility. The *Rochellers* took up Armes, because a Garrison was there placed. The *English* enter *France* and *Scotland*, and burn part of *Edenbrough*: such like Actions as these were done during the twenty years intervall of the last, and this *Conjunction* which now succeedeth.

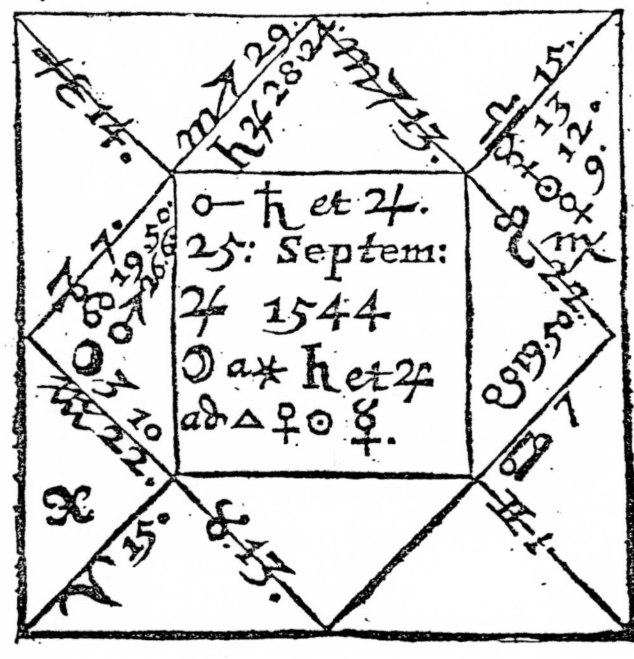

The seventh Conjunction of Saturn *and* Jupiter, *but the sixth lesser.*

The

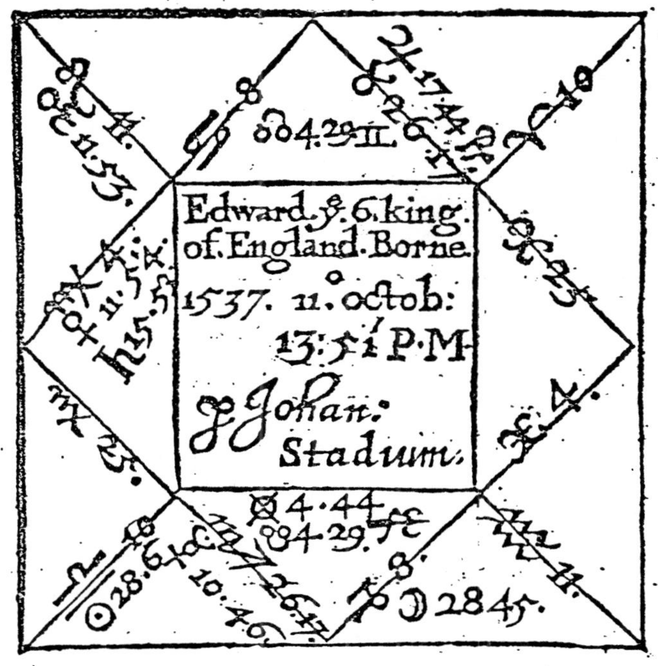

The *Pleiades* culminating and *Saturn* in the Aſcendent, 4 *Planets* in their fals or detriments, might give cauſe to ſuſpect this King ſhould neither live long, or have any quietneſſe in his Raigne: the *Conjunction* preceding is in oppoſition to his tenth houſe: and *Mars* in the *Conjunction*, is in the place of the *Moon* at birth: I conceive pure *Melancholly* killed him, and that he was not poiſoned: is not *Saturn* Lord of the ſixth in the Aſcendent; cannot Kings dye upon bad directions without poiſon? *Aſcendens ad* Saturn & Luna *ad* ... may be *Abſciſſor*, to any living, ſo placed as here.

The *Conjunction* was in the eleventh houſe of heaven, but in the moſt viperous ſigne, a *manifeſto* to the world, that what miſchief was then in Action, would not eaſily be concluded; and that the Clergie both with ſwords, words, treachery, and ſubtile deviſes would endeavour the maintaining of their Rights and the Tenents they held in Religion, though all the world periſhed thereby.

The *Dragons taile* in *Cancer*, might have warned *Scotland* of troubles enſuing, and alſo *Rome* her ſelf that miſchiefe was approaching.

Anno 1545. The Councell of *Trent* began, the laſt generall Councell that ever was, or perhaps that ever ſhall be; and yet it cannot properly be called generall, becauſe many Chriſtian Princes ſent not any *Suffragans* thither, yet whoſoever ſhall read the Acts of it and conſider its continuance, ſhall finde matter to wonder. *Henry* the 8. dyeth 1546. to whom ſucceeded his ſon *Edward*, of whom *Cardane* an *Italian* hath given an excellent Character. 1547. Religion was altered in *England*. The *Neapolitans* make inſurrection in contradiction of the accurſed Inquiſition. The *Scots* are overthrown at *Muſcleborough*. Nothing but diſputation about Religion, and con-

troverſie

troversie for Religion all this Kings Raigne all over *Europe*, the Councell of *Trent* still sitting. 1553. *Edward* dyeth and *Mary* comes with a little trouble to Raigne.

She dyed when the *Sun* came to the body of *Mars* the 8. of *Decemb.* 1554. the *Sun* was almost totally Eclipsed in 27. *Gemini*, the *Sun* being in 27. *Sagittary* the place of *Saturn* at her birth, *Saturn* then by transit being in *Pisces*, also 1555. the *Moon* was totally darkned in light being in 23. of *Gemini*, *Saturn* by Transit being in *Aries*, which might bring sorrow enough to this Queen, and affliction to the City of *London* and Kingdome of *England*: *Gemini* being the Ascendent of *London*, and *Aries* of *England*: an Ecclipse in either of those, but especiall in *Gemini* is fatall to *England*.

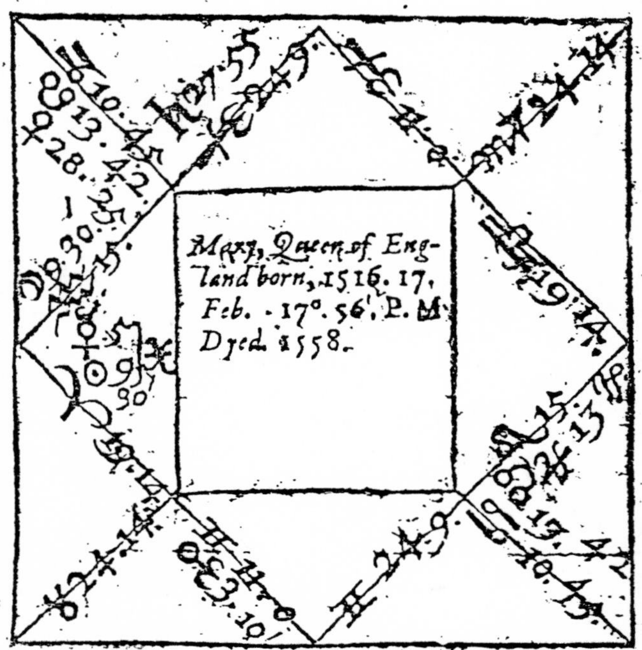

The *Moon* in *Opposition* to *Jupiter*, who is Lord of the tenth, give this Queen no honour or fame, the *Moon* being also diminishing in light, addeth to the former infelicity. The place of the *Sun* in her *Radix*, is the place both in signe and degree of the *Conjunction* of *Saturn* and *Jupiter* subsequent to her birth: *Ex inde Regnum acquisivit.* The Nativity doth not declare her to be of so monstrous a condition as some have branded her with: she did permit the *Roman* Clergie to burn many of her *English* Subjects, for which to this very day the Nation doth not relish that name, *viz.* *Mary*; Naturally they love that Prince most, that is sparing of their bloods and purses: and what King soever followes the advise, *Henry* the fourth gave to his son *Henry*, shall never loose their loves, but he that suffers them to be tyrannized over by insulting Officers, or permits Monopolies, he shall finde it a hard task to regaine their affections.

The

The time this Queen raigned was short, to the great content of the *English*, although the *Spaniard* is a gallant man, yet her people were not well pleased with that Match; for if *Spain* be subject to *Sagittarius*, *London*, and much of *England* is to *Gemini*, signs opposite one to another, and this is an Astrologicall reason, why for the most part, we love not that majesticall people.

In 1557. we lost *Calis*, but could never since obtain it: In the year succeeding Queen *Mary* died, and with her all the sorrows of the *English* ended, God giving us in her room, the vertuous, and prudent *Elizabeth*: That very year Reformation began in *Scotland*.

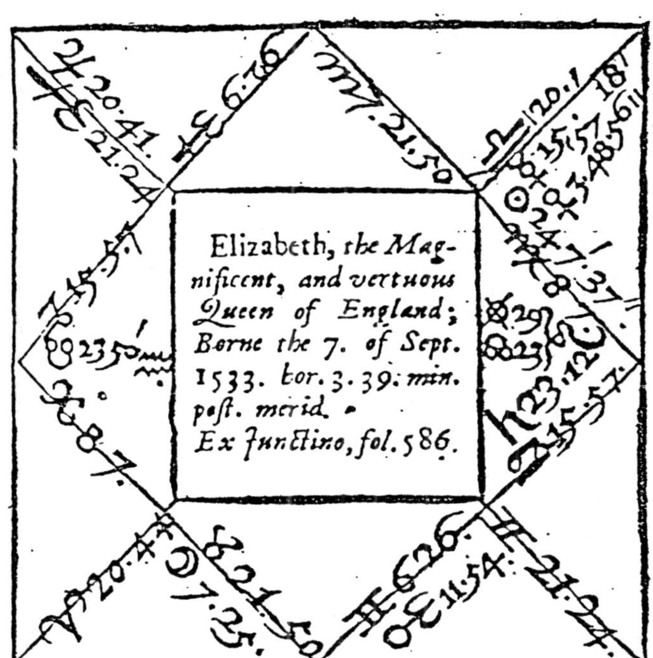

Elizabeth, *the Magnificent, and vertuous Queen of England*; *Borne the* 7. *of Sept.* 1533. *hor.* 3. 39. *min. post. merid.* *Ex Junctino, fol.* 586.

This Queen died when the Ascendent came to the Pleiades. I know no reason why she should have been angry with any Astrologer, that should have said; Madam, about your 69. year the Ascen. comes to the Pleiades, which denotes, not onely sicknesse unto your person, but disturbance in your government. Her M. C. about that time came to the Conjunction of *Saturn*. The *Irish* warre was not very successefull, which much afflicted her.

This Queens enemies are signified by *Saturn* in the seventh House, who having no essentiall dignity there, could not much hurt, yet had she lived the years of *Mathuselah*, she could not have wanted detractors, and powerfull Adversaries, for *Saturn* seldom is reconciled, and the *Dragons-tail* in *Aquarius*, a fixed Sign, stirred up the many slanders cast upon her honour; having three Planets in essentiall fortitudes, she feared no man: no enemy, no adversary could ever have advantage of her. How that Conjunction of *Saturn* and *Jupiter* in 1484. as *Junctinus* would have us beleeve, could prognosticate any

 honour

honour unto her, I see not. The agreement of her *Genesis*, with the *Scheame* of the Conjunction in 1544. I confesse did portend glory, and renown unto her; as any that examine both the Postures may easily perceive.

1558. Religion is established in *England*, and conference was had between Papist and Protestant; *Calvin* and *Westphalus* the Lutheran they contend, nothing but contention and variance about Religion: But I hold it needlesse to write more in an historicall way; for here followed for some years, nothing but Controversie upon Controversie, still, Religion being the thing pretended to be the occasion of all disturbances: but in the year 1563. the Councell of *Trent* ended, and toleration of Religion was granted to the Protestants in *France*; the same year there was

The eighth Conjunction of *Saturn* and *Jupiter*, but the seventh lesser.

Mars in *Taurus*, the Ascendent of *Ireland*; *Shan Oneal* rebelleth.

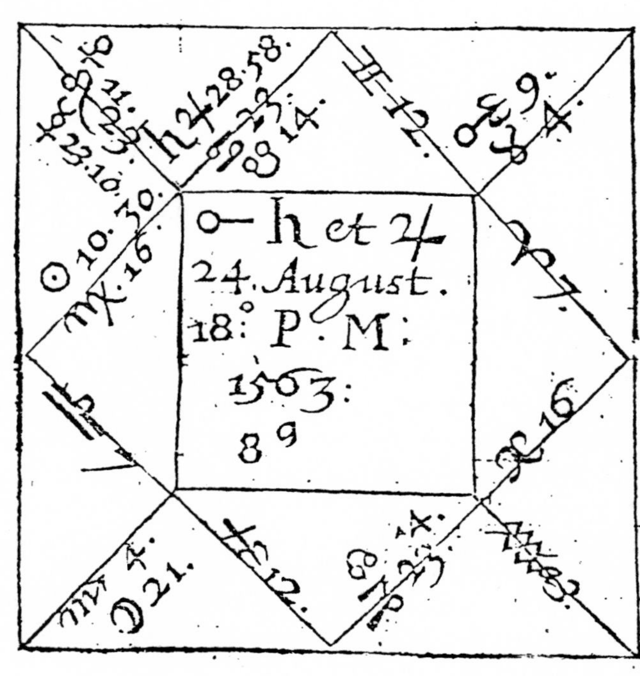

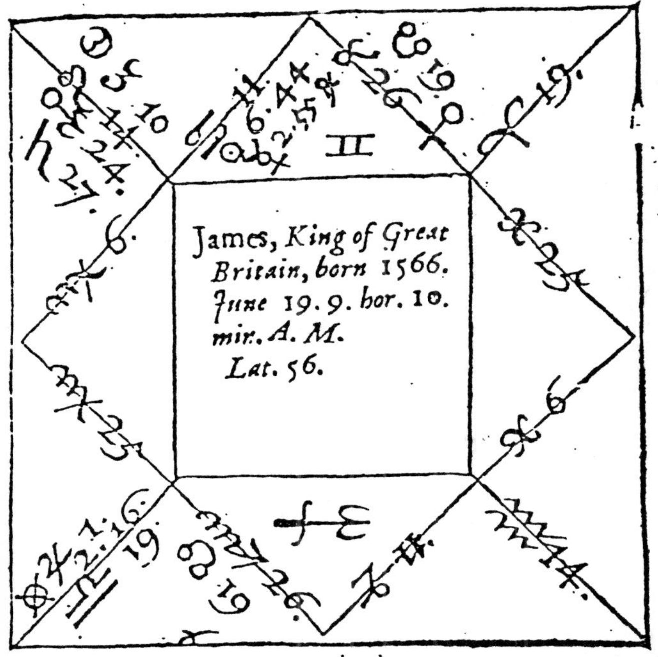

Venus culminating with eminent fixed Stars, & the mutuall reception of the *Luminaries*, the harmony betwixt his Scheame and the Conjunction preceding his birth, gave him that fame and esteem hee had in the world; and would God hee had lived to our times: The *Sun* is Hyleg. and therefore hee died when the *Sun* came to the body of *Saturn*: I also wonder, he never received hurt by falls from horses, or by fire: Its true, *Saturn* in the twelfth doth there most good, if ever any; least hurt I am sure he doth. *Saturn* and *Mars* in *Leo* gave him that eminent mole on his side.

1569. Is a Councell at *Millain*; two *English* Earls rebell: *Scotland* afflicted extreamly; the *Dragons-tail* in *Cancer* gives that Nation trouble. A year full of misery to the *Netherlands*, by means of Duke *D'alva*. The *English* began to flourish in all parst: See what it is when the Ascendent of the Conjunction and the Princes are of one Triplicity, no generall fate impending. Queen *Elizabeths* Ascendent being 15. of *Capricornus*, this in 1563. the 16. of *Virgo*, and although it was in the seventh of her birth, yet *Jupiter* being well signified, gave her victory over *Saturnine* enemies; the truth is, the Conjunction of the superiours being near the radicall place of *Saturn* in her birth, excited her own Subjects to rebell, *viz.* the *Irish*; and many intestine troubles in *England*: God gave all her enemies shame, but no reputation that molested her, yet was shee seldome quiet during the continuance of the effects of this last Conjunction.

1582. The *Gregorian* Kalender was first instituted, in which year King *James* was detained by the *Ruthens* as a prisoner. Many and sundry were the actions of these times, which I omit, and hasten to the next Conjunction of *Saturn* and *Jupiter*.

The ninth Conjunction of *Saturn* and *Jupiter* in the watry Trygon, but the eighth lesser.

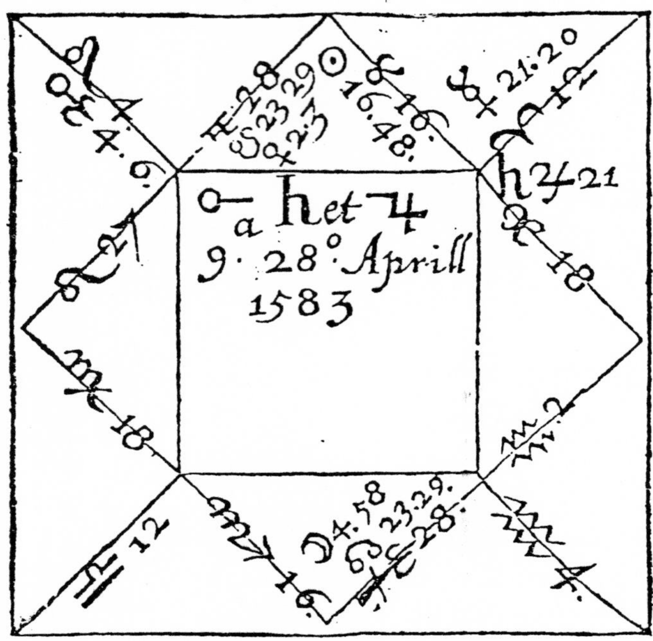

This Conjunction falls in the second House of Queen *Elizabeth*, importing much consumption of her Treasure: Having the *Moon* at her birth in *Taurus*, which is now the signe Culminating, it prenoted her Victorious atchievements; the *Sunne* also in this Conjunction is in *Trine* to his place at her birth. All things now being in the memory of man, I give every man leave to peruse Histories.

Merlinus Anglicus Astrologicus.

WHat now succeeds, was formerly in the year 1643. a little before the Conjunction in *February*; written, and intended to have seen the World ere this time, but because, *Difficile est judicium; de quo caremus exemplis multarum radicum in nostris temporibus: Rigel. Apho. 46.* Its very difficult to judge of those matters, concerning which we have few or no Presidents in our Age: I was inforced therefore to look behinde our times, and to procure, as well as I could, the nine Conjunctions of the watry Trygon, which preceded this, of which I intend my Discourse; of all which, the curious Astrologer may make better use, then is fit for mee to expresse: If there be either errour in the true place of the Planets, or in some of the Scheames, let it be remembred that of *Roger Bacon, De mirabilibus, fol.* 10. *Pluribus modis contingit deviare, quam signum attingere, & ubi plura requiruntur facilius erratur.* Its more easie, saith he, to erre, then hit the mark, and where many things are required, the more easily we may fail. Perhaps, my writing may stir up either some more able man to convince me of errour, or to take more labour to amend my imperfections, with either of which I shall be well contented: in the mean time, receive this Discourse as I formerly composed it.

The Authors former intentions, now published.

THat I may not exceed the memory of man, we are to remember that, in the year of our Lord God, one thousand five hundred eighty and three, there was a Conjunction of *Saturn* and *Jupiter* in the signe of *Pisces*; of which one Master *Harvy* did write: What effects there then followed, let either the Annals of *England*, or of forraigne Nations informe you; Yet let not us forget the *Spanish Armado* in 1588. which threatned no lesse then destruction, or subversion to the *English* Nation, and yet one *John Harvy*, a Physician, in contradiction of *Regiomontanus*, an admirable Astrologer, who designed that year for a strange one, was pleased to publish his own folly, and indeavoured to maintain, It would be a year as others; but the actions of the year, which he lived to see, confuted his erroneous judgement,

The

The entrance of *Saturn* and *Jupiter* into the fiery Trygon, calculated exactly with Instrument, by Sir *Christopher Heydon* Knight.

Before I can come to handle this last Conjunction of the watry Trygon, I must speak something of the two Superiours first meeting in the fiery Trygon, 1603. for I must leave nothing behind me: and of that Conjunction in 1623. I intend hereafter to be more copious in writing my judgement upon this Triplicity; yet slight not what now comes from mee.

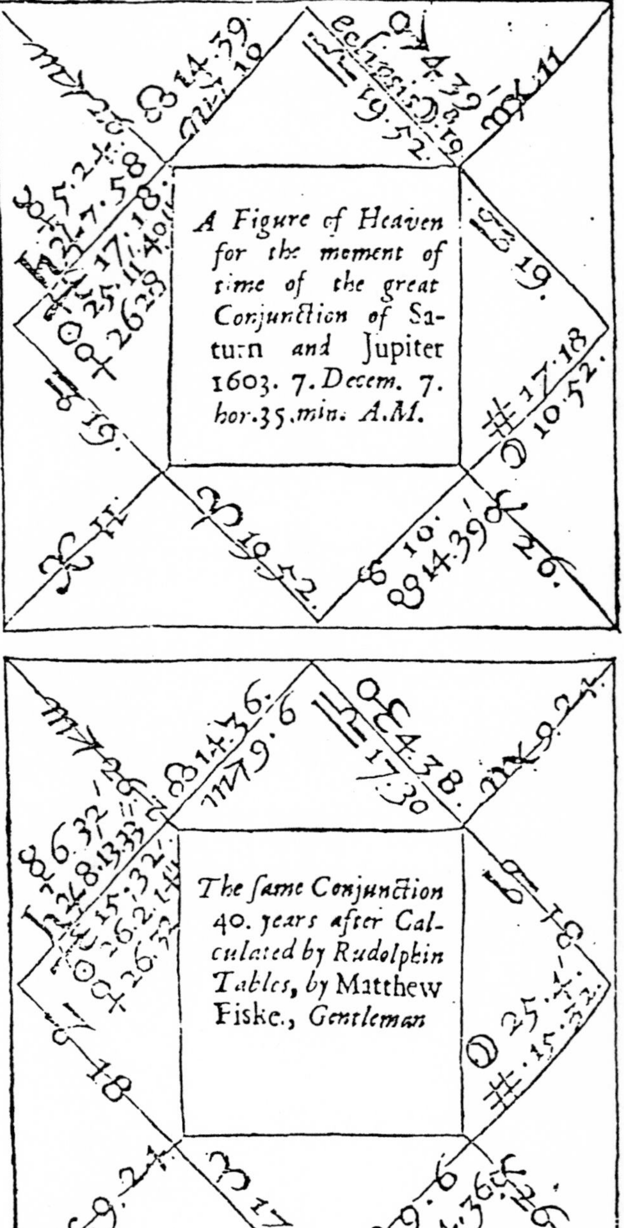

7. December 1603.
19. hor. 21. min. P.M.

Having

HAving intreated my loving Friend, Master *Matthew Fiske*, to give me the true Scheame of the great Conjunction of *Saturn* and *Jupiter* in 1603. (for it was so) hee gave me the Positure aforesaid, exactly done by the *Rudolphine Tables*: Some dayes after, I had occasion to peruse a letter lent me, which was wrote to Doctor *Foster* of *London*, 40. years before, wherein I found the Scheame as you see Calculated by Sir *Christopher Heydon* with Instrument; At which I wondred, and was not a little joyfull, that the Tables of *Kepler* were so exact, and my friend Master *Matthew Fiske* should be so able; for in truth, he hath as perfectly performed the Calculation, by the Tables of *Kepler*, as Sir *Christopher Heydon* did by his curious observation; which, in a word, makes good the Calculators exactnesse, and the verity of the Tables, being directed by an able hand.

Of the great, or, rather greatest Conjunction of Saturn *and* Jupiter, 1603. *it being their entrance into the fiery Triplicity.*

THis Trygon is called by *Ptolomey*, The first of the *Zodiacke*; and by the *Arabians*, The fiery Trygon: And we are to know, God hath alwayes innobled, and adorned these Trygonall returns with some memorable, and notable changes in the Church and Commonwealth; Amongst which, this of the first, hath ever carried the prerogative from the rest, both for that the world was first created, and the chief Epoche of great Actions, and alterations have happened under it; and also because this Trygon beginneth with *Aries*, the chief of the *Cardinall* Signes.

The first restitution of this Trygon, after the Worlds creation, happened in *Enochs* time; the second, in the universall Deluge; the third, in *Moses*, and the children of Israels delivery from the bondage of *Ægypt*; the fourth, in the Monarchy of the *Meds*; the fifth, in Christs, and the *Romans* Empire; the sixth, in *Charles* the Great, and the translation of the *Western* Empire to the *Germans*: And now this seventh, hath a secret mystery of Sabbatisme in it, and it promiseth something of more singular moment to the World then the other: For as *Johannes Anglicus, fol.* 13. *tractat. prim.* saith; *Et propter hoc evenit, quod prima vice quum junguntur in Trygono, & cum de alio se mutatur hæc Conjunctio, virtutem habeat magnam, & majorem quam alia conjunctiones, viz.* For this cause it commeth to passe, when they are first conjoyned, after the leaving of one, & entring into an other Triplicity; such a Conjunction hath great vertue and operation, yea and greater then any other.. What those effects may be, and what in a full measure of time may be expected, if wee beleeve the *Arabians*, or *Cardane*, they are set down by *Campanella, de sensu rerum. fol.* 358. *Sub Arietis Triangulo sunt monarchiæ ingentes, leges justæ, sapientes divinorum, pietas bona cœli & Europes in nostro hemisphærio.* Under the fiery Trygon mighty Monarchies arise, just Laws, the *Europeans* in our Hemisphear will bee more conversant, and greater searchers of divine things, &c, But the same Authour, in his Astrologicall *Tract. fol.* 64 delivers the matter more fully: *Dum fiunt magnæ Conjunctiones in Trygono primo, quæ durant annis* 199. *& singulis* 20. *fiunt annis, nascuntur orbi inferiori monarchiæ, tranquillitas, pax, ex Solis & Jovis dominio, item sapientes insignes sterilitates magnæ ob triangulum igneum: Viz.* Whilest the great Conjunctions of *Saturn* and *Jupiter* are in the first Triplicity, which continueth 199, years, and are every twenty years once, in our inferiour world there arise Empires, Monarchies, tranquillity, peace, by reason of the dominion of the *Sun* and *Jupiter*, great barrennesse also, because its the fiery Trygon.

All men know, that in this year 1603. *James* the sixth, came to be King of *England*: Could a more memorable thing bee in this world, then for a *Scottish* King to become Monarch of the *English*, and that without blows, considering the former Antipathie betwixt both Nations: Was not this in effect a new Monarchy, yea, and a great one to be King of *England*, *Scotland*, and *Ireland*?

Did not that prudent King bring Peace, not onely to the *English*, but in effect, was the sole procurer of it over all *Europe*, which not long after followed? And had wee not in 1603. a great plague in *London*, and during his raigne, many years of great scarcity? All which, verifie the *Arabian* Doctrin exactly: If we examine the Conjunction, we shall find *Mercury*, that in the Conjunction was King *James* his Significator, in our Horizon was Combust, but separating; and was not that good man miraculously delivered from the fury of the Powder-plot in 1605. But I passe by these things, and do deliver my judgement, what may in time bee expected under the fiery Triplicity, this being the fore-runner of part of those many accidents, yet are remaining to be compleated. I say, and judge: That God will restrain Monarchicall Pomp, and reduce all to an Aristocraticall mediocrity, both in the government of the Commonwealth, and of the Church; But before this be effected, *Omnia nutu*

unius

unius regentur, as *Cardano* long since predicted: After which, God will give so long a Peace, and such tranquillity to the Earth, as shee never yet enjoyed the like; In the mean time as *Mercury*, *Jupiter*, and *Saturne* in this Scheame of their first return, are in the twelfth House, I conceive that privately, and underhand by lies, by treachories, by faigned and dissembled Treaties, and Ambassadours, and by the policie of the Jesuiticall faction all over *Europe*, the true Protestant Religion shall infinitely be distressed, and the heavenly intentions impedited, and all those Countreys that professe Protestantismne exceedingly be molested, by so secret and close a compact of Villains, and false hearted traytors, lurking in the bosomes and closets of Princes, as that many will think Popery and Papisme shall return to its old seat in every Countrey, but that it never will in our Kingdomes, for *Jupiter* being in his chief House, cannot but in fine overcome, and the rather, because he receives the *Sun* and *Mercury* in the Ascendent; which shew, that God will miraculously by meanes of some young Prince, or Commonalty of people, discover and bring to light, the close mystery of those Plots, that from the year 1603. untill almost 50. years be accomplished, shall involve all at sometimes, and part at other of Christendom in most bloudy broiles; but of this anon.

The actions performed during these 20. years, are fresh in the memory of every man: I therefore come to the next Conjunction.

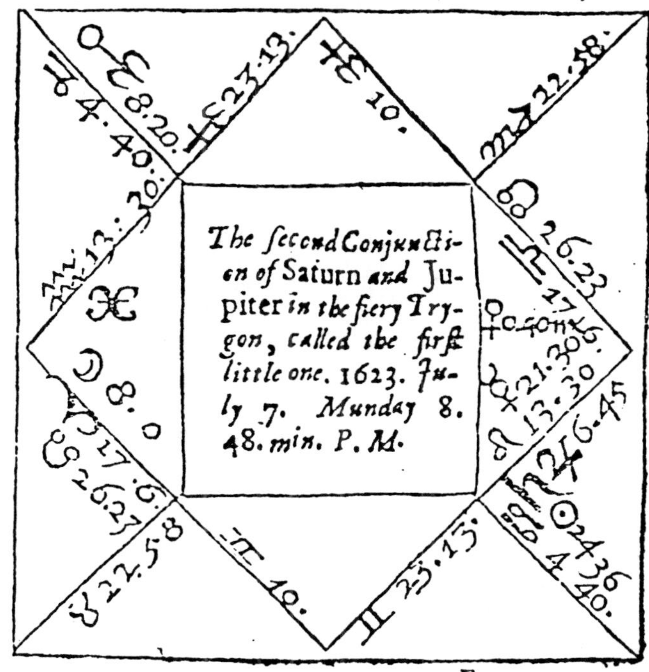

The second Conjunction of Saturn *and* Jupiter *in the fiery Trygon, called the first little one.* 1623. *July* 7. *Munday* 8. 48. *min. P. M.*

We may see things are not yet mature, to put the will of the Celestiall bodies, and in them the Decree, I hope, of the Almighty into full action. This Conjunction, is locally in the sixth House, in opposition to the precedent in 1603. God retards his Decrees for a time; hee is scarce born to this year 1643. that shall see the beginning, in any full measure, of what this Sabbaticall return of the Planets intend. The effects of this Conjunction, and the principall Sticklers do all their deeds of darknesse under-hand, in as much as concerns Religion: Is not *Jupiter* Lord of the House of Authority, and *Sol* generally the significator of Kings in the sixth House, and subterranean, and in *Cancer* the twelfth from *Leo*: Are Princes deluded, and will they not see? After 17. years the *Moon* comming to the *Suns* Quadrature, will either give sight of former misgovernments, or else puzzle them, & *forsan*: Here's *Venus* in the seventh, and *Mercury*, and the Conjunction it self is in the signe of the seventh House: Shall women rule, or men of feminine constructions, and constitutions, crosse all the *Europian* designes, and make us all sick of the infinite misery they bring upon us; Let *England* beware when either *Aquarius* is the Ascendent of a Conjunction of the Superiors, or of an *English* King or Queen, witnesse this Conjunction, and the Ascendent of Queen *Mary* 1516. And forget not that King *James* his death succeeded this Conjunction some few years, and a great plagve after his death, carrying away 50. thousand soules to accompanie so noble a Prince.

We in *England*, have had two of our best Princes deaths followed with two great plagves, *viz.* Queen *Elizabeth* 1603. and King *James* 1625. There's a mystery in it, if I durst unfold it; I hope we shall no more such great plagues, I wish such Princes. But because occasionally I shall touch other matters of this Conjunction, in my immediate succeeding Discourse, I omit any further relation, and come to this Conjunction which was in 1642.according to the *English* account, which must of necessity be the Designatrix of some memorable Actions, in regard it is in a signe of contrary nature to the two preceding.

The

The ninth lesser Conjunction of Saturn *and* Jupiter, *and the last of the watry Triplicity.*

209. 31.

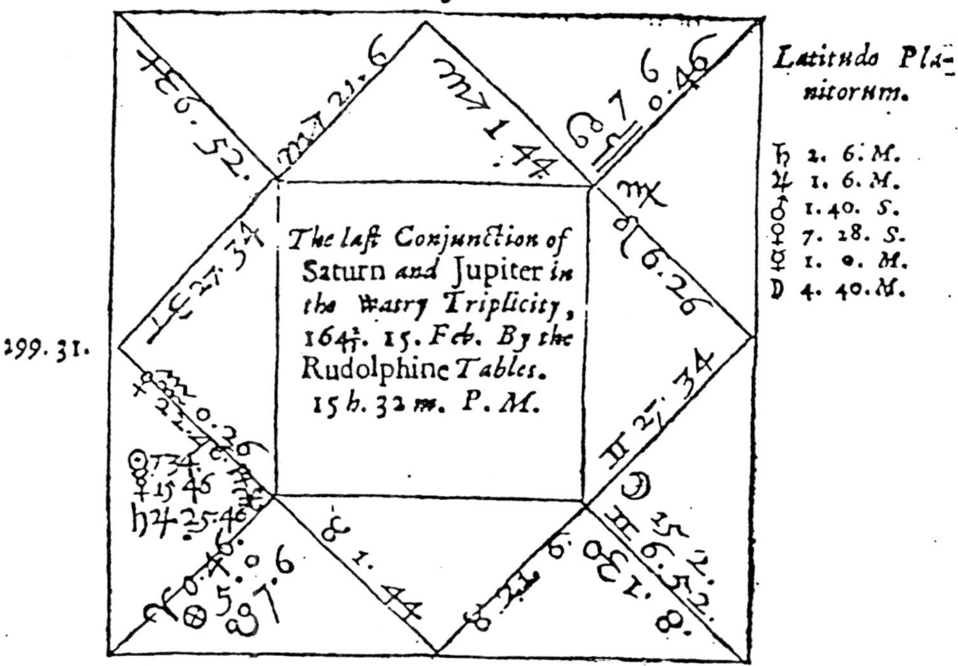

This is the *Conjunction* of which I intend now, and first did intend, to write of, it happens, or is in a signe contrary to the two former *Conjunctions, viz.* in 1603. and 1623. they convening in signes of the fiery Triplicity, and this in the signe of the watery, the former two in Regall and diurnall signes Masculine and Cholerick, this in a Feminine, Nocturnall, Watery, Moyst and Flegmatick, oblique and by corporeall, vitious and crooked signe, obedient and of divers proportions; quite contrary to the two former.

Let the inhabitants of Europe in generall observe, that as this *Conjunction* is in an aquaticall signe, so the effects proceeding from hence will be such, and of such like quality and operation, as fire is to water, or water to fire: for as water allayeth and abateth the extraordinary hotnesse of fire in naturall operations, so this *Conjunction* foretelleth that what either is now, or hath been illegally obtained by any Prince against his vassails, or by the Nobility and Gentry against their Tenants in the former fiery or Commanding times (when Will and

 Pleasure

Pleasure, were positive Lawes) shall now by the effects depending on this Conjunction, receive a quenching or abatement of their heat, violence and oppression, proportionable to the quality of the Patient or undergoer of former sufferings: *Albumazer Diff.* 2. *Cap.* 1. *Cum mutatio fuerit in aquaticis vel signis terreis, significat vulgi & mediocrium hominum equalitatem eorum cum regibus in ordine, viz.* When mutation or change of any of these *Conjunctions* is either in watery or earthly signes, it denotes the estate of the common or mean man to be equall to that of Princes. An Aphorisme if judiciously observed and pithily understood, not much deviating from truth.

Let the Kings, Princes, and Magistrates of Europe observe and carefully beware, that if they have by any hostility, subtilty, treachery, or any Court by unwarrantable meanes prevailed or incroached upon their inferiours, I say here will be a time of recovery offered, here will a day of retaliation appear, before the effects of this *Conjunction* surcease, so that the same tyranny that any Prince hath used against his people, or the same measure of injustice any Court of Justice, and its Officers have executed against poore offenders or Complainants; the same proportion of hardnesse of heart in the Subject against his Soveraign, and of the weeping Client against the insulting Officer shall now be retorted, and with excesse in the execution thereof.

And further as the two precedent *Conjunctions* in 1603. and 1623. were both in Regall signes, and so thereby the Prerogative of Princes the power of the Magistrate, and authority of many Courts was elevated to an exceeding height in greatnesse, so by this *Conjunction* in the year 16$\frac{42}{43}$. the contrary may, or ought to happen, and a suppression of those exorbitancies in each severall calling, may fortunately be expected, for this *Conjunction* shall be as a bridle to the two former. The appearance of this *Conjunction*, as I observe, is contrary to that of former times; for usually those *Conjunctions* did successively and in an orderly progresse succeede each other in signes of the same Triangularity, for the space of 198. years, and 265. dayes, and when they had run over that Station the Almighty had decreed them in that *Trigon*, they entered into the subsequent *Trigon*, and therein accomplished the like number of years and dayes as aforesaid. But now in *Anno* 16$\frac{42}{43}$. as if the divine Providence, were about to change the constant order of nature, and the whole Fabrick of the Universe, these two most waighty or ponderous Planets (after two *Conjunctions* in the fiery *Trygon*) come to their tenth and last *Conjunction* in the

signe

signe of *Pisces*, the last signe in number of the *Zodiack*, and perhaps the last that shall ever be in this *Trigon*, being in a signe which is the most weak and impotent of all the twelve; but yet a *House* wherein *Jupiter* hath much power. The Celestiall bodies whether guided by the immediate finger of God, or whether so appointed by the *Secundreian* Intelligences or Planetary Angels, who move and direct our earthly affaires, as the more *secret learning* informeth us, have given permission to two precedent *Conjunctions*, in the Regall Triangularity, before they would permit a perfect conclusion of the watery. Times have no Presidents of the like excursion, or mutation (that ever I could read of) nor shall the ages in future see the like. It may justly be doubted and in an Astrologicall way divined, that there shall be a sensible disturbance, if not a finall subversion, to those Common-wealths and Monarchies, that had originally their beginning either in 1603. 1623. or neer, or since those times. For let that be granted, which is most certain, that the first *Conjunction* of the fiery Triplicity was in *Sagittarius* 1603. and this now is *Pisces* in perfect Quadrature in respect of Signe, but in most exact partill *Quadrate* to the place of the *Sun* and *Venus*; if the *Moon* in that was in *Opposition* to the *Sun*, in this she is in a *Square*; the Positure of *Saturn* and *Jupiter* then was in 7. *deg.* 58. *min.* *Sagittary*, that degree now is the cuspe of the twelfth house; shall tribulation and affliction be brought upon us, after so long a time, by the malice of those times or Action of those men that then lived, or shall we disturbe the preposterous oppressions which then and since had life and support.

Sub quarto Trigono, qui primum respicit hostili radio, Monarchia prima frangitur; incipiunt hereses dire, armisque protecta, ob Martem & Lunam, fides plus armis quam miraculis ampliatur, surgunt nova Religiones, priscam austeritatem (sive superstitionem) mollientes, ad bonum tamen usum, quoniam syderum est inclinare, libertatis est uti inclinatione bené vel malé. Campanella fol. 70. lib. 2. de Astrolog. Under the fourth Triplicity, which respecteth the first Triplicity with an hostile Aspect; the Prerogative of the first Monarchy will be shaken; direfull heresies begin, protected with Armes, by reason of *Mars* and the *Moon*, faith is more inlarged by the Sword than miracle: new Religions or Tenents arise, checking the former austerity (or rather superstition) and yet to a good intent, because the property of the stars is to incline, but the use of Liberty is to use that inclination well or ill. I shall speak more amply of these things when I come to handle the Agent in this *Conjunction*; Let us now observe the face of all

all or most part of Europe at the moment of this *Conjunction* in *Feb.* $16\frac{42}{43}$. It is nineteen yeers and 223 dayes, since the last meeting of *Saturn* and *Jupiter* in *Leo*, who list, in any histories may see the story of those times, but now it findeth us in *England* in this posture, His Majesty *Charles* King of *England*, the son of *James*, who came to the Crown of *England* 1603. by the decease of *Elizabeth* Queen of the *English*: I say this *Conjunction* findeth him engaged in an uncivill and unnaturall War against his own Subjects, the *English* Nation, and in particular against the Parliament, the representative body of the Kingdom, against the most famous City of *London*, the Kingdomes *Metropolis*, and almost against the whole Commonalty and Yeomanry of *England*; his Majesty in defence of his own Rights, and of the persons of severall delinquents and Malignant Counsellours so Voted by both houses; the *Parliament* stand in opposition of those Malefactors, and in defence of themselves, Protestant Religion, Liberties of the Parliament and Subject. I wish we had been better employed, that is, had not been in Armes one against another. *Quo semel est imbuta recens, &c.* *France* is in action against the *Spaniard*; *Portugall* wrested about a year before from the *Spanish* crown, hardly ever to be recovered from that brave Prince enjoyes it; its his right, God keepe him safe in his Kingdome, and let his off-spring long enjoy it.

Catalonia, where fierce people inhabite, in Armes against their Soveraigne, for oppressing them with too heavie burthens.

The *Swede* in the bowels of *Germany*; * *Denmark* quiet and secure, not yet molested. *Scotland* in great tranquility by the blessing of God and vertue of the prudent Nobility, and yet carefull of the *English* Parliament; The United *Provinces* (*statu quo*) in Armes against his Majestie of *Spain*, as yet having made no * *adresses* to us, that sometimes were their good friends. The Irish in Rebellion against the King of *England*, pretending subversion of their fundamentall Laws and Popish Religion was intended by the English. The Pope at odds with the Duke of *Mantua*, and some petty *Italian* Princes. I heare not but that the *Turke* is quiet, and so the *Polonian*, the *Cossack*, the *Transilvanian* and *Muscovites* are all in peace; be it so, and I pray God it may be so, but I fear peace is such a blessing they shall enjoy but a short space.

It was quiet at the time of the conjunction

In May 1644. they did.

This is the true condition of *Europe* the 15. *Feb.* $16\frac{42}{43}$. at the true time of *Saturn* and *Jupiter* their *conjunction*. The State of *Venice* is quiet.

When

When I had well considered our manifold troubles, and that they preceded the moment of this *conjunction*. I was enforced to look backward, and so I did to the *conjunction* in 1603. and that in 1623. and to all the Eclipses since those times, and to the one hundred and twenty Conjunction, of which *Ptolomy* forewarneth the Astrologer diligently to consider in generall accidents, all these exactly considered. yet did they not give my mind satisfaction, but incited me to a higher Scrutiny: for though I well know, that every visible Eclipse in our *Horizon* of the *Sun* or *Moon*, and every of those lesser *Conjunctions* afore mentioned have in one kind or other speciall and materiall significations in their influences upon the bodies and actions of men, yet because the effects of any Eclipse of the *Sun* cannot last above three yeers, nor of the *Moon* a far shorter time, I was induced to consider, if there were not some Comet or blazing star, whose effects were not as yet fully determined, and which as yet I had not remembred, and which might happily coöperate, or had prepared matter for this present Conjunction to work upon; for the Conjunction could not begin to operate so long before its being: the effects we know must alwayes succeed the causes.

The last Comet which appeared in *Europe* was in *Anno* 1618. excellently observed by *Longomontanus* in *Astronomia Danica*. There are a people that do too much slight the appearance and effects of Comets, as if they signified nothing, but let them consider, That God doth not alwayes speak unto men in expresse words and sillables but many times extraordinarily, admonishing us by the Motions and apparitions of the heavenly bodies (which are the works of his owne fingers) is sufficiently testified, both by that star which led the *Magi* in the Gospell to the knowledge of our Saviours Nativity, and by the words of Christ himself, presaging the destruction of *Jerusalem*, forewarned the *Jews* to lift their heads to heaven, to behold the signes that should be in the *Sun* and in the *Moon* and in the stars, before that day. Neither did the events fail his prediction (for as *Josephus* a Captain no lesse famous in those Wars, than a true Historiographer) reporteth, besides the great and fearfull Eclipses preceding, there appeared a terrible Comet in form of a flaming sword over the City, by the space of a whole yeer together, as you may read *Lib. 7. cap. 12. de bello Judaico.* And surely I doubt not, but it pleaseth God by these heavenly Prodigies, no lesse to participate to, and communicate, and confer with men about his secret determinations, then he was wont of old by dreames and visions. It was excellently spoken by the Philosopher

Hero-

Herodotus, When God is to punish a Nation or City, he first signifies his intention by Prodigies. It was also as well said of that Christian, who delivered this sentence. *Loquitur cum hominibus Deus non modo lingua humana, per Prophetas, Apostolos & pastores, sed nonnunquam etiam ipsis elementis in formas & imaginas diversas compositis, viz.* God doth not onely deliver his will unto us by Prophets, Apostles, and Pastors, but sometimes in the Elements composed into severall formes and Images. I am informed by *Ptolomy* in *Aphoris.* 98. *Trajectiones atque crinitæ secundas partes in judiciis ferunt, viz.* Comets and blazing stars, carry a second part in judgements. And by *Guido Bonatus, fol.* 592. *Omnes Cometæ significant bella, terrores, & magnos eventus in mundo.* All Comets signifie Wars, terrours, and strange events in the world; we are commanded by *Cardane in Segment.* 2. *Aphoris.* 133. *In constitutionibus generalibus etiam Cometas & reliqua incidentia observare oportet:* In giving judgements upon generall Constitutions, consider the Comets and the rest of the judgements incident thereunto: of which opinion *Ptolomy* is *Lib.* 2. *Quadripartiti, fol.* 105. *Observandæ sunt Cometæ in universalium eventuum consideratione, etenim effectus hæ pariunt, quales a Marte cientur ac Mercurio: ut bella, æstus, motus turbulentos, & alia quæ ista sequi consueverunt*; Comets in consideration of generall events are to be observed, for these produce effects, and are known by *Mars* and *Mercury, viz.* wars, droughts, violent commotions, and other enormities which usually accompany: *Rigel*, addeth *Aphoris.* 137. *Mutantur Regna per apparitionem Cometarum in signis regiis, dum movetur motu sensibili & de uno in alio signo, & magis quando plures una in uno anno erunt:* Kingdomes are altered by the apparition of Comets in regall Sines, (why not houses?) more especially when they sensibly moove out of one Signe into another, or when at one time and in one year many appear: There were seen 1618. three Comets, the first began and ended in the Signe of *Leo*, a Regall signe, and chiefly concerned by its verticality *Bohemia* and *Hungaria*, and those Countries there adjacent, but by reason of the Signe *Italy*, and *Rhetia* neer the *Alpes, &c.*

The second Comet did not appear to us, nor was there any thing seen in our Horizon but the *Tayle*, it principally threatned those parts of the *Indias*, which the *Spaniard* and *Portugals* have obtained by their industrious Navigations.

The third is that which I must make use of in this discourse, as being exactly observed, and passed through three Signes, &c.

The

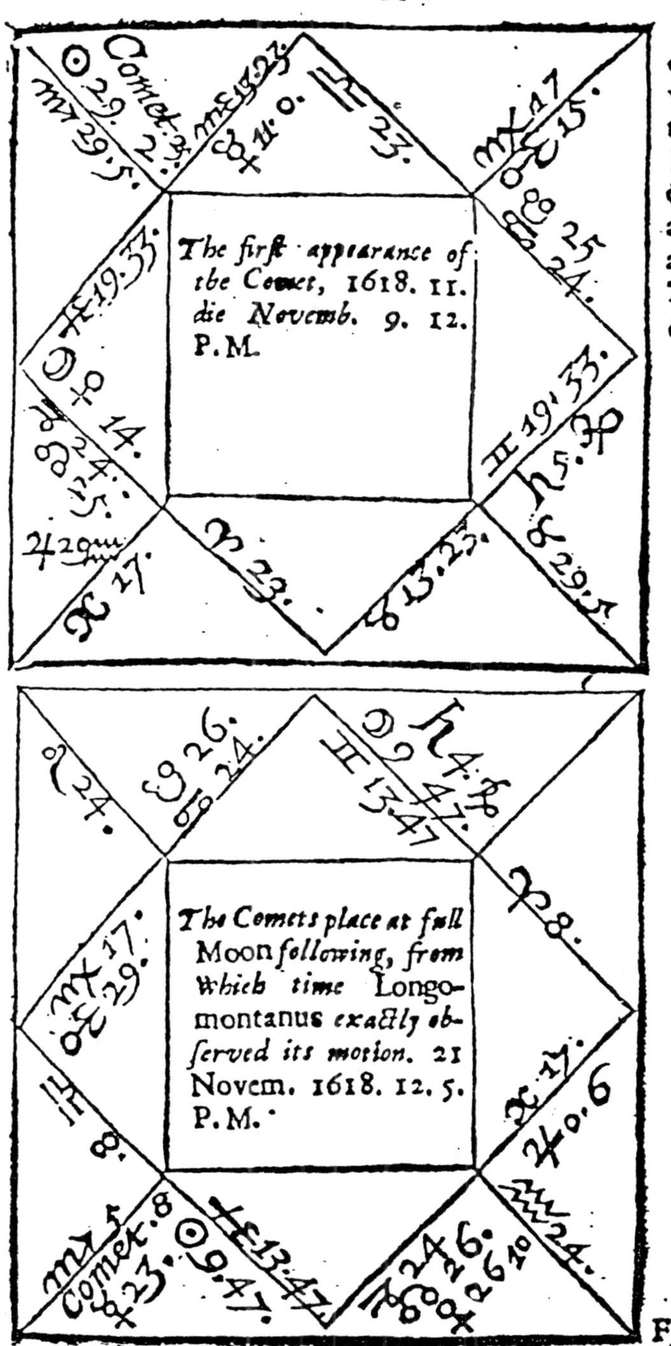

The last *Aphorisme* quoted in *Rigel* is not vaine, for hath not there been one new Monarchy already erected, *viz. Portugall*: and may there not be another before 1648. *Tale aliquod forsan, &c.*

F

It is conceived the Comet began the day above named, but in regard of the thick mists and clouds which over-spread that part of *Denmarke*, *Longomontanus* lived in, he could make no observation before the 21. of *Novemb.* although D. *Bainbridge* in *London* observed it the 18. of *Novemb.* being Wednesday, and finished his observation the 16. of *December* following, the Comet being after 28. dayes not visible in *London*. As there was a speech many dayes and a rumour of the appearance of a Comet, but no exact visibility thereof, so it may be well observed, that the mercy of Almighty God is infinite, that did as it were consult with himself, whether this direfull Comet should not be recalled, and adde some more years of Repentance to the world.

The Astrologicall judgement which succeeds, I frame according to the observation of *Longomontanus*, from the time of the full Moon succeeding the Comet. And I do conceive as it was 28, days observed by my Author, and also by Doctor *Bainebridge*, and so many dayes was for the most part altogether visible, so I say, (*salvo judicio aliorum*) the effects shall shew themselves 28. yeares, and be so long time, ere the accidents signified by it, shall surcease: See its motion in Longitude, and its Declination.

Ephi-

Ephimeris Cometæ.

Moneth.	*Dayes of the Moneth.*	*Its dayly Motion.*		*Its Motion in Longitude.*			*Declination.*		*Anno Dom.*	
		G.	*M.*	*G.*	*M.*	*Sig.*	*G.*	*M.*		
Novemb	21	3	20	9	25	♏	3	20. *Mer.*	1618	
	22	3	17	7	55	♏	0	35. *Mer.*	1619	1
	23	3	14	6	25	♏	2	20. *Bor.*	1620	2
	24	3	11	4	55	♏	5	30. *Bor.*	1621	3
	25	3	9	3	7	♏	9	0	1622	4
	26	3	6	1	20	♏	12	0	1623	5
	27	3	3	29	30	♎	15	20	1624	6
	28	3	1	27	45	♎	18	10	1625	7
	29	3	0	26	10	♎	20	40	1626	8
	30	2	57	24	10	♎	23	15	1627	9
Decemb.	1	2	47	22	0	♎	26	10	1628	10
	2	2	38	20	0	♎	29	10	1629	11
	3	2	24	18	0	♎	32	0	1630	12
	4	2	19	16	20	♎	34	20	1631	13
	5	2	16	14	40	♎	36	30	1632	14
	6	2	14	12	30	♎	38	40	1633	15
	7	2	12	10	20	♎	40	50	1634	16
	8	2	10	7	40	♎	43	0	1635	17
	9	2	8	5	0	♎	45	0	1636	18
	10	2	6	2	20	♎	47	0	1637	19
	11	2	3	29	30	♍	49	0	1638	20
	12	1	59	26	40	♍	51	0	1639	21
	13	1	55	23	40	♍	53	0	1640	22
	14	1	50	20	50	♍	55	0	1641	23
	15	1	43	18	0	♍	56	40	1642	24
	16	1	33	14	40	♍	58	10	1643	25
	17	1	18	11	10	♍	59	35	1644	26
	18	1	8	7	45	♍	61	0	1645	27

The Comet, as you may obſerve, was not fixed, (as that Star in 1572. whoſe effects this age ſhall ſcarce live to ſee) but in 28. dayes ran through part of *Scorpio*, all *Libra*, and 22. *deg*, and 15. *min.* of *Virgo*, in all the degrees of its motion were according to its Longitude, 77. *deg.* and 50. *min. Cometæ mobiles bella indicant ab externis. Cardanus, Seg.* 3. *Aphoriſ.* 117. *In Cardinibus Regum mortes, in nono loco religionis jacturam, in octavo vel duodecimo peſtilentiam, aut jacturam segetum, in undecimo Nobilium mortes:* Mooving Comets shew war from Forraigners: if the Comet shew its self in the tenth house, it portends the death of Kings, if in the ninth, the hazard of Religion and spoil of the Church, if in the twelfth or eighth, a pestilence or the spoil of corn; if in the eleventh, the death of many Nobles follow. *Cardanus* ends not so, *vide Seg. 5. Aphoris. 15. Cometes valde clarus ac conspicuus, tum etiam mobilis ac diuturnus, mutationem alicujus Imperii decernit.* When a Comet appeares clear and conspicuous, and also quick in his dayly motion, it pre-notes a mutation or change of some Empire. *Cometes mutantes leges, si in nono, vel undecimo apparuerint, seditionem in lege, non legem ostendunt, nec erit in illa unum caput, Card. Seg. 2. Aphoris. 206.* Comets that altar Laws, if they appear in the ninth or eleventh house of heaven, they rather shew controversie in points of Law, than the dissolution of the Law; yet they shall contend upon many points of the Law. Whether these profound *Aphorismes* have not been exactly verified, even upon the *English* Nation in particular, and upon almost every Country in Europe since this Comets appearance, I leave it to every honest Reader to consider: Have an eye to the pressures of *France, Germany, Denmarke,* and *Ireland, &c.*

Not onely the swiftnesse of the Comets Motion, but its Retrogradation or course in motion might have induced any versed but meanly in the principles of Art, to judge some more than usuall accidents to be forth-comming into the world; and if we would know of what Nature these actions should be, heare Doctor *Dee*, *Aphoris.* 88. *Planeta Retrogradus natura constans decretum quodam modo perfringere videtur, periodum suam diurnam breviori absolvendo tempore quam ipse Æquator, &c.* A Retrograde Planet doth seem to break the constant order of Nature, finishing his diurnall period, in shorter time than the *Æquator* it self. So that it seemes some Princes and Potentates, many Noble men and Ecclesiasticall have ever since the appearance in 1618 been steared in the course of their lives by the influence of this Retrograde Comet, *viz.* They have laboured hard by a strict hand, and an awing domineering authority to oppresse their Neighbours Tenants and Subjects, esteeming that the safest for them, whereas in truth it first undid them in the good opinion of the people, and lastly when the Comet came to be Verticall over the afflicted Countries, very necessity inforced them to rise in Armes for destruction of their Retrograde Lords.

At first this Comet had Meridionall declination from the Æquator, as as if God would willingly have spared us, that are on the North side the *Æquator*, and live in Northern Latitude; and sent out his punishing Angell to more remote Countries, *viz.* the *Indies*, *&c.* But our sins encreasing, he gave direction to the Comet to point out *Europe*, and in *Europe*, *England*; yet his clemency was such, as that he permitted not the Comet to be Verticall over any part of *England*, untill it had been visible and verticall to many other places 21. dayes, which in measure of time, give, according to my limitation, twenty one yeares.

By which his long forbearance, it appeareth, that God did reflect upon the many intercessions of some *Abrahams*, *Samuels*, *Davids*, and *Daniels*, that then lived amongst us: who, with weeping, fasting, and mourning, like so many *Hezekiahs*, obtained these 21. yeares longer, for us to repent in. After the Comet, I say, had been visibly apparent, 21. dayes, it had by the exact observation of *Longomontanus*, 49. *degrees* of Northerne Declination, and then entred the signe of *Virgo* the Common ascendent of the *English* Kings and Monarchy; for many conceive *William* the Conquerour obtained *England* presently after a *Conjunction* of *Saturn* and *Jupiter*, in *Virgo*; I am certain it was during the earthly Triplicity: and we finde by experience those Kings of *England*, that have any signe of the earthly Trigon their Ascendent, have been fortunate to the *English*, *& sic è contrario*; Queen *Elizabeth*, King *James*, *Henry* the 8. and *Edward the* 6. had so. As then it entred *Virgo*, it came neer to be Verticall and perpendicular over *England*: *Quo magis ad perpendicularitatem super aliquam elementarem superficiem accedit axis radiosus alicujus stellæ, eò fortius circa talem suæ incidentiæ locum, suas vires illa stella imprimet; directo quidem modo, propter majorem agentis vicinitatem: reflexo autem, quia reflexi tales radii, ad incidentes, viciniùs conduplicantur. Dee, Aphoris.* 54. By how much greater the *Axis* or radious beames of any star doth come to perpendicularity upon any elementary superficies; by so much the more forcibly he doth imprint his influence upon such a place of his incidence, in a direct manner, by reason of the greater vicinity of the Agent: but in a reflexed way, because such beames bowed or turned back are neer conduplicated to the incidents. *Stellæ verticales magnam habent vim, & sunt illæ, quæ tantam habent declinationem ab Æquinoctiali, quanta est elevatio poli illius Regionis; Dasipodius, Aphoris.* 68. Stars that are Verticall have great power, and are those which have as much declination from the *Æquinoctiall*, as the elevation of the Pole of that Region: If we adde 21. years to 1618.

we

we shall arive to the year 1639. Who is ignorant of our then approaching troubles? And yet because the Comet was not then Verticall fully over *England*, no great mischiefe then happened: a cloud was falling upon us, but did not; yet from the time it had 49. degrees of North Declination, it began to exasperate and stir up matter in the English Nation, and so as its declination increased, our courages were stirred up, and it was much augmented, I mean the effects of the Cometary influence by that great Ecclipse of the Sun, 22. *May* 1639 in *Gemini*, for the *digits* Eclipsed were 10. and 40. *min.* It began in the ninth house, its true Eclipse or middle, was in the 8. its conclusion in the 7. Church men began our misery, war, and death shall end it. I was ever fearfull of the effects of that Eclipse: for he that observes it, shall finde that the Sun is Lord of the tenth, and he is Eclipsed by the Moon in the eighth: *Per solem reges dupliciter intelliguntur, per Lunam populus, sive vulgus:* an easie Artist may put this into sense.

The Comet now in 1639 came close home unto us: it was four dayes or somewhat more verticall over all *England* (for after it had 56. degrees of Northern declination, it passed farther Northward towards *Scotland*) so it had then time to leave its impression more deeply upon us, according to that 55. *Aphoris.* of Doctor *Dee, Quó stellæ ejusdem mora, super horizontem major fuerit, eó ad suæ virtutis fortiorem faciendam impressionem per directos suos radios, est accomodatior:* By how much the greater or longer the mansion or abiding of the same star is above the Horizon, by so much the more is he fitted by those his direct beames over those parts, to make a more strong impression of his influence: had some Europeian Princes seen the judgement I gave upon that *Solar* Eclipse in 1639. it might have frighted them, or exhorted them to look to themselves. But *Principi ne magnum malum unquam prædixeris, sed periculum:* which in effect saith; Never tell your Prince truth, an horrid basenesse.

The 12. of *Decemb.* 1618. the Comet passed 26. *deg.* and 40. *min.* of *Virgo*, which is the degree within one, opposite to the *Conjunction* of *Saturn* and *Jupiter* in 25. *Pisces.* Adde 22. yeares to 1618. and it answers 1640. Consider the Declination of the Comet, you finde it 51. The Comet was then Verticall over many places of *England* and in speciall manner to *London* it selfe; This year 1640. Our Parliament began at *Westminster.*

I take

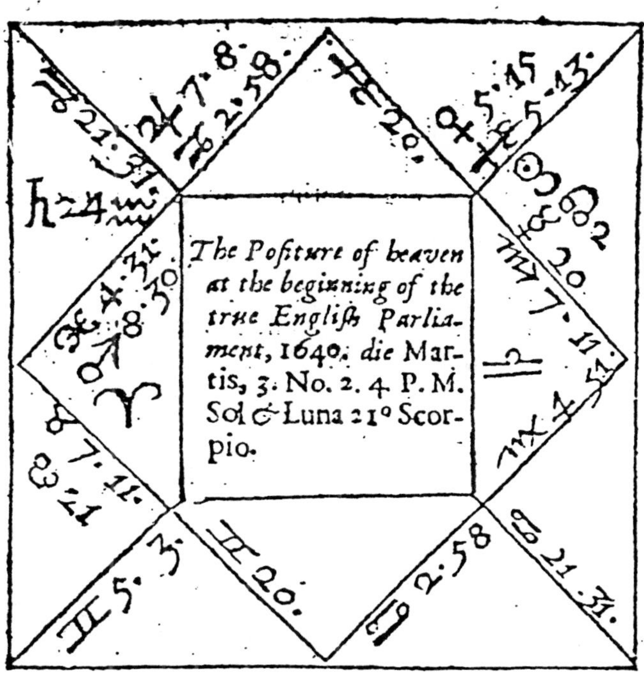

I take that time for the moment of its beginning, at what time his Majesty went after Sermon into the Parliament house, and began his speech, which was 2. *ho.* 4. *min.* P. M. *diei prædicti.*

Far be it from my thoughts Astrologically to judge, and publish my judgement, what successe may be expected from the scheame aforesaid betwixt his Majesty and the Parliament, I desire so to carry my discourse,& in so equall a ballance,as I may not offend either his Majesty, whom I do honour as my Prince; or the Parliament, under whose protection I now live,and whose just rights I am bound to maintaine by Protestation.

The angles of the figure are double bodied, common, or called by corporeall; the Sun is a little Eclipsed and in *Scorpio*, the most viperous Signe of the *Zodiack*; *Mars* possesseth the East Angle in *Pisces*, a Signe of his own *Trigon*; *Jupiter* is Lord of the Ascendant, but not of the tenth house, because he beholds not the house: *Saturne* the supreamest of Planets, represents his Majestie, he is in the twelfth house,

House, the *Sun* and *Moon* applying to a Quadrature of him, the Aspect is in fixed signes, and out of the worst Houses of Heaven: Absolutely there's a cunning spirit that pretends fair, and yet impedites both King and Parliaments reconcilement, a spirit that will not let His Majesty see the Parliaments realty to him, nor suffer the Parliament to beleeve His Majesty intends fairly to them.

Fear to offend silenceth my further thoughts, onely I will be bold to conjecture, death or, some untimely accident may cut off three of the greatest enemies both King and Parliament have, ere the Moneth of *December* 1644. or it will bee then perceived openly who they are, and they questioned and imprisoned; if they run not away; the reason is, because both *Mercury*, *Sun*, and *Moon* are in square to *Saturn* in the 12. house. they in the 8. house, and being disposed by *Mars*, it may bee hoped Divine Justice will find them out, because *Mercury* wanteth 4. degrees of the Aspect, I judge 4. years (*a tempore inceptionis*) to determine the discovery of these grand Machivillians. And herein I point at men, or the like in generalls, and not aime at any in particular; whether man or woman, both are guilty. Adde 23. years to 1618. which answers the 13. *December*, and it answers to 1641. The Comet then, had 53 degrees of Northern Declination, and was Verticall over most of our inland Counties of *England*, *viz.* *Leicestershire*, *Northamptonshire*, *Rutlandshire*, *Nottinghamshire*, *Warwick*, *Derby*, and *Stafford*, and many adjacent Counties, which have more then fifty one, and lesse then fifty four degrees of North Latitude: Did not our miseries steale upon us, and the cursed rebellion of the *Irish* begin 23. *October* 1641. And did not many of our inland Connties begin to smart: But to see how God concatenateth worldly affairs with Cœlestiall apparitions: All *January* 1641, *Stilo Anglicano*, was full of fears, mistrusts, jealousies, and what not: for then *Mars* by Transit, passed the ninth degree of *Sagittarius*, directly opposite to the place of the *Sun* Eclipsed 1639. and in that degree of *Sagittarius* he was in perfect square to *Saturn* in the ninth degree of *Pisces*: So that at one time, and in one day, the two unfortunate Planets beheld themselves with *Quadrat* Aspect, and the one by *Opposition*, and *Saturn* by *Quadrat* the degree Eclipsed 1639. This their *Quadrat* was the first of *January*, at what time, and upon which day, as I remember, or neer it, many Apprentices came to *Westminster*. The tenth of *January* His Majestie wen to *Hampton* Court, but returned not to this day: The eleventh of *January* 3000. *Buckinghamshire* men, came in behalf of themselves and their honest

honest Countrey-man *John Hambden* Esquire. The 18. of *January* the *Essex* men came in abundance to *London.* Ten Bishops were questioned in Parliament, for now both the Comet passed the ninth in the Radix, and also the Eclips in 1639. was in great force.

When the Comet had been observed 24. dayes, and cut the 20. degree of *Virgo*, which was on the 24. of *December* 1618. and in proportion of time, points out 1642. having then 55. degrees of Northern Declination, it became perpendicular or verticall to *Yorkshire*, part of *Lincolnshire*, Bishoprick of *Durham*, *Lancashire*, *Cheshire*, *Westmerland*, *Cumberland*, *Northumberland* and *Wales*: whether those Countreys then suffered, and were quiet, let the *English*, whom it most concerns, judge. From those Countreys especially, proceeded that Army of men wherewith his Majestie gave battell to the valiant Patron of his oppressed Countrey *Robert* Earle of *Essex*; I am not certain, if any got by that field, the losse fell upon His Majestie, by losing some thousands of *English* men; for not a man, or youth perished, whose King and Soveraign he was not, and of whom he might not have expected better service against the inhumane *Irish*; and therefore I use to say, when I hear His Majesties forces have killed so many of the Parliaments, That His Majestie hath still the worst, for he hath a speciall interest in the life or death of any that is slain, or otherwaies perisheth; and when we are all killed, by these unkind divisions, if it happen His Majestie, or his posterity to survive, Over whom shall He, or they raign? The earth is the same, but where, or whither are the men gone? Queen *Elizabeth* was used to say, She would beleeve nothing against the meanest of her Subjects, which a father would not against his child. By these her loving words, and actions answerable to her promises, she was really Queen of *England*, and *English*-men, but I transgresse too farre; One *William Cecill* now at Court, was to be prized at as great a rate as the Horse *Richard* the third cried for, at the losse of his Crown and Kingdom in *Leicestershire*.

According to the former proportion of time, let us observe what part of *Virgo* the Comet cut the 15. of *December* 1618. and wee shall find it was the 18. of *Virgo*, almost the degree of the ninth House at the Comets apparition, and of the Ascendent the postventionall full-Moon; Did not our Parliament, and also the Synod of Divines for Reformation concur, and also put in action their agreement, by discussing points of doubt in Doctrin and Ceremony, the year 1643. for if wee adde 25. years to 1618. doth not the Comet then cut the degree of the ninth House, by which Religion is principally signified; the Comet had then 56. degrees, and 40. minutes of Northern Declination, and then became Verticall to that part of *England*, and *Scotland* which lieth betwixt *York* and *Edinborough*, and to *Edinborough*, and somewhat beyond it; I pray God no trouble or disturbance may arise in that Kingdom, or in those parts, this year 1643. perhaps it may be retarded untill 1644. or 1645. how ever *Mars* in *Gemini*, in the *figura mundi*, portends much warre and bloudshed in the West part of *England*.

When *Scotland*, and our Northern Countries have had their share, the effects of this Comet must go farther Northward, it cannot leave that wise Nation without trouble; The Comet worketh slowly, but it failes no where; *Quaecunque lentius operantur, diutius protrahunt suos effectus, neque enim delitescere vis syderis potest nec aboleri. Card. Seg. 1. Aph. 55.* Those Stars, or Comets that work gently or slowly, protract their effects the longer; for the efficacy, or operation of a Star can neither be obscured, or abolished.

The 16. of *December* 1618. the Comet had appeared 26. dayes, answering to 26. years, and our 1644. The Comet then passed the 14. degree, and 40. minutes of *Virgo*, the place of *Mars*, at the Comets appearance. The year 1644. by the *figura mundi*, and the potency of *Mars* in *Aquarius*, and the whole Figure, and his opposition to the Moon in the tenth House, is probably like to bee very full of action, and many battells to bee fought in the North, and North-west of *England*; and so also South-West, and full West from *London*, &c. Both the Comet, and the *figura mundi* signifie the year to bee extream ill. &c. And it threatens the death of a great Queen, or Lady, and also of an Ecclesiasticall person, and persons; nay it portends sudden death to some great King, or Prince; God blesse His Majesty of *England*, &c. The Pope can find no leasure to die.

When the Comet cut the 14. degree and 40. minutes of *Virgo*, it had 58. degrees and 10. minutes of Northern Declination; If *Denmark*, *Norway* and some parts of *Swethland*, have so much Northern Latitude, as it is most certain they have, then may they expect the same proportion, and trouble, at home, and abroad, both in warre, and its subsequents that their neighbour Countreys undergo; for 1644. it will bee Verticall to *Denmark*, *Norway*, and some other Countreys subject to the *Dane*, and to *Swethland* and its Territories, as also to some Confines of the *Polacks*, and *Muskovites*: The excursion of the *Tartar* into *Poland*, or *Walogalia*, *Muscovia* may be feared

the

the year 1644. and the *Turks*, or some others into *Germany*, or his Confines.

The 17. of *December* 1618. which was 27. dayes after the Comets visibility, and in measure of time answers 1645. the Comet cut the 11. grad. and 10. minutes of *Virgo*, and had 59. degrees and 35. minutes of Northern Declination. It will then be Verticall to those Tracts of Land which have so much Latitude Northerly, and they are some parts of *Muscovia*, adjoyning to the *Crimensian Tartar*, and that part of *Tartaria*, where the *Mordway Tartar* liveth, or to any Region habitable, that lieth under the same Paralell, or Latitude: Let those Princes living there, look both to the *Turk* and *Tartar*: for the time hastens, the enemy approaches.

The 18. of *Dececember* 1618. answering our 1646. the Comet entred, or passed the 7. degree and 45. minutes of *Virgo*, having 61. grades of North Declination from the *Æquator*; It then became Verticall to those people that have or live under the Elevation of the Pole 61. *viz. Finland*, and then to *Swethland* it self, and those that inhabite near the *Baltique Sea*; *Livonia* may begin the Dance, allotted for beginning those remote peoples troubles: After 28. dayes, neither did Doctor *Bainbridge*, or *Langomontanus* observe, or could have sight of the Comet any more; So that if we find my measure of time to hit right, then the effects signified by that Comet, shall have no conclusion untill 28. years from its first apparition are compleated: now if we adde 28. to 1618. it will be in the year 1646. but I rather say, 1647, before the generall calamity threatned by that Comet in 1618. shall surcease.

I have no president from Astrology, that hath guided my fancy, to give for every day of the Comets appearance, one year in measure of time. When *Olaus* the *Dane*, wrote of the Comet in 1585. and came to write of the time, when, and how long the events should continue; *Ab Astrologis hac doctrina sufficienter non sit declarata.* This Doctrin (quoth he) is not sufficiently handled of Astrologers: Being therefore doubtfull of the successe of my precedent judgement, I laid aside my foule papers, and went to St. *Peters* at *Westminster*, the last Wednesday in *April* 1643. to hear the Fast Sermon preached before the Parliament. One Master *Greenall*, or *Greenhill*, a learned Gentleman, amongst many observations said; *That God had often warned us of these times, by his Ministers, and by signes from heaven; and in particular, by that Comet in* 1618. *whose effects, he said, would continue, from the time of its beginning* 28. *years, as one* Herlicius *wrote*: This

Herlicius, or any of his works I never saw, (but I understand that he was a *Dane*, and wrote *Almanacks*) His, *viz.* Master *Greenhills*, words gave me incouragement, so that I conceived, I was not single in my judgement, and thereupon I collected my dispersed Papers, and put them into that form, thou that readest these Lines, dost see.

The tail of this Comet, all the time of its being, pointed out the West, and North-west parts of the World; if we beleeve *Charles Piso* the *French* Physician: *Cæterum quibus locis minitentur & intentent effectus suos, ostendunt Zodiaci partes sub quibus collectæ ipsæ & incensæ, primum exarserint: tum inclinationes comarum crinitæ pro ratione formæ, Ptolomeus lib. 2. fol.* 103. *Quadripartiti.* What places are principally threatned, and intended to feel the Comets influence, the parts of the *Zodiack* where first the matter was collected, and appeared, do manifest: as also the inclinations of the scattered haires, according to the form of the Comet. *Austria* certainly, the seat of the *Roman* Empire, was chiefly pointed out by the Comet, to be either the seat of war, or the place from whence much mischief should come. The passage of this Comet through the forms of the fixed Stars is most to bee admired, and wanted nothing but a tongue, and an audible voice to expresse articulately the ends why God did illuminate the same.

The generation of this Comet in *Scorpio*, under the Sun-beames, did plainly expresse, and shadow out unto us Virulent and Scorpion-like Counsels, and Confederacies of those who in the 19. chap. of the *Revelation* are described to have the faces of men, but the stings of Scorpions in their tails; I mean, the Jesuites, and Legates of the Pope, out of whose mouth they are sent, and by their Vow of mission are bound to go, whither he shall send them, and to execute whatsoever he shall employ them in: Being in this Emblematicall generation of the Comet, described to lurk in the Courts of Kings, and Emperours (as it were under the Sun-beams) thereby more importunately to solicite and incense them to take any opportunity to sting and extinguish such as professe the true Protestant Religion in their Dominions. Do Kings and Princes harbour such monsters, and will not beleeve it: will they not beleeve there are Bees in the Hive, unlesse they feele their sting first? when they are undone, and their Kingdoms, and Subjects destroyed, some belief will bee given to what I write, but *Post est occasio calva*; The axe is laid to the root, a few more blows cuts down the Tree: but this is *Ænigma*: *Semper autem videntur, quæ contra ordinem signorum feruntur, mutationem legis significare*;

nificare; quod motus is primi cœli sit. atque ob id a Deo vel supremo Rectore; leges autem permissione Dei sunt habitus vero ad solem declarat ipsius effectus initium: nam si orientalis extiterit Cometa, brevi initium est habiturus effectus. Cardanus 272. lib. 2. Ptol. Its ever observed, those Comets which move in a Retrograde course, do signifie the mutation of Lawes; because that motion is of the first Heaven, and therefore from God, or some supream Rector of our Affairs, (perhaps he means, the Planetary Angel presiding at this time) but Laws are by permission of God: the habit of the Comet to the Sun, shews his beginning to be quick and sudden, if hee be Orientall, &c. And so it was, for *Matthias* the Emperour survived not the Comet three Moneths: He had the 16. of *Scorpio* the Ascendent in his Nativity; he lived when the Comet blazed, but when the Comet cut the 16. of *Scorpio* he sickned, and not long after died: the Empresse died a little before, so did Queen *Anne*, in *Anno* 1619. and yet Comets have nothing to do with Princes, or signifie any thing, as some erroniously hold.

As the Comet first appeared in *Scorpio*, and was disposed by *Mars*; *Multos labores in genere hominum, inter principes contentiones gravissimas iras inter populares; summorum virorum mortem, inopiam & caritatem Annonæ, metum bellorum, regum furorem & ab illis multorum defectionem, non sine civili motu & intestinis cædibus. Mizaldus in Cometog. lib. 2. fol.* 179.

Many shall be the labours of mankind, (when a Comet is in *Scorpio*) fearfull dissention betwixt Princes, tumults amongst the vulgar, the death of Prime, and Eminent men, scarsity and dearnesse of provision, fear of warres, the anger of Princes, much defection from them by their Subjects, not without civill discord, and intestine slaughter. As the Comet passed through *Libra*; *Mortem principum in tractu occiduo, cædes occultas cum conjuratione formidandas, censiis plurimorum jacturam*: If the Comet passe through *Libra*, Princes of the West part of the World shall die, fearfull murders occultly carried, and mens estates consumed they know not how. The Comets passage through *Virgo*; *Mercatoribus damnum, & mutuas inter homines injurias cum omni injustitia, nec non virorum proborum vexationem & captivitates indicere plurimum solet. Nec in armorum strepitu otiosa erit & principum cæde. Mizaldus in Comet. fol.* 168. The Comets passage through the signe of *Virgo*, (who Enigmatically represents Religion and Justice, under whose title the Church and Spouse of Christ is figured) and over whom the Comets tail did bow

five

five dayes, intimates that for some years the Church of Christ should be afflicted by the Pope, Emperour, King of *Spain*, and others Jesuitically addicted; But when the Church hath over-passed those afflictions, they shall fear no more persecutions to follow, but enjoy a perpetuall peace and tranquillity in this world. It further denotes, that the industrious Marchant shall make ill Voyages, and men shall prosecute each other with all kind of injustice; good men shall bee vexed, and imprisoned; a rumour and fear of warre to no purpose; but great persons made away suddenly. Let us observe Historically, if these axoimes of the learned, have not been true in our age, and Common-wealth.

From the time of the Comets appearance, which was 1618. untill it became Verticall to *England*, which was 1639. wee did not miserably suffer; but all men know, matter hath been preparing for these very times ever since: How did the *English* groan under the pressures of the Monopolists, about 1618. 1619. and 1620. How much treasure did we spend, and how much disgrace was it, that simple employment to *Algiers*, in the latter end of King *James* his raign, our brave Sea-men, and the brave spirited Sir *Robert Mansell*, muzled up with a blank Commission: To number the Sea-men captivated in those times, or recount the unvaluable losse of the *London* Marchants, were *Infandum renovare dolorem*; tears, but not words best expresse it; And immediately, or few years after, the Conjunction of *Saturn* and *Jupiter* in 1623. wee lost King *James*, whose raigne was spent in peace; what a monstrous plague afflicted the City of *London* that year 1625. and all, or the most part of the Kingdome the next year; Now, or near this time, was our unfortunate attempt to relieve *Rochell*, after our owne Ships had undone them, and then we fight in the mud at the Isle of *Rees*, where wee lost the best men we had then living, not in fight, but by treachery in the Ouse and Dirt, &c.

The destruction of the *Rochellers*, and in them of the Protestant party in *France*, and the innocent bloud of that Protestant party, cries aloud to heaven for vengeance against the Authour, and procurer of their finall destruction: A City, Queen *Elizabeth* loved; nor did the victorious *Henry* the fourth King of *France* distast it. To this day, the *Rochellers* beleeve *Buckingham* was the Authour of their undoing; Was he so? He was exceedingly to be commended, for advancing his kindred; but in this, he hath left a blemish to his posterity, which time will not wipe off, and yet I really beleeve, it was not so much

hee

hee as that Jesuiticall counsell too conversant with him; How ever, he was the first on whom all Laws depended, for the Laws speak nothing, but what he and his Parasites would have them say; and had not an untimely death swept his Ambition away, we had questionlesse ere this been contented slaves, or imbrued our hands in each others bloud. But there's a Yeomanry of *England*, indures no slavery, its hard to root it out, they breed their sonns excellently well, and its an ill bird defiles his owne nest; their sonnes prove excellent Lawyers, and best know the estate of every County they live in; are a valiant and discreet people: of this the Duke thought not of, nor the reverend, but unfortunate, *William Laud*, Archbishop of *Canterbury*, in all his undertakings; nor *Thomas* Earl of *Arundell*, in his mercilesse Court of Honour, the Advocates abusing that honourable man; where it was a greater offence to call an idle Gentleman a Knave, (when perhaps one might have added, Thief, and Beggar) then to have stollen an Ox, and answered the Indictment at Sessions: But I digresse, and doubt not but to live, and see vengeance in full measure powred and distributed upon him, them, and their families, that had any hand in furthering the oppression of the *Rochellers*, and the poor *French* Protestants, or in the miserable losse of the 12000. men Count *Mansfield* had.

All our Parliaments have been unluckely, and by sinister Counsels dissolved, since 1625. what reason can be given, none certainly; onely it pleased a prevailing faction to cloud His Majesties grace from his Subjects, rendring him unkind, but themselves worse then *Achitophel*. Were not many of our brave Gentlemen, whom their Countrey sent up for the Publique benefit imprisoned? Did not some die in prison, Gallant men, of the House of Commons, of the representative Body of the Kingdom? Oh *Elliot*, well spoken, Sir *John Elliot*, I ever expected the unmercifull usage of thee in the Towre, should be returned, and the same mercy (which was none at all) inflicted upon every private Counsellor, or Actor in thy miseries; they that advised thy strict indurance, neither of God or man deserve favour: what was done to thee, had it been possible, should have been inflicted upon the whole Comminalty of *England*: But *Elliot* is dead, his death will have no nay, no mercy on his offenders, or afflictors: Others suffered also: But to the Comet. How many Noble men suddenly died? Who knew the disease, whereof either the Honourable *Lodowick* Duke of *Richmond*, or the very Noble *Marquesse Hamilton* died; and how suddenly was valiant *Oxford*, the

Heroick

Heroick Earle of *Southampton*, and his valiant son, and many other men of excellent birth and Nobility, taken from us: We have had many Princes in the West part of the world, dead since the Comets appearance, many a dear yeer; Wheat I have seen at 12 shillings a bushell; honest preaching Ministers, I have seen captivated and oppressed; enforced to fly into forraigne Countries, or else silenced; I have seen the Laws speak, not law, but fancy: I wish there had been no errour in the Clergie; Their pride began when the Dean of *Westminster* was made Lord Keeper; *William Laud* Archbishop of *Canterbury* augmented their insolency: not a Sexton must sweep the Church unlesse put in by the Parson: a Vestery is no Vestery unlesse he confirmed it: Parochiall priviledges and customes were invalid, notwithstanding antiquity and personall oathes of as good mens sons as himself, confirmed the truth thereof.

Richlieu of *France* was the onely wise Courtier and Clergie man that ever lived.

While *Finch* was Lord chiefe Justice of the *Common Pleas*, to obtaine a Prohibitian, was an Herculean task, yet Justice *Hutton* in his absence would do it: such times, such Officers. But I am too tedious, yet let me be excused, sith I do it not to blemish any man, or to cast a false aspersion upon the honour of any one: I repeate these things onely to make the Cometary *Aphorismes* better understood, and to shew their verity, I might be more copious, but should I so do, I might the more offend, and therefore I conclude what I intend to speak of the Comets effects, unlesse occasionally a word or two hereafter drop from my pen; this which is wrote will give the more light to the succeeding discourse, which now orderly follows.

The effects of the present Conjunction prosecuted.

BEfore I speak of this *Conjunction*, by some (falsely) called great I must acquaint you with that *Aphorisme* of *Ptolomy, viz.* 50. *Ne preteremittas centum & viginti conjunctiones; In his enim posita est cognitio eorum quæ fiunt in mundo & generationis & corruptionis*: In your generall judgement passe not over the 120. *Conjunctions*: For the knowledge of Mundane affaires is posited therein, as well of generation as corruption: that which I now handle is the first in order of the 120 but because few there are that understand *Aphorisme*, or what those one hundred and twenty *Conjunctions* are, I will orderly in a subsequent Table put them down, as also the dignities and debilities of all the seven Planets in this present *Conjunction*, 164$\frac{2}{3}$.

The

The Dignities of the Planets in the Conjunction, 1 6$\frac{11}{41}$.

Saturn *his Fortitudes.*		*Debilities of* Saturn	
Free from Combustion.	5	Occidentall.	2
Direct in Motion.	4	Peregrine.	5
Increasing in Number.	2	Diminishing in light.	2
In *Conjunction* with *Jupiter*.	5	In Termes of *Mars*.	2
Swift in Motion	2		
In reception of *Venus*.	4		11
In the second House.	2		
	24		
Jupiter *his Fortitudes.*		Jupiter *his Debilities.*	
In his own House.	5		
Free from Combustion.	5	Occidentall.	2
Direct in Motion.	4	Diminishing light.	2
Increasing Number.	2	In Termes of *Mars*.	2
Swift in Motion.	2	In *Conjunction* with *Saturn*.	5
In second House.	2		11
	20		
Mars *his Fortitudes.*		Mars *his Weaknesse.*	
Free from Combustion.	5	Occidentall.	2
Direct	4	Slow in Motion,	2
In the fifth House	3	Peregrine.	5
	12		9
Sol *his Fortitudes.*		Sol *his Debilities.*	
Swift in motion.	2	Peregrine.	5
In the 2°.	2	Face of *Saturn*.	1
In Termes of *Venus*.	2		
	6		6
Venus *her Fortitudes.*		Venus *her Debilities.*	
Free from Combustion.	5	Retrograde.	5
In the 2. House.	2	Slow in Motion.	2
In Termes of *Jupiter*.	2	Face of *Mars*.	1
	9	Orientall.	2
			10

Mercury *his Dignities.*		Mercury *his Debilities.*	
Swift in Motion	2	In Detriment	5
Occidentall	2	*Sub Radiis*	4
In the second	2		
Direct	4		
Face of *Jupiter*	1		
	11		9

Luna *her Fortitudes.*		Luna *her Debilities.*	
Free from Combustion	5	Peregrine	5
Increasing in light	2	Slow in Motion	2
In Termes of *Venus*	2	In 6 House	3
		Face of *Mars*	1
	9		11

Latitude of the Planets.

Saturn,	2. *deg.*	6. *min.*	M. D.
Jupiter,	1.	6.	M. D.
Mars,	1.	41.	S. D.
Venus,	7.	28.	S. D.
Mercury,	1.	11.	M. D.
Luna,	4.	34.	M. D.

The Diurnall Motion of the Planets.

Saturn,	7. *min.*
Jupiter,	14.
Mars,	31.
Sol,	1. *deg.* 13. *seconds.*
Venus,	26. *min.*
Mercury,	1. *deg.* 55. *min.*
Luna,	11. *deg.* 57. *min.*

The Antiscia of the Planets.

Saturn,	4. *deg.*	34. *min.*	*Libra.*
Jupiter,	4.	34.	*Libra.*
Mars,	28.	52.	*Cancer.*
Sol,	22.	26.	*Libra.*
Venus,	7.	14.	*Scorpio.*
Mercury,	14.	14.	*Libra.*
Luna,	14.	58.	*Cancer.*

Contrantiscias.

Saturn, Jupiter,	4.	34.	*Aries.*
Mars,	28.	52.	*Capricor.*
Sol,	22.	26.	*Aries.*
Venus,	7.	14.	*Taurus.*
Mercury,	14.	14.	*Aries.*
Luna,	14.	58.	*Capric.*

Saturn hath Fortitudes	13	*Venus* hath Fortitudes	1
Jupiter hath	9	*Mercury* hath	2
Mars hath	3	*Luna* hath Debilities	2
Sol hath no Dignities.			

The

The 120. Conjunctions in Ptolomey, Aphoris. 50°.

2
♄ ♃
♄ ♂
♄ ☉
♄ ♀
♄ ☿
♄ ☽
♃ ♂
♃ ☉
♃ ♀
♃ ☿
♃ ☽
♂ ☉
♂ ♀
♂ ☿
♂ ☽
☉ ♀
☉ ☿
☉ ☽
♀ ☿
♀ ☽
☿ ☽
21

3
♄ ♃ ♂
♄ ♃ ☉
♄ ♃ ♀
♄ ♃ ☿
♄ ♃ ☽
♄ ♂ ☉
♄ ♂ ♀
♄ ♂ ☿
♄ ♂ ☽
♄ ☉ ♀
♄ ☉ ☿
♄ ☉ ☽
♄ ♀ ☿
♄ ♀ ☽
♄ ☿ ☽
♃ ♂ ☉
♃ ♂ ♀
♃ ♂ ☿
♃ ♂ ☽
♃ ☉ ♀
♃ ☉ ☿
♃ ☉ ☽
♃ ♀ ☿
♃ ♀ ☽
♃ ☿ ☽
♂ ☉ ♀
♂ ☉ ☿
♂ ☉ ☽
♂ ♀ ☿
♂ ♀ ☽
♂ ☿ ☽
☉ ♀ ☿
☉ ♀ ☽
☉ ☿ ☽
♀ ☿ ☽
35

4
♄ ♃ ♂ ☉
♄ ♃ ♂ ♀
♄ ♃ ♂ ☿
♄ ♃ ♂ ☽
♄ ♃ ☉ ♀
♄ ♃ ☉ ☿
♄ ♃ ☉ ☽
♄ ♃ ♀ ☿
♄ ♃ ♀ ☽
♄ ♃ ☿ ☽
♄ ♂ ☉ ♀
♄ ♂ ☉ ☿
♄ ♂ ☉ ☽
♄ ♂ ♀ ☿
♄ ♂ ♀ ☽
♄ ♂ ☿ ☽
♄ ☉ ♀ ☿
♄ ☉ ♀ ☽
♄ ☉ ☿ ☽
♄ ♀ ☿ ☽
♃ ♂ ☉ ♀
♃ ♂ ☉ ☿
♃ ♂ ☉ ☽
♃ ♂ ♀ ☿
♃ ♂ ♀ ☽
♃ ♂ ☿ ☽
♃ ☉ ♀ ☿
♃ ☉ ♀ ☽
♃ ☉ ☿ ☽
♃ ♀ ☿ ☽
♂ ☉ ♀ ☿
♂ ☉ ♀ ☽
♂ ☉ ☿ ☽
♂ ♀ ☿ ☽
☉ ♀ ☿ ☽
35

5
♄ ♃ ♂ ☉ ♀
♄ ♃ ♂ ☉ ☿
♄ ♃ ♂ ☉ ☽
♄ ♃ ♂ ♀ ☿
♄ ♃ ♂ ♀ ☽
♄ ♃ ♂ ☿ ☽
♄ ♃ ☉ ♀ ☿
♄ ♃ ☉ ♀ ☽
♄ ♃ ☉ ☿ ☽
♄ ♃ ♀ ☿ ☽
♄ ♂ ☉ ♀ ☿
♄ ♂ ☉ ♀ ☽
♄ ♂ ☉ ☿ ☽
♄ ♂ ♀ ☿ ☽
♄ ☉ ♀ ☿ ☽
♃ ♂ ☉ ♀ ☿
♃ ♂ ☉ ♀ ☽
♃ ♂ ☉ ☿ ☽
♃ ♂ ♀ ☿ ☽
♃ ☉ ♀ ☿ ☽
♂ ☉ ♀ ☿ ☽
21

6
♄ ♃ ♂ ☉ ♀ ☿
♄ ♃ ♂ ☉ ♀ ☽
♄ ♃ ♂ ☉ ☿ ☽
♄ ♃ ♂ ♀ ☿ ☽
♄ ♃ ☉ ♀ ☿ ☽
♄ ♂ ☉ ♀ ☿ ☽
♃ ♂ ☉ ♀ ☿ ☽
7

7
♄ ♃ ♂ ☉ ♀ ☿ ☽
1

It is time I enter upon judgement, which I would willingly do, but that in prosecution hereof I must first explain some curiosities, not vulgar to many English Astrologers; my intention after that being to proceed methodically:

First of the Agent, *viz.* a *Conjunction* of *Saturn* and *Jupiter.*

Secondly, the Patient or subject matter in which the Events shall happen.

Thirdly, the place, Countries, or Kingdomes, the events shall appeare in.

Fourthly, the space of time the effects shall continue.

Fifthly, the nature of those effects, whether good or evill.

Some reduce all to this Latine Verse,

> *Cur? ubi, seu quando, quibus & quid provenit do:* others thus,
> *Ubi, quando, in quo genere rerum: cujusmodi.*

Where? when? in what kinde of things? the nature and quality, *viz.* good or ill.

Of the Agent, viz. *a Conjunction of* Saturn *and* Jupiter.

Those that are not versed in Astrologie must know, that *Saturn* and *Jupiter* are the two chiefest Planets, and do once, and but once in 20. years, or more truely in 19. yeares, 318. dayes and twelve houres, come to *Conjunction* in some one of the twelve signes; when they are both in one signe, degree, and minute of that signe, then they are said to be in *Conjunction.*

They do also usually make ten severall meetings or *Conjunctions* in signes of the like nature, called a Trigon, Triplicity, or Triangularity; these ten *Conjunctions* they perform in 198. years, 265. dayes, &c. and then they desert that Trygon, and fall to their *Conjunctions* in the subsequent in an orderly processe, as out of the fiery Triangularity into the earthly, &c.

The ancients formerly wanting those exact Tables the latter ages have produced, were of opinion that *Saturn* and *Jupiter* might and did make 12. and sometimes thirteen *Conjunctions* in one Triplicity, of which minde was *Guido Bonatus, Albumazar, Abraham Avenaris, Alcabitius, Haly Rodoan,* and many others. The reason of their mistake was, because they did proportion eight signes, two degrees, and

and thirty minutes, to be the true processe of *Saturn* and *Jupiter*, betwixt one *Conjunction* and another, *viz.* if at their leaving of the watry Triplicity, they first met by *Conjunction* in no degrees of *Aries*; by adding 8. signes, 2. *grad.* and 30. *minuts*, in their next *Conjunction* they should meete in the second degree and 30. minutes of *Sagittarius*, for so many signes, degrees and minuts it is from 00'. 00'. *Aries* If to 2. *grads*, and 30' of *Sagittarius* you againe adde 8. signes, 2. *grad.* and 30. *min.* the third *Conjunction* in the fiery Triplicity shall be in the fifth degree of *Leo*, and so you should do in all the rest. By this account, the two superious must make 12. *Conjunctions* in each Triplicity, or ever they could go through the 3 Signes of that Trygon.

For if you multiply 20. *viz.* the space of time betwixt *Conjunction* and *Conjunction* by 12. *viz.* the number of *Conjunctions*, they will produce 240. for the measure of time, or the revolution of the two Planetary *Conjunctions* in one *Trygon*, and then it will be 960. years, ere they compleatly finish their severall *Conjunctions* in the foure Triplicities, for if you multiply 240. by 4. the number of *Trigons*, it makes the result 960.

But this *Hypothesis* is fals, for the modern Calculators do say, and that with more verity, That the years betwixt one *Conjunction* and another, are nineteen, 318. dayes and twelve houres: so that the two superiours come to *Conjunction* 47. dayes, and some houres sooner then former Astrologers conceived: and the processe of degrees they run from one *Conjunction* to another, is not so little as 8. signes, 2. *grad.* and 30. *minutes*, but somewhat more, *viz.* 242. *grad.* 59. *m.* 9. *seconds* or 8. *signes*, 2. *grads*, 59. *min.* and 9. *seconds*, which is 19. *min.* more than the Ancients allowed. And yet I do not finde that this manner of proportion doth exactly concur in that *Conjunction* of *Saturn* and *Jupiter* in 1603. 14. *Decemb.* at what time by *Origanus Saturn* and *Jupiter* were in *Conjunction* in 9. *s.* 36. *m. Sagittarius.* Let us make experience for example sake: If I adde to 1603. 19. years, it brings me to 1622. the 14. of *Decemb.* being a Common yeere is the 348. day of the yeer, to which if I adde 318. dayes, the number allowed more then 19. years, it makes 666. dayes, from which if I substract 365. the complement of a whole year, there remains 301, for the day wherein, according to the rule aforesaid, the second *Conjunction* should happen, *viz.* 27. day of *October* 1623. the *Conjunction* of *Saturn* and *Jupiter* was by *Origanus* his Calculation, the eight day of *July* 1623: one hundred and eleven dayes sooner: but let us examine the signe and degres of the two former *Conjunctions* by adding eight signes 59. *min.*

 to

to the signe and degree of the *Conjunction* in 1603. Place of the *Conjunction* after 8. Signes, 9. *grad.* and 36. *minutes* of *Sagittarius*:

Sign. 8.	*grad.* 9.	*min.* 36.	
Sign. 8.	*grad.* 2.	*min.* 59.	
Sum.	16.	12.	35.

From 16. signes being more then the	*Sig.* 16.	12. *grad.*	35. *min.*
Zodiack, I substract the whole	*Sig.* 12.	00. *grad.*	00. *min.*
Circle, and there remaines ————	04.	12.	35.

By this reckoning the *Conjunction* in 1623. should have been in the 132. *grad.* of the *Zodiack*, or after, 4. signes, and so in 12. *grad*, 35. *min.* of *Leo*, for *Aries*, *Taurus*, *Gemini*, *Cancer*, being numbred *Leo* succeeds; but the true *Conjunction* according to *Kepler*, was in 6 *grad.* 45. of *Leo*; and so also by *Origanus*.

By meanes of this addition of so many Signes, it came to passe that *Alstedius* did mistake, when he said in *Thesauro Chronologiæ*, *fol.* 482. *Anno* 164$\frac{3}{4}$. *Accidet Conjunctio*, Saturni & Jovis *in Ariete*, (the *Conjunction* was in *Pisces*) *quæ portendit novi alicujus imperii revolutionem.* In the year 164$\frac{3}{4}$ there shall happen a great *Conjunction* of ♄ and ♃ in *Aries*, which portends a Revolution of some new Monarchy.

That excellent Mathematician *Kepler* did also, by some such rule without further Calculation, say the same in: *Lib.* 2°. *Epito. Astronomiæ*, *fol.* 188. *Anno* 1603. *Coiverunt* Saturnus & Jupiter *in* Sagittario, *Anno* 1623. *in Leone. Anno* 1643. *in Ariete*; *Anno* 1663. *in* Sagittario: *Saturn* and *Jupiter* made *Conjunction* in 1603. in *Sagittary*. In 1623 in *Leone*. In 1643. they meet in *Ariete*: and in one thousand six hundred sixty three in *Sagittario*, &c.

I have the rather been tedious herein, to shew that there is not any certain rule can be made, whereby without Calculation the true *Conjunction* of *Saturn* and *Jupiter* may be had, for there will be variation in degrees, if no worse errour happen. The best Tables now extant are *Keplers*, I conceive them to be so exact, as its possible for the Art of man to frame, and they perform the motion of the Planets with much verity, being handled by an able Artist: to conclude then I say, as ten times two degrees, make 20. degrees, and ten times 59'. doth make ten degrees wanting ten minuts; nay not so much, because ten time nine *seconds* make 90. *seconds*, a minute and a half, all these put together make up, 29. *deg.* 51. *min.* 30. *seconds*. Therefore this being the Complement of a Signe, the two superiours can make but 10. *Conjunction* in one *Trygon*, and no more, &c.

When

When one of the Conjunctions of Saturn *and* Jupiter *is called greatest, great, mean or the least.*

THe latter Astrologers, as *Cardan, Naibod, Origanus, Haghen,* and since their death, *Campanella* say, That there are three kinds of *Conjunctions,* which in Latine they tearm *Maximam, viz.* the greatest: *Mediam, viz.* the mean or middle: *Minimam, viz.* the least of all. *Maximæ vero Conjunctiones appellantur, quæ in Trigono igneo fieri incipiunt, inprimis Ariete, primo Zodiaci signo; Cum enim in illis ex aqueo in igneum signum, quæ qualitatibus primis sibi maximé adversantur transitu fiat, maximæ quoque mutationes in illis temporibus in toto mundo accidunt, Orig. fol. introduct.* 449. They are called the greatest *Conjunctions* which begin in the fiery Trygon, and especially in *Aries,* the first signe of the *Zodiack;* for when a Transit is made out of the watry Triplicity into a fiery signe, which are contrary to each other in their first qualities, then are there in the whole world the greatest mutations and alterations, &c.

And that this is the true sense of all Authors, *viz.* that that onely *Conjunction* is called *Maxima* or *Magna,* and no other, which is the first *Conjunction Saturn* and *Jupiter* make in the fiery Trygon, and especially in *Aries,* I prove by many examples. *Alcabitius, diff.* 4. *Major autem omnibus Conjunctionibus est Conjunctio* Saturni *&* Jovis *in initio Arietis.* The *Conjunction* of *Saturn* and *Jupiter* in the beginning of *Aries,* is greater than all the other *Conjunctions*; of which opinion is *Naibod, fol.* 353. *In Com. sup: Alcab. Etenim prima, omniumque maxima* Saturni *scilicet &* Jovis *Conjunctio in principio Arietis celebrata, tempora generaliter disponere videtur.* The first *Conjunction* of *Saturn* and *Jupitir* celebrated in the beginning of *Aries,* seemes generally to dispose of the times, and of all *Conjunctions* is the greatest. *Maxima conjunctio dicitur cum permutando se ex aqueo, signo Arietem ingreditur:* Its called the greatest Conjunction, when the change is out of a watry signe into *Aries, Card. Seg.* 1. *Aph.* 67. Of the same judgement is *Johannes de Saxonia:*

Paulus Prassicius sacerdos Aversanus is more plain. *Quod Triplex quum sit* Saturni *&* Jovis Conjunctio, *remotissima illa quæ noningenis annis* (it should be 794. *&* *diebus* 331.) *contingit maxima dicatur; quæ autem per singulos vigenos annos ex quo conjuncti jam fuerint, minima: Atque post singulos feré ducentos & quadragenos circuitus* (vult potius 198. *Annos &* 265. *dies*) *quod inter minimam hanc ac maximam remotissimamque illam contingit, media:* Sith the *conjunction* of *Saturn*

and

and *Jupiter* is threefold, that which is most remote and happens but once in 900. years, is called the greatest (it should have been in 794. and 331. dayes) that which is from the time of their last meeting once in 20. years, is stiled the least: but that which is after a progresse, circuit or compasse of 240. years (it should have been 198. yeares and 261. dayes) and is between as it were the greatest and the lesser, is called a mean or middle *Conjunction*. *Sed Ptolomeus & Haly in Centiloquio & proposit*, 58. *& 64. volunt intelligi per conjunctionem majorem, conjunctionem*, Saturni & Jovis *in Ariete, & media conjunctio eorum est, cum mutatur in novam Triplicitatem, & conjunctio minor cum conjunguntur in reliquis signis. Johannes Anglicus dist.* 2. *fol.* 16. But *Ptolome* and *Haly Rodoan* his Commentator in 58. and 64. proposition, will have us understand by the greater *conjunction* of *Saturn* and *Jupiter*, that it is onely when they enter *Aries*: their mean *conjunction*, when they remove into a new Triplicity, and so the least *conjunction*, when they are joyned together in severall parts of the signes of the same Nature.

Avenaris a learned Jew translated out of *Hebrew* into *Latin* by *Henry Bate* 1281. Shall conclude all, *Conjunctio autem magna* Jovis *est cum* Saturno, *in signo Arietis, quod est, quia sunt stellæ graves & tardæ, & non significant super particularia, imo super communia: & quia signum Arietis est signum primum inter signa, ergo hæc conjunctio vocatur magna, sed quando vadunt a Triplicitate ad triplicitatem, tunc vocatur hæc conjunctio media, conjunctio vero ipsorum de* 20. *in* 20. *Annos in signis Triplicitatis, quæcunque sit illa vocata, est conjunctio minor, Avenaris, fol.* 79. *de conjunctionibus*. But, saith he, the *conjunction* of *Saturn* and *Jupiter* is called great when its in the signe of *Aries*, because they are pondrous and slow Planets, and signifie no small matters, and *Aries* is the first amongst the signes, therefore such a *Conjunction* is called great: and when they remove out of one Triplicity into another, that *conjunction* is called *media* or meane: but their *Conjunction* every 20. yeares in signes of the same Triplicity, be it in what signe it will, it is called the least *Conjunction*, or a lesser and no other, &c.

By what I have collected, I gather thus much, That when the two superiour Planets remove out of the watry Triplicity, and enter the fiery, and do therein make their first *conjunction* in *Aries*, that is, properly by all antiquity called *maxima* or the greatest *Conjunction*, and no other, unlesse improperly was so called, but that: Now if upon their mutation of Triplicity they first convene in *Sagittarius* or *Leo*, as in 1603. their first *Conjunction* was in *Sagittarius*; that *conjunction* may properly be called *Magna*, and was no other, but it had been absurd to have called it *Maxima*, it was a great *Conjunction* because it was their first *Conjunction* in the fiery Trigon and in a fiery regall signe; but it was not *Maxima*, because it was not at that time in *Aries*, which is the first of the *Zodiack*, a Cardinall signe, the house of *Mars*, the exaltation of the *Sun*, a signe where *Jupiter* hath both a Triplicity and a Terme: when they *viz. Saturn* and *Jupiter* leave the fiery, and first meet in the earthly Trygon, be the *conjunction* in what signe it will, it shall be called a mean *conjunction*, all the nine *conjunctions* they make after in that Trygon, are called little ones; in this sense *Alstedius* spoke *fol.* 482. *Chronologia*, and calls the *conjunction* of *Saturn* and *Jupiter* in 1603. *Magnam: Hanc secuta est Anno* 1623. *conjunctio minima Saturni & Jovis in Leone, signo regio & itidem igneo.* After the great *conjunction* of *Saturn* and *Jupiter* in 1603. there followed another little or the lesser *conjunction* of *Saturn* and *Jupiter*, in *Leo*, a Kingly or regall and fiery signe; but whereas he goeth on & saith, *Hujus conjunctionis ignis consumet omnes scorias & faces urbis Romæ*, Anno 1635. *quo ad finem decurret revolutio Romani Imperii sub Trigonis*: That is, the force or fire of this *conjunction* shall destroy all the refuse or dreggs of the City of *Rome*, &c. In this I differ from that learned man, and do say, that By any Constellation I can finde, the overthrow of Popery is not so near, the first beginning of sorrow and disturbance to Popery in *Italy* will be about the year 1654. 1655. or 1656. but not a generall subversion for some ages: neither shall the Empire of *Germany* come to finall period, or the Illustrious house of *Austria* in that measure of time, some have fondly conceived: it will yet hold up his head, but not flowrish in that vigour it hath done many will be the afflictions, losses, and enormities that stately family shall undergo, and that suddenly, but not such as shall bring it to confusion, &c.

I am not ignorant that *Messahalah* a learned *Arabian* thinketh otherwayes of these *conjunctions*, and onely calleth that of *Saturn* and *Jupiter* the greatest, that of *Saturn* and *Mars* the middle or mean *conjunction*, that of *Jupiter* and *Mars* the least *conjunction*, but because all antiquity and reason is against his opinion, and he stands single in that matter, I forbear further answer, and come to the proper nature of each Triplicity, and signe of every Trigon. &c.

You must understand that *Aries*, *Leo*, and *Sagittarius*, make the first Trigon, vulgarly called the regall or fiery Triplicity, *Trigonus hic*

 igneus

igneus est Christianorum : Dasipodius, Aphor. 54. This Trigon represents Christianity, saith he. Those actions performed under the dominion of this Trigon, do farre in honour and glory exceed all the rest: *Conjunctiones in signis igneis, si fiant, tum mundi imperia & monarchia constituuntur propter Solis, & Jovis dominium : qui significant tranquillitatem in mundo, apparent etiam sapientes & insignes viri, magnæ sterilitates propter dominium planetarum calidorum parumque humidorum : Dasipod. Aphor.* 64. If Conjunctions be in fiery Signes then Empires, and Monarchies are erected, because *Sol* and *Jupiter* do rule that Trygon, and they signifie tranquillity in the world; many wise men and famous appear in the world: generally barren years, because the Planets are rather hot and dry, then moist.

Fiery Triplicity.

THe *Aphorisme* is generall, but for the most part, when *Saturn* and *Jupiter* make their first Conjunction in *Aries*, God suddenly raiseth up some new Monarch of great force and command, that by warre, and the destruction of some neighbouring Princes enlargeth his Dominions, and quite destroyeth the former Dominion they had, and the Laws they lived under. For many ages the posterity of this Princely man continues, and rather rules with strict hand, then with a gentle rod, and yet after fourty Conjunctions, his off-spring decayeth in fame and repute, and by little and little diminish, so that in fine, his own Subjects do parcell out his Inheritances, and convert them to their proper uses.

If *Saturn* and *Jupiter* have their first Conjunction in *Leo*, some sturdy Prince, of an *Herculean* Valour, but not *Cressian* Purse, troubles all his Confederates, and all Princes grow favorious, and exercise tyrannie some one thrives, and gets by all his indirect means, yet in the height of all his greatnesse, vanisheth by sudden death, or is much molested by his Vassails, leaving no perfect conquest to his Posterity, who may much brag of a valiant Ancestor, themselves never after performing any service deserving the name of his kindred: That Trygon breeds valiant men, but extreamly unfortunate, and generally under that Trygon, the first position beginning in *Leo*, the evils are fixed, and every Prince doth then vainly conceit of himself to bee the onely *Alexander* for Magnanimity, when as in truth, the perfections of that great man are buried, and these upstarts have but the shadow of him.

If

If the first Conjunction of *Saturn* and *Jupiter* happen in *Sagittarius*, the world seems weary of former warres, and upon small intreaty will be ready to hearken to peace: some ancient family is decaying, and a new one repairing and exalted: an appearance of Schisms, and new Doctrins, but none priviledged by authority: the Church much troubled with curious niceties, men stumbling at straws, and striding over blocks: the majestie of *Jupiter* is such in *Sagittarius*, all things tend to peace, and do the Devill and Jesuits what they can, there will bee tranquillity upon the most parts of Christendom, during the first twenty years of that Trygons government; All the actions of those years ending in Treaties, Leagues, Messages, and the like. Many men will be in hope to aspire to greatnesse, the end crowns onely one. But because *Sagittarius* is a double bodied Signe, two generations passe not without superlative discord to the actions, or beginnings of this Conjunction. Wee must not poize down our judgement with example, lest wee be thought partiall,. Let it passe; I come to the Earthly Triplicity.

Earthly Triplicity.

THe affairs of this world, which most flowrish under the earthly Trygon, or are most principally agitated in the world during these severall Conjunctions in *Taurus*, *Virgo*, and *Capricornus*, are the displacing of unfaithfull, and perfidious Viceroys, Governours of Armies, Towns, Forts, and of all manner of men, of any quality, that are either entrusted by any Emperour, King, Prince, or any Principality, or private State, or that have great Offices under them, and in this generall Catastrophe, they suffer most, whose Ascendents in their Nativities are *Scorpio*, *Cancer*, or *Pisces*.

Then doth it happen, and usually it never failes, but there are great Inundations, Earthquakes, many Comets, and Blazing-stars, much Idolatry, and Superstition in the Religion every people professe: It also commeth to passe, that the Revolution of this Trygon, or during the Conjunctions of *Saturn* and *Jupiter* in *Taurus*, *Virgo*, or *Capricornus*, that, that Kingdom is dissolved and brought to nothing, which had its originall in *Cancer*, *Scorpio*, or *Pisces*. Much famine, and scarcity of provision for man and beast.

If the first Conjunction in this earthly Triplicity, begin in *Taurus*, many stately Palaces, and curious Structures, brave and Princely Monasteries, Noble mens Houses, admirable in Architecture, and delightfull

 lightfull

lightfull in Situation are erected; Men wallow in luxury, and wantonnesse overspreadeth those Climates subject to *Taurus*, or those are the men especially that most actively manage the great affairs of the World: the Husbandman hath many times excellent crops of Corn, but no great successe in his Cattle, the Murrain destroying his bigger Cattle, and the Rot, or such like disease many times the lesser Cattle. I shall relate a story, within the memory of man, out of *Assuerus in Jatromathematicis, fol.* 206. *Refert Diomedes Cornarius, cum Anno* 1598. *&* 1599. *per universam Germaniam quedam boum pestis immaniter grassaretur: ex decreto Archiducis Matthie, a Collegio Medico Viennensis archigymnasii: Que nam tanti contagii causa esset, quesitum fuisse; Medici responderunt communicatis consiliis, Duas potissimum occurrere, unam remotiorem nempe Astrologicam, alteram propriam Physicam, quasi prior non esset vel maxime physica: Astrologicam quidem allegarunt hanc, Quod Anno* 1597. *in Tauro visus esset Cometa, tum etiam Conjunctiones multa in signis ruminantibus; Deinde & hanc addiderunt rationem physicam, quod diuturna precessisset nebulosa cœli constitutio, & humiditates terre ob inundationes inducta; unde pascua infecta essent ex ejusmodi humiditatibus, atque Aer contagiosus redditus ex demortuorum pecorum decubitu. Cedo, vero, lector quis uspiam esse possit tam obtusa ingenii acie, qui non videat hanc posteriorem rationem esse longe communissimam; que si valeat, jam non soles boves, sed & eves, porcos, capras, equos, aliaque id genus animantia communibus & pascuis & Aere utentia, pestis promiscuo corripere debuerit: Consectaneum igitur est, ut quanquam cause illa & pandemie, & endemia, denique & epidemie simpliciter malum auxerint; vera tamen & propria istius pestis in solos boves grassate causa non statuatur, post Deum, alia, quam cœlestis illa a syderum Syzygiis deducta.*

Diomedes Cornerius relateth, That in the years 1598. and 1599. there being an universall Pestilence, which unmercifully consumed the Oxen of *Germany*, the Archduke *Matthias*, commanded the Colledge of Physicians in *Vienna*, to shew the cause thereof. The Physicians returned their answer; That there were two causes, one Astrologicall, but that more remote; the other more near, and that was Physicall; As if the first cause were not more Physicall: They said, The Astrologicall cause was; because in 1597. there was a Comet seen in *Taurus*, and there were also many Conjunctions of the Planets in ruminating signes. (Astrologers call *Aries, Taurus, Capricornus*, signes ruminating, because they represent those creatures that chew the cudd) The Physicall reason the Colledge gave was, That there

there had preceded a cloudy constitution of heaven, and the earth very moist, by reason of inundation of waters; whereby the Pastures were infected with surplusage of moysture, and the ayre made contagious with the death of the dead cattle: Give me leave, Reader, (saith my Author) was ever any man such a blockhead, that perceives not the latter reason to be a common one,&c? Thence it would have proceeded, that not onely Oxen, but Hogs, Sheep, and Horses must have perished with the infection. The true cause therefore, saith *Assuerus*, after God, is no other, then that which is drawn from the Aspects of the Planets, and Constellation of heaven.

If the first Conjunction of *Saturn* and *Jupiter* bee in *Virgo*, the effects materially fall upon men; their quality Kings, and Potentates; much affliction and great dammage to Archbishops, Bishops, Priors, and Clergy men, they are disgraced, and displaced, but for what cause none know; the Civilian and inferiour Lawyer, and many Judges unjustly handled, for *Mercury* having much to do in *Virgo*, he imployes mens wits to nothing but treachery, when *Saturn* and he have any Aspect to each other, either of them being therein, *viz.* in *Virgo*: And it sometimes comes to passe, that under this Conjunction, some Princes, meerly by a trick of wit, lose all their fortunes without fighting, and so are fooles all the rest of their lives. Many dearths.

If *Saturn* and *Jupiter* make their first meeting in *Capricornus*, it portendeth a great variation in the Ayre, and the weather: it argueth a change of government in those Churches, or Countries subject to *Capricornus*, and that then much silly Superstition shall bee intruded upon the common people; It lightly in Christian Common-wealths erects some superstitious Orders of Friers and affords them large possessions:

And if there bee any dying sinner in those times, in such a good condition, as he would willingly erect some Pest-house, for sinning Friers, its alwayes observed, the good confessing Priest will have the pleasantest Mannour he hath, wherein the whole Fraternity may have freedom at large, to perpetrate their close devotions: *Saturn* in *Capricornus* loveth the most profitable and usefull places, and grounds; but the *Moon* and *Venus* having to command in the Trygon, have a little, if not most regard to pleasure, luxury, and good honest feeding.

A Conjunction in this signe inventeth many admirable inventions in Mineralls, and many enrichments to cultivate the earth: it afford-

eth.

eth plentifull increase of all manner of grazing Cattle, but not much Corn, or Wine. It changeth the fashions of men in their attires, and makes men reserved, austere and grave; it procureth much sobriety, and temperance upon earth, and its inhabitants, and it enclines the Kings of this World to accumulate wealth for an unthrifty posterity; It sheweth the exaltation of many families to great preferments, though themselves were descended of mean parents. The Yeoman in *England*, and the Peasant in *France*, and the *Flandrian* Boor breed up their children gallantly, &c. But those words are mysterious and not explicable.

Airy Triplicity: under which

THere are generally flowrishing in the World excellent learned men, both in judgement and Science: Its a time, wherein all Arts have countenance, and all Artists encouragement, by which learning increaseth, and excellent Mechanicks are cherished. The World, or the affairs of Princes Courts, and Kingdoms are subtilly, and closely governed, for the most part, by Princes meanest servants. If *Saturn* and *Mercury* give them their Character, those fellows are directly Rascalls, Atheists, perjured Villains, that do all for their own advantage; Dissemblers they are, not fearing God, or loving their Prince, whose ears they do not onely inchant, but stupifie with forged lies, advancing their own proper ends. Will not *Mercury* procure men to speak much? and *Saturn* to dissemble much? *Saturn* was never yet found an enemy in jest, nor *Mercury* a friend in good earnest.

If so be *Saturn* and *Jupiter* have their first Conjunction in *Gemini*, the learned that then flowrish, write more words then matter, and indeavour with Logick and Philosophy to maintain dangerous positions, which should rather be concluded with verity and honesty. This is understood in Divinity; But I conceive the point may bee stretched out to an other kind of learning.

If the first Convention of *Saturn* and *Jupiter* be in *Libra*, Divines then living, handle matters with great profundity and learning, and their works remain famous to succeeding Ages: Divinity is now handled like Divinity, saving that sometimes they strain too high a point. Magick is earnestly sought after, which this foolish age condemns; though King *James* said; *Magus* (was) *rerum humanarum divinarumque perscrutator*; A meer searcher into Divine and Hu-

mane

mane Learning: And *Agrippa* in his Epistle to *Trithemius*, maintains; *Magum apud literatos viros, non maleficum, non superstitiosum, non dæmoniacum sonare; sed sapientem, sed Sacerdotem, sed Prophetam.* That a Magician amongst learned men, was not accounted a Witch, a superstitious or devillish fellow, but a wise man, a Priest, a Prophet. But let an Angell preach this doctrine, twill not be received. Under this Conjunction so beginning, great actions are done in the world: The Marchant thriving by Sea, and by Land: If a Monarchy, an Heresie, or Order of Friers, or a Common-wealth begin now, it endureth very long; not so much supported with Armes, as Wisdome, and dexterity in Treaties, by which surreptitious kind of prudence, immunities are obtained from such, or such a Common-wealth, as afterward are never to be regained.

If so it chance, that *Saturn* and *Jupiter* bee in Conjunction, their first time of leaving the earthly Trygon, in the signe of *Aquarius*, which is the joy and delight of *Saturn*, not onely famous men in life, learning, and conversation arise, but also in honesty, integrity, and Religion; *Saturn* is so over-joyed in *Aquarius*, he permits *Mercury* but little dominion to do ill; wherefore excellent Schoolmen, Mathematicians, Astrologers, and men learned in every kind of learning, do find great encouragement in the world, so that the composition of all manner of excellent learning, comes usually from men living in these times, as born under a Conjunction in this Trygon.

Of the Watry Triplicity

LAst of all, when the two Superiors make their return into the watry Triangularity, which *Mars* doth principally rule; There are stirred up for Religion, and by the Clergy, many most dreadfull warres, as also many contrary Sects, and opinions in Religion, strange Engines for warre, and the destruction of mankind are framed, many plagues, and pestilences afflict the Earth. Yet if *Saturn* and *Jupiter* make their first Conjunction in *Cancer*, the Common-people make some gentle Commotion, or desire to have some reformation in Religion; and rather then fail, they crave help of the Nobility, by whose means they obtain their desires with moderation, and without blows: And, although it might be otherwise doubted because *Saturn* in *Cancer* is in detriment, and *Mars* in his fall, yet I do conceive, *Cancer* being the onely House of the *Moon*, the signe where *Jupiter* is exalted, and where *Mars* hath the onely govern-

ment,

ment, by Triplicity, all things go on in a loving way. unlesse *Mars* at the time be unluckely placed in *Libra*, and then nothing but change of opinion, new found Tenents in the Church, and what not? Not any Sectary knowing his owne heart: for let his Prince give him leave to broach one errour, and he will perform it with proclaiming twenty.

Certainly if *Mars* have no hostile radiation to the then Conjunction, the power of *Jupiter* will perform wonders.

Si qua fides astris, aut si quid ab alto
Æthere cognatum nostris in mentibus haeret.
Crediderim fas, ac lege, & jura, piumque
Et rectum manare, & amica fœdera pacis.

If any faith in stars there be, or from the heavens so high
We knowledge do derive, when Jove *doth rule the skie*
Beleeve me then, both Law, and Rights, or what is just we have,
Leagues friendly, blessed peace besides: what more can we then crave?

Many Churchmen of inferiour Rank, come to great fame, and fat Benefices in the World, and admirable preferment in the Church; Private grudgings betwixt the ancient Nobility and the Clergy, &c.

If *Saturn* and *Jupiter* have their first Conjunction in *Scorpio*, upon leaving one, and entring this Trygon, wherein neither *Saturn* or *Jupiter* have any materiall dignities: An egge is not so full of meat, as the Church of factions. Princes Courts are the Seminaries of sedition, faction, luxury, and lechery; ill government follows, feeble Princes, and masculine Queens, bloody warres, pestilentiall diseases: Now one of *Mars* his lying spirits hath licence to make the Prophets preach untruths, and the Priests to babble vain words for sound Doctrine. *Post Conjunctionem Saturni & Jovis in Scorpio, surrexit secta venenosa, quæ tanquam lues totum pervasit orbem*: After a Conjunction of *Saturn* and *Jupiter* in *Scorpio*, an untoward Heresie arose, troubling all the world. *Campanella.*

If *Saturn* and *Jupiter* begin in *Pisces*, Reformation of Church and men; is talked of, and much expected; its long in agitation, unwillingly prosecuted; a generall Councell amongst Christians; Heresies and novell opinions vex the Church: The signe is common, Men are double tongued; Can Authority settle they know not what? In an other sense, *Stultus interrogator facit sapientem deviare*; Things done now, continue not a whole age; Its good to be sure.

The

The Agent handled, viz. *a Conjunction of* Saturn *and* Jupiter.

THe present *conjunction* of which I now treate, doth happen in 25. degrees and 26. minuts of *Pisces*, the Ascendent of the Scheam is *Sagittarius* : *Neque enim ex signo conjunctionum duntaxat effectus cognoscimus, sed ex coorientium figura* : For onely by the signe of the *conjunction*, we do not judge the effects, but by the figure ascending at the time of the *conjunction* : *Sciendum autem est minus esse mali in aspectibus signorum, quam partium, sic enim inevitabiles sunt effectus* : so *Prolus* upon *Ptolomey* : had I treated of some aspects of these two planets, *viz.* either of the *Sextile*, *Quadrate*, or *Opposition*, there had been lesse matter or mischief to be thought on, but it being a *conjunction*, the events will be very strong and inevitable; this is spoken with too much aggravation. *Jupiter & Saturnus mutant res & convertunt, eritque variationis initium, cum mutantur ex una figura in aliam in conjunctionibus* : *Almansor*. 127. *Jupiter* and *Saturn* convert and change matters; when in their *conjunctions* they change out of one form into another, there is the beginning of variation. This *Conjunction* beginneth in a perfect *Trine*, to the last Comet we saw, *viz.* In 1618. that began in 25 *Scorpio*, the signe wherein the first *conjunction* of *Saturn* and *Jupiter*, was in their last return to this Trigon: this *conjunction* is in *Pisces*, the last signe of the *Zodiack*, and of this Triplicity. It may please God after some cruell stormes and with much vexation to the whole Christian Common-wealth, this Conjunction may perfectly conclude such things, as shall remaine imperfectly begun by the Comet, when the effects of it are determined, this Conjunction being an assistant to execute Gods decree, intended by that former heavenly apparition, but in a milder execution, and not so violently. But if any shall say, Why did not the little Conjunction of *Saturn* and *Jupiter*, 1623. seeing it was after the apparition, work and cooperate as well as this present Conjunction? I may answer easily; That matter was not then prepared, but preparing, that Conjunction having no affinity, with either the signe of its first apparance or almost with any it passed through, during its continuance: for the Conjunction then was in a fiery signe, and rather stirred and fitted materialls for the building, then otherwayes: we know the progresse of the Comet was in *Scorpio*, *Libra*, and *Virgo* : And yet that Con-

 junction

junction, I am sure, passed not away without a heavy touch of its malice, which came fully upon us, when in a due measure of years, it was Gods will, the effects should break forth upon *England*, viz. 1625. But now *Pisces ob Jovis domicilium, aquas dulces nobis suppeditat, Pro. fol.* 70. Being *Pisces* is the house of *Jupiter*, let us hope he will supply us with sweet and pleasant waters, we have had too much bitter: *God grant us better dayes.*

In the Scheam of this present Conjunction, *Saturn* is absolutely the strongest, *Majus infortunium* Saturni *est, cum fuerit in signis foemininis*; Martis *cum fuerit in masculinis, Almanson. proposit.* 83.

Saturn doth most mischiefe in Feminine signes; *Mars* in Masculine: in our Scheam they have such a position: *Insuper, si* Saturnus *sit in loco, in quo dignitatem habet; significat quod gens antiqua locum inhabitans quemcunque, devicta non erit, neque de loco suo extracta, & propter naturam* Saturni *multiplicabuntur per mundum odia, rancores, turbationes, fames, & infirmatatum species, Avenaris, fol.* 80. Moreover if *Saturn* be in the figure where he hath dignity, an ancient people shall not desert their habitations, nor be drawn out of their own soyle; hate, rancour, trouble, famine, and severall sorts of infirmities shall be multiplyed all over the world: *Saturn, Jupiter, Sol*, and *Mercury* are in their motions very swift, exceeding their mean proportion very much, which may be one reason, why the effects hereby signified, shall quicklier begin and go forward with greater vigour during their continuance: *Quanto sydus majus est, ac motus velocior, eo etiam opera syderis sunt manifestiora, Dasipod. Apho.* 8. The swifter a star is, and the greater, the more eminent are his operations, *Climatum differentia facit, ut celerius aut tardius eventus proveniant, & ut planeta in angulis sunt vel cadentibus vel succedentibus; Carda. Seg.* 5. *Aphoris.* 98. The difference of *Climates* causeth the events to come sooner or later, and according as Planets are placed in Angles, cadent houses, or succedent.

Et generaliter, si fuerit infortuna fortuna cadenti copulata, aut infortuna elevata, fient due infortuna; nihil fermé juvantes & multum nocentes, Generally if an infortune be joyned to a fortune, either cadent in house or otherwaies, both become infortunes; helping firmely nothing, but impediting much. *Car. Seg.* 5. *Aphoris.* 123. *Quod si fortuna elevatur, infortuna juvabit quidem; sed & nocebit, quoniam detrimenta magna facilius est inferre, quam felicitates, impediuntq; detrimenta felicitates, felicitates autem detrimenta impedire non solent:* If a fortune be in Conjunction with an infortune, and in a cadent

house,

house, and the fortune be elevated, the infortune may do good; but he shall also do mischiefe: for its easier to infer or produce great dammages or losses then blessings: detriments do impeach happinesses but very seldome that happinesses do impeach or keep back mischiefes, *Card. Seg. 5. Aphoris. 124.*

I judge *Saturn*, *Jupiter*, and *Mars*, wholly Lords of the Conjunction; and although *Mars* is not very powerfull, yet being Lord of the tenth, and having exaltation in *Capricorn* an intercepted signe in the ascendant, and in longitude neer *Oculus Tauri*; I do allow him a Prerogative in judgement, and not without just grounds in Art. Some and those very good Astrologers, have esteemed *Jupiter* to be most strongly fortified in the Positure, and that he was directly Lord of the Conjunction, he hath the signe for his, and is elevated above *Saturn*, as having 60. minutes lesse South Latitude then *Saturn*: how much elevation is of consequence in this matter, and what it is, I handle hereafter. Thus much I say, Had *Jupiter* been so powerfull, we might have expected from so benevolent a Planet, that which *Aratus in Phene. fol. 49.* saith in another sense: *A Jove principium, &c. Plena vero Jovis omnia quidem compita; Omnes vero hominum cetus: plenum vero mare & portus: ubique autem Jove indigemus omnes: Hic veró benevolus hominibus commoda significat*: All places are full of *Jupiter*; man, the Sea, heavens, what not? This benevolent Planet signifieth all manner of emoluments to man, but heare it by *Pontanus* excellently and to the purpose in *Urania, fol.* 2903. Its *Jupiters* property being sole Ruler.

——————Fœlicibus addere seclis
Secula, perpetuumq́, annis extendere in avum,
Tanta Jovis placidi clementia,

But being corrupted by the predominancy of *Saturn*, the same Author tells us what may be expected.

——————Ni malus Atro
Sydere torpentes Saturnus *funderet ignes,*
Funderet & lethi causam infelicis, & omne
Morborum genus, & misera mala plurima vita:

viz. Jupiter being chiefe, he makes this age as happy as the former, or gives addition of blessings, and extends his benevolence many yeares.

So much is the clemency of the mild *Jupiter*: but having affliction by *Saturn*, one mischiefe comes in the neck of another, unhappy causes of mens deaths, every kinde of ill and unwholesome diseases, and the many miseries of mans life are increased. I desire every Reader to picke out my meaning out of short sentences and Aphorismes, my intention being not to make a Comment. *Benefica si superata fuerit: efficatia ejus minuetur, & imbecillior fiet. Proclus. fol.* 74.

If a fortune be overswayed by an infortune; his efficacy in working his effects is diminished, and is more imbecill.

The Planets are all subterranean, *viz.* under the earth, certainely Gods Providence is wonderfull; the Conjunction in 1603. was in the twelfth house, that Conjunction in 1623. in the sixth house, this in the latter part of the second, if not part of it in the third: All men know, the two former houses mentioned, have no affinity with the ascendent, the one intimates the obscure managing of mundane affaires since 1603. by a close hand not visible; but if you will know who it is; observe *Mercury* is neer *Jupiter* and *Saturn* in consultation; who is he; *Mercury* is Lord of the ninth, its Religion, or the Religious; *Mercury* in detriment signifies counterfeit.

Religion or the politikly Religious, or superstitiously Religious, had, or were to mannage the actions of that first Conjunctions Rule and Dominion.

Come we to the Conjunction in 1623. observe, *Mercury* is then with *Cor Leonis*, as if the Clergie should get Regall Countenance and support to maintain their errours; if that will not serve; observe, *Mercury* is in the seventh house; he will stir up war and bloodshed: By whose means and procurement? Is not the seventh house the place of heaven signifying women? why then, the female Sex shall be furtherers of an erronious Clergie, & of the Apostate Jesuits, I say, of all their private designes, which have, or shall involve all Christendome in blood and slaughter. But if some say *Mars* being in the *figura Conjunctionis*, 1623. in his exaltation, how comes it to passe, Episcopacy and the Clergie now faile in 1642. or 1643. First, I say, that since 1623. for many yeares their power was great and formidable, but at what time the Comet came to touch the ninth house of his figure; and when *Mars* by due direction came to the *Opposition* of the *Sun* in the sixth of the figure 1623. as you shall see, if you substract 8. *deg.* 20. *min.* the place of *Mars*, from 24. *deg.* 36. *min.* the place of *Sol*, there remaines 16. *degrees* and 16. *minutes*, which put into time, make 16. years and 3. moneths. Adde 16. years and 3. moneths to the 8. of *July* 1623. and it brings you to the yeer 1639. and moneth of *October*. Who knows not that, to be the year of the Prelates first sense, that they should forsake their lusty Benefices and fat Bishopricks, and of the sensible dislike the Nobility and Commonalty took against them, for it was much about that time, they would have imposed a new Common Prayer Book upon the Scottish Nation, and some Inquisition-like Canons on the patient *English*. This present Conjunction 1643. is also subterranean, as if God would not yet give light to mortall men, what really he intends by the return of *Saturn* and *Jupiter* into the fiery Trygon; some glympses we have now and then, either by Eclipses, or the like; but if we observe things rightly, matters are not carried as apertly as in former times: *Latet anguis in herba*: All the affaires of Christendome are managed by a Cabinet Counsell, by almost an invisible society, which lurk in every place and are every where, and yet no where: The actions intended by some, during the continuance of this Conjunction, are such, as God would not suffer a Planet to be above the earth to countenance them; such like affaires being so detested by man, and so punishable by God, as in thought a righteous soule detesteth naming the least part.

The *Sun* (that is *Lux mundi*) is in a watry signe, as if he shed tears at the rehearsing, and so is both *Saturn*, *Jupiter*, and *Mercury*, as if young and old should weep their fill; the *moone* being the goddesse of the night, is in the sixth house, and in an ayrie signe, as if she intended to fly into the desarts, and give no light at all, rather then to such foul intendments.

It had been good, that either the actions or the contrivers of these calamities had been strangled in their cradle and infancy. But againe to my figure, which when I have adorned with those fixed stars, which are neer the Cuspes of the twelve houses, and the Nature and quality of every house, not orderly, but somewhat confusedly, I then shall handle the effects, although I give in every line almost a little light of what may be expected.

Sciendum porró est, stellas fixas dominari: fixas sumemus tum splendidas quæ sunt angulares, tum quæ sunt in parte Ecliptica: Proclus fol. 67.

We know the fixed stars have also power; those we take which are either Angular, or of great magnitude, or those which are in the Eclipticк.

I begin with the tenth house first, for if Kings and Princes be not first remembred, they will take it in pet, scorne, and derision: *Arcturus* a noble fixed star culminateth, he is of prime magnitude and nature of *Jupiter* and *Mars*, his Latitude which is much, brings him to mediate heaven with almost the second degree of *Scorpio*: the Longitude of *Arcturus* is in 18. *deg.* 56. *min.* in *Libra*. In the name of God why do Princes shoot so far from the mark? all men know *Libra* is a humane signe; had it not been better to have rested therein; then to make transmigration into *Scorpio*: a signe which presents falsenesse, vaine oathes, treacherous Protestations; yet they would be reputed notwithstanding gods, and Saints; if they would really be so; *In Divis nihil est quo angantur, sed omnia aequali quadam felicitate transigunt; Cardanus de Intelligentiis*. The gods or Intelligencers never are molested; they do all things justly, or with equall Justice. With the Cuspe of the fourth house, a small star of the nature of *Saturn* and *Mercury* descends.

The tenth house represents Kings, Emperours, Princes, Dukes, Marquesses, Lords, Viscounts, Sir *Thomas* and Sir *John*, both Knights, &c. Authority; Magistracy, Courts of Justice and of Princes, and Lord chiefe Justices, Judges of all Courts, or any man in command, or exercising power over another, all offices, the profession any man lives in, be the quality or trade what it will: if either the *Sun* or *Jupiter* be in this house, or command that; its a signe of happinesse in the matter in question, provided, they not onely aspect the house, but have essentiall dignity where they are, either *Saturn* or *Mars* herein mar all the rost.

The fourth house naturally signifieth our predecessours, as Fathers, or Lands, Tenements and hereditaments, also pastures, fields, woods, towns besieged, treasures under ground; *in figura mundi*; it signifieth Kings wives, great persons wives, and Concubines, and being rightly understood it tells Kings who are their enemies, what Nation or people do love or hate them, but this is *In judicio magnarum, mediarum & minarum Conjunctionum, & in Eclipsium tam solarium quam Lunarium, medium Cali, Regis, legisque Dominos, judices, & etiam praeliorum dominos, Angulus autem, terrae partes, & terras, locum etiam, in quo natus est infans. Almansor, proposit.* 89. It agreeth with my former signification of the houses.

Upon the Cuspe of the 11. house called the good Angell, there is a fixed star of the third magnitude, being the formost star in the palme of the left hand of *Ophiuchus*, of the nature of *Saturn* and *Venus*, having 17. degrees of Boreall Latitude, and with the Cuspe of the fifth house there descends an obscure star of the nature of *Mars* and the ☽, and its placed in the brest of the Bull, and hath 8. degrees of Meridionall Latitude; very neer unto it doth descend the *Pleyades*, of a stirring, active and seditious nature; shall our eyes behold the father against

gainst his son, and the son in arms against the father? Shall the assistance and aids one Prince sends another, either be unseasonable, or of no concernment? Shall the forraigner seldome finde the way home againe, unlesse he can devoure a Canon, or wade thorow the Sea? Can *Saturn* and *Venus*, that represent Kings favorites, be good counsellours to their masters, the one being old, the other not so, there being perfect antipathy betwixt them? Do not these villaines betray their Princes secrets, each in opposition to other, while the poor Potentates study and admire how their Counsells are detected: all men know *Venus* is youthfull, and *Saturn* cynicall or churlish. This hard fate will follow the Courts of Kings, for many yeares yet ensuing.

By the eleventh house, we meane Kings servants, Favorites, their assistants, good name and fame; friendship, the provision both of men and money for them, their amunition, &c. their Exchecquer or Treasury.

By the fifth house, I understand, Embassadours, (which in our climate will play their Prankes.) Children, Playes, Banquets, Ale-houses and Taverns; Messengers, Agents for Republiques, &c.

Upon the Cuspe of the twelfth house there ariseth with the seventh of *Sagittarius*, which was the degree almost of the great Conjunction of *Saturn* and *Jupiter*, 1603, two fixed stars of the nature of *Mars*, *Jupiter*, *Saturn*, and *Venus*, and these are on the right knee of *Ophiuchus*: The house it self is the house of imprisonment, of Witchery and Sorcery, all underhand practises; of those enemies which work all manner of mischiefe and yet are not visible; of whispering Rascals, of malice, dissention, private revenges and quarrels, of Horses, Cowes, and Oxen, Asses, and Camels; it tels the fate of the Kindred of Princes, is it not the third from the tenth: I mean not this in Kings Nativities, but in Eclipses, Conjunctions, and *Sol* his ingresse into *Aries*.

So many Planets neer the Cuspe, and *Mars* in opposition to the Cuspe of the twelfth: shall we have Souldiers, Church-men, Nobles, and the whorish *Venus*, and now and then a Kinsman to a King, all in fetters, or imprisoned; or shall *Mars* in vaine afflict that house, and destroy none of these Creatures at one time or other: Can these whisperours live alwayes so clandestinely, that neither a halter, a sword, or musket can finde them?

Upon the Cuspe of the sixth we have two fixed stars descending, of the nature of *Saturn*, *Jupiter*, and *Mars*. This house signifieth all manner of ſickneſſes, and Servants both Male and female: all little Cattle as Sheep, Hogs, Goats, &c. Shall Saturnine diſeaſes, as the Spleen, old aches in mens bones and joynts quartan Agues, Surfets by colds, Rhumes and Palſies, a dry Coughs. Lameneſſe, &c. afflict?

Shall the Conſumption or waſting of the Lungs, a *Joviall* diſeaſe; Pluriſies, diſtemper in the blood, and much ventoſity, or Fluxes in both kinds, torment us? Or ſhall the running of the Raines, ſharpe Feavers, and madneſſe be upon us; which are Martiall diſeaſes? I omit to repeat wounds in the head, face, and thighs, &c. Shall the Servant ſtrive to be equall with his Maſter, nay, to beare rule over him: this ſounds like the dream of *Joſeph*, ſo much contemned by his brethren, but ſo fully afterwards verified.

The Cuſpe of the aſcendent, or firſt houſe, hath two ſtars co-ariſing with it, of the nature of *Mars* and *Luna*, *Saturn* and *Venus*; of the Scorpion, the firſt chine or joynt next the body, the other is of the two ſtars, of the North part of the ſting of the Scorpion, without forme the Southermoſt: *Hinc Lachryme*: the unruly multitude ſtir up ſudden commotion, and involve themſelves in Labyrinths: and as the fixed ſtar neer their aſcendent is without form, or is a Chaos; or *rudis, indigeſtaq; moles*; ſo it may be conceived their judgements being unrefined, they labour for, they know not what; can neither digeſt matter or form, for what they will pretend: and yet they will ſtir up matter to gravell the moſt parts of *Europe*; nor will beleeve, they know any thing, till they are well beaten: which in fine they will be. Old men alſo and young Melancholy maids, will helpe to foment, and put forwards the effects of this *Conjunction*.

This firſt houſe is called, the Horoſcope in Nativities; the Aſcendent in Eclipſes, Conjunctions, and horary queſtions; it ſignifies in our *Conjunction*, the State of the Commonalty of *England*; the State of the people; how it ſhall go with them, well or ill: In Nativities, it repreſents the life and beginning of man; and partly his complection, and condition &c. With the Cuſpe of the ſeventh houſe, which generally ſignifieth, women, war, contention, publique enemies, there doth deſcend divers ſtars of the nature of *Mercury* and *Venus*; theſe two Planets ever repreſent youth, witty facetious men, jeſts, and ſuch like: Papers, libels, pamphlets, or vaine books; young men and maids ſhall have a ſhare in ſetting the world at variance, and ſhall alſo ſuffer by the effects of this diſmall *Conjunction*, and the calamities thereupon depending.

Mercury repreſents Secretaries, and Clerks of Councells, Meſſengers

gers, or Nuntio's, Embassadors, Factors, or the like, such as agitate with the pen in State affaires; *Venus* sheweth us, women and children shall as well Act their parts, as men their *Conjunctionall* Tragedy.

A Star of the quality of *Saturn* and *Mercury* ariseth with the sixth of *Aquarius* in the second house: much Legerdemaine will be used by the interloping Officer, or covetous Lawyer; and yet not so much by the Lawyer as shirking Clerk, and dull Country Gentleman, to obtaine the estates and fortunes of other men: for plodding and restlesse knaves are never quiet, or weary of doing mischiefe. This house presents the fortune and estate of the Country man in generall, which is not like to be good, because *Saturn* is without essentiall fortitudes, and *Venus* is *Retrograde* in the second, which signifieth diminution of the husbandmans fortunes, his houshold-stuffe, his money, plate, corn, and what ever he sustaines himself by.

Upon the cuspe of the eighth house, representing the inheritances of the dead, and the death of mankind in generall, I finde divers stars of the condition of *Saturn*, *Mars*, *Mercury*, and *Sol*, of very malignant influence; which intimate mens estates and inheritances shall be violently wrested from them by kingly hand, or gift of Kings, because *Mars* is one significatour; or by the insulting Souldiour or Commander; the worm-eaten Pettifog, or unjust Judge: colourable pretences being accepted for strong evidence; many Tenants will seek to informe against their Landlords, &c. Such a connexion of fixed Stars on the cuspe of the eighth house, denoteth the severall manners death useth, to bring men to their end: is there not the *Aselli* both North and South, and *pectus Cancri* within the limits of the house. Do not these denote violent and unexpected death, by sword, water, and halter.

With no degrees of *Aries*, no fixed star ascends, the third house is ascendent with ☋ now brother against brother, kinsman to kinsman envious; the enemies of ones house are the worst: *& sic ad infinitum*: Neighbour against neighbour.

With the first of *Libra* descends no fixed star: ☊ is in the ninth, but its not a Planet but a Node: this is the house of Religion, Clergie men of all sorts, so that Religion for a long time will not be fully setled; because *Jupiter* is lesse powerfull then *Saturn*, and *Venus* Lady of the ninth *Retrograde*. Its fit to regulate that first, yet the *Conjunction* saith, It will not be so: Oh the many disturbances the Synod shall finde.

The Cuspes of the houses finished and Illustrated with fixed stars, I come to the Planets: *Saturn* and *Jupiter* being in the 25°. *Pisces*,

L have

have with them a Star of the third magnitude and nature of *Saturn* and *Mercury* : its an addition of strength to *Saturn*, that he hath a star of his own nature joyned with him; and *Jupiter* is in strength somewhat diminished, to have a fixed star of the nature of his enemie, in Conjunction with him ; he's the more invalid to resist the Potency and malice of his insulting enemie : for that Axiome is not ever true, *Quicquid ligat Saturnus, solvit Jupiter* : what ever *Saturn* hinders, *Jupiter* helps : thats onely to be understood, when *Saturn* is lesse predominant than *Jupiter*; for at all times, and in every signe and house of heaven, this is not true. If he mean Magically, it is true, with its proper limits : For let one be bewitched by *Saturn*, or by a man or woman of *Saturn* his conditions; the cure must be by observing the progresse of *Jupiter*, by hearbs to him appropriated, gathered and applyed when he is *valdé potens*, in his houre, &c.

With *Mars* are the *Lampadas*, *Succulæ*, or *Aldebaran*, all of the nature of *Mars*, *Jupiter*, and *Luna* : from hence arise sudden tumults, commotions, much bloodshed, and want of duty in servants, and inferiour sorts of people; the one to their Masters, the other to their Soveraignes.

With *Sol*, who represents the equipage of Princes, are some (*stellæ juvantes*) and but some, of *Jupiter*, *Saturn*, *Mercury*, their natures; the Sun may cry out for more helpe, himself being peregrine; and *Almansor* in *proposit. suis* saith, *Planeta* Peregrinus, &c. is like a man thrust out of all : *Venus* is joyned with a fixed star of the Nature of *Mercury* and *Saturn*, as also *Jupiter*, but *Jupiter* comes in last of all: *Post est occasio calva*. *Venus* signifies Ladies, Queenes, and she is also significatrix of the Clergie.

Mercury having particular signification in our Scheam of such as make strife and contention, and of faithlesse servants, is accompanied with a fixed star of his own influence; we may note, Birds of a feather will flock together. *Luna* is with a fixed star, of the nature of *Mars* and *Mercury*, generally she signifieth (*omnem hominem plebeium*) when *Mars*, *Mercury*, and *Luna* are together (without a miracle) they incline a man to be a knave, false, and treacherous : what shall be the result of a consultation, where *Mars*, *Mercury*, and *Luna* meet, *Insanum vulgus*, never pleased: In this position, the significatrix of the commonalty in generall is so ill placed, so weak in fortitudes, they have great cause to mourn, weep, howle, and lament ; but little neede of a paire of Bag-pipes, &c.

Of

Of the patient, or subject matter, in which principally, the events shall happen; and whether good or evill.

IN treating hereof, I find at first some repugnancy, and difference amongst the Learned: *Haly Rodoan*, in his Comment of the 63. *Aphorisme* of *Ptolemy*, hath these words. *Oportet aspicere in conjunctione* Saturni *&* Jovis, *in eodem minuto ad elevationem unius eorum super alterum: & judica cum fortitudine naturæ ejus; scilicet elevati in hoc mundo, & similiter fac:* Consider in every Conjunction of *Saturn* and *Jupiter*, who is most elevated, and judge according to the nature of him that is most elevated in the heavens, or in this World: do likewise so, &c. He goeth further; *Habent itaque effectus mirandos, sed superat elevatus; est autem judicium validum, cum fuerit conjunctio in ascendente, vel in Alchirem, vel in Eclipsi Solis vel Lunæ:* These Conjunctions have marvelous effects, but the elevated Planet superates, The judgement is firme, if the Conjunction be in the Ascendent, or in the degree wherein any of the 21. principall Conjunctions was, or in the degree, of an Eclipse, *Solar* or *Lunar*. Of this opinion, *Almansor in pro.* 60. seemeth not clearly to be, *Ea quæ accidunt in hoc sæculo, sciuntur & investigantur ex magna fortitudine superioris significatoris & ex sua elevatione:* Accidents of this world may bee found out, by the great strength of the superiour Significators, and from his Elevation. *Trapezuntius* tells us, what he conceives to bee intended by Elevation in this place; *viz.* in 63. *Aphor. Ptol. Qui propinquior est maxime longitudini suæ in Epicyclo, in eum elevari dicitur, qui a sua remotior est.* The Planet, saith he, that is nearest to his Longitude, in his Epicycle, is elevated above him, who is more remote from it, *viz.* his Longitude. That the *Arabian* Astrologians intended onely in these Conjunctions to judge the effects by that Planet most elevated, I do verily beleeve; and that they meant by elevation, according to *Trapezuntius* the *Greek*. There are many other wayes not explicated, whereby one Planet is said to be elevated above another; and yet I cannot conceive, that the sole elevation, in that sense, most speak of, shall be of such force, as to judge the effects of any Conjunction, by which of the two Planets is most elevated; or to speak more near to common capacity, hath least South Latitude, if it bee South; or greater North Latitude, if it bee North; To conclude a sollid judgement hereupon, I hold it altogether absurd: but the Ancients wanting those exact Tables which wee now enjoy,

 whereby

whereby they were made uncapable of the exact time of the two superiour Conjunctions, and so of having a right Ascendent of the true Conjunction, we are content to take the signe, and degree, and the latitude of the Planet, without further consideration: And hereupon it was that *Cardane*, who lived in the dayes of *Edward* the sixth, wanting those conveniencies, which this age, by the industry of *Tycho*, and others enjoy, burst out into these speeches, when hee spake of these Conjunctions, and how impossible it was to have the exquisite Conjunction of *Saturn* and *Jupiter*, because *Jupiter* doth exceed *Saturn* in diurnall motion, sixe minutes, seldome seven; *Ad hoc discrimen nullus mortalium, nec instrumento, nec aliter discernere potest: in Coment. lib. 2. Ptol. fol.* 215. The disadvantage is such, quoth he, no mortall man, either with Instrument, or other wayes, can discerne the time of the true Conjunction. But since I had the Conjunction of *Saturn* and *Jupiter* in 1603. so exactly performed, by Sir *Christopher Heydon* with Instrument; and the same (*de novo*) calculated by the excellent and industrious, Master *Matthew Fiske*, out of the *Rudolphine Tables*, betwixt whom there is no sensible variation, but in place of the Moon: I say, I conceive it possible, and I do beleeve I have the Conjunction of *Saturn* and *Jupiter* in 1643. exquisitely done by the same learned hand: and that either he, or any, as able as himself, may compasse the true moment of any Conjunction. But because the word Elevation is of great extent, you shall see more fully, how many wayes a Planet is said to bee elevated above another:

1. The Planet that is lesse distant from the *Apogeon* of his *Eccentrick*, is more elevated, then he that is more remote. 2. A Planet above the earth, is elevated above one below, or under the earth. 3. A Planet in the midd heaven, or near it, (or tends from the Horizon to the tenth House) is above him that is in the eleventh House: hee that is in the eleventh, is elevated above him in the twelfth: hee in the twelfth, above any in the Ascendent. 4. If all are above the earth, the nearest the midd heaven. 5. If all are under the earth, then the next to the Ascendent. 6. The Latitude is considerable, *viz.* the elevation of a Planet, according to the Latitude of the *Zodiack*. In Conjunctions, North Latitude is preferred before South; and therein the greater Latitude North, the greater elevation; if both have South Latitude, he that hath least, is most elevated: for in truth hee is neerest the Ecliptique.

Notwithstanding this Elevation, of which the Ancients so much ſtood upon, I ſhall make it appear by the conſent of later Authors, and Reaſon it ſelf, the beſt Author, that ſomething elſe beſides elevation, is conſiderable in judgement of theſe ſuperiour Conjunctions, and that the eſſentiall and accidentall Dignities are of more concernment then ſublimity, &c.

Pontanus in Coment. 63. *Aphor. Ptol. Quum autem fieri poſſit, ut pari ſublimitate aut declinatione ferantur, quid tunc ſervandum eſſet, non expreſſit Ptolomeus, relinquens nobis conſideranda permulta, quibus examinari vires utriuſque, atque invicem penſitari debeant:* But ſith, it may ſo happen, as both Planets are carried with one and the ſame ſublimity and declination; *Ptolomey* doth not then direct what is to be done, leaving us to conſider many things, and amongſt the reſt, the ſeverall fortitudes of either Planet, are to be penſitated, or looked after.

Cardanus reſolveth the queſtion more perfectly, in *Seg.* 2°. *Aphor.* 2. *In omni planetarum conjunctione eum planetam dominatorem conſtitue, qui ſublimior fuerit in Eccentrico, & parvo circulo, & qui in loco plures habuerit dignitates, & qui plures ſtellas ſua natura ſimiles habuerit.* In every, or any Conjunction of the Planets, conſtitute him Ruler, who is higheſt in his Eccentrick, and in his leſſer Circle, and who hath moſt Dignities in the place of the Conjunction, and hath moſt Starres of his own nature with him.

Doctor *Dee*, a learned *Britain*, and one of the acuteſt Aſtrologers the laſt Age produced, in *Aphoriſ.* 116. conſenteth with *Cardane*; *Circa illas* 120. *conjunctiones, generaliſſimam nos hanc proponimus methodum; quando ſolum duo ex ſeptem copulantur,* 21. *variæ eſſe poſſunt conjunctiones, & in illarum ſingulis quis duorum planetarum erit fortior conſiderari debet.* Concerning the 120. Conjunctions *Ptolomey* ſpeaketh of, we deliver this generall Methode; When two onely are in Conjunction, there may be 21 Conjunctions, in every of which conjunctions, we ought to conſider which is ſtrongeſt. So ſaith *Theodoricus Haghen*; *Eorum effectus ſecundum fortitudinum convenientiam evenit:* The effects of the Planetary Conjunctions do come to paſſe according to the convenienciе of their Fortitudes. By all which, I do affirm it the ſafeſt way, whereupon to ground a certain judgement, to examine the fortitudes and debilities eſſentiall, and accidentall of the two Planets, at the time of their Conjunction, according either to the Methode of *Darius, Leovitius, Junctine,* but eſpecially of *Origanus, fol.* 539. And I conceive the meaning of *Ptolomey* in that 63. *Aphoriſ.* was this; That when both Planets in a Conjunction have equall

equall fortitudes or debilities, that then wee are to consider, whic of the two is in the highest part of his Epicicle.

In our present Conjunction, *Saturnus transit Apogeon*, 20. *Martii*; & *Jupiter in Epiciclo superiorem partem* 23. *Martii*. By this meanes, *Saturn* is nearest his Absis: *Origanus in fine Ephemerid. Anno* 1643.

Its therefore certain, *Saturn* hath most dignities, and *Jupiter* more elevated; by which I conceive, what Religion, Law, or Justice would have effected, shall again finde impediment by *Saturn, viz.* cunning plotting, treachery, falsehood, &c. The subject matter, upon which this Conjunction shall have most influence, shall therefore be of the nature of *Saturn* first, then of *Jupiter*, and last of all, *Mars* shall claim his part in the Tragedy, for it will be one. Wee usually say, Labour is from *Saturn*, Religion from *Jupiter*, Fire and Sword from *Mars*.

If we consider the signe ascending, or of the Conjunction it self, or the signe where *Mars* and *Luna* are, its *Bicorporeall*, *Bicorporea hominibus & Regibus judicium prabent, ob duplicem affectionem: Rex enim respectu subditorum, & subditi respectu regis dicuntur. Proclus fol.* 68. Double bodied signes give judgement upon men and Kings; A King in respect of Subiects, and Subiects in consideration of a King, are so called, upon a twofold affection. *Pisces* is an Aquaticall and flegmatique signe, but very near to the Equinoctionall, and Cardinall signe *Aries*; it will not be long ere matters appear in farre different course to former times, in a more majesticall straine. The signe is appropriate to *Jupiter*, and is his House: *Si Conjunctio sit in Scorpione vel Piscibus, quæ sunt domus altiorum planetarum, significant longitudinem temporum, quam signa inferiorum planetarum. Albumazar diff.* 2. *cap.* 1. If the Conjunction of the superiors is in *Scorpio* or *Pisces*, they being the Houses of the weightier Planets, shew a longer time of the duration of effects, then if the signe had been of the inferiour Planets.

If the place of heaven be considered, as *Cardane* will have it, *Aphor.* 89. *seg.* 5. *In omni Conjunctione considera locum, & quis eorum sit superior.* In every Coniunction, consider the place of the Coniunction, and who is superiour of the two Planets. If this bee true, as I doubt, it is, the Coniunction it self is in the second House, or in that part of heaven, which signifieth riches, estate, goods of fortune, money, plate, houshold-stuffe, Corne, Jewels, or in plaine words, such things, or livelihoods, as without which one cannot live, and are the

proper

proper personall estate of every man. And this *Escuidus fol, 17. In quo genere rerum apparebit effectus, hoc scitur ex qualitatibus & formis:* And more punctually, and to purpose. *fol. 41. Conjunctio Saturni & Jovis in secunda domo, muta erit venditio & emptio, & acquisitio census, & erit multa concupiscentia in illis.* From the quality and forme of the signes, we know the manner of the effects. A Conjunction of *Saturn* and *Jupiter* in the second House, there will bee small buying and selling, and as little enriching ones estate, notwithstanding many shall much desire it. Here are no lesse then five Planets posited in the second House; *Mars* and the *Sun* in square Aspect, the *Moon* in the sixth, applying, or rather separating, or in partill Quadrature with *Mercury*, &c. I cannot but iudge from hence, the sudden undoing of many a man, by rapine, theevery, taxes, legall, or illegall, *Mercury* makes any thing legall. I must Prognosticate great impoverishment to the estates, and inheritances of the Nobility, to the Clergy, to the Gentleman, to the Lawyer, and the industrious Yeoman, and hard labouring Farmer, the *diurnall* operating labourer, the curious, or idle Mechanick, the Collier, Tincker, and the most sordid of all Professions, except the hangman.

To the Merchant I divine great losse by Piracies, Shipwracks, and by broken Creditors, or bankrupt Debtors: I cannot imagine by this Coniunction, who, or what kinde of man, or of what nature, and profession he shall be of, that in these turbulent times, shall either thrive, or keep his own. As there are many Planets in the House of riches, and they in a common signe; so also shall bee the meanes whereby men shall bee impoverished; Hee that is rich to day, is not certain to abound to morrow; Hee that kept servants this Moneth, may be servant himselfe the next: An universall poverty in estate, in Cattle, Corne, and what not. A time most uncomfortable, I see, for some succeeding years, bad to all, good to a few.

If the tenth House signifie Kings in generall, or particularly in our Scheame, you shall finde *Mars* but moderately dignified, as ill as Cadent, and worst of all, having no Aspect to the eleventh House, that signifies the support of Princes. Consider their part of fortune, projected from the tenth house; its then in *9. grad. 12. min. Aquarius:* who disposeth of *Saturn*, Lord of *Aquarius*, doth not *Jupiter*? and is not he Lord of the twelfth, of the Ascendent, and disposer of the Coniunction it self? With what difficulty, labour, and discontent shall the Grandees of the World, supply their necessary disbursments for part of the years alotted to the conclusion of this *Conjunction*. In the next

place

place let me make *Jupiter* the generall significatour of Nobility, Gentry, Episcopacy, Lawyers. *A Jove Prelatura, a Saturno austera Religio.* Prelacy is from *Jupiter*, Munkery from *Saturn*: So that Cloisters of Fryers, as well as Benefices of idle Bishops will smart, and come short of their revenues; for as much as *Jupiter* is in the second house, in a particular way he must signifie according to his position therein; but because he is there personally, he may and doth in generall signifie the persons above named, and then admitting that house for the ascendent, the subsequent house demonstrates their fortunes and estates, but therein you behold the *Dragons taile*, then which there is no greater argument of either wasting all, or a remedilesse impoverishment, or vast and unnecessary expences, and expending their private stocks: as *Mars* is Lord of their house of substance, so is their part of fortune in *Conjunction* with him; what may that signifie, but consumption of their revenues, and devastation of their moveables: for *Gemini* is an humane signe: if you will know by whom this shall be, *Mars* being Lord of the tenth, points out by Authority and strong hand, by the Souldier: the *dragons taile* denoteth vulgar persons, clownes, day labourers, vagabond fellows; their own tenants as forward as others: what either the Souldier, Regall commands, or Magistracy leaves, the Peasant will in time lay hold of the rest.

Let us consider the Yeomanry and Farmers of *England*, they are generally represented by *Saturn* and the *Moon*; and together with them is involved the generall fortune of the whole Commonalty; their part of fortune is in *Aries*, in company with the *dragons taile*, and *Venus* being Retrograde is neer the Cuspe of the second, *Sol*, *Mercury*, *Saturn*, and *Jupiter*, all posited partly in the house; here's every one catching and snatching a part, and yet harken what *Guido Bonatus* saith, *fol.* 551. *Si Jupiter fuerit corporaliter junctus Saturno, erunt opera quæ homines faciunt cum silentio, & operabuntur per modum religionis, & cum apparitione fidei & observatione preceptorum justitiæ*: if *Jupiter* be corporeally joyned to *Saturn*, men do their actions silently, cloking all their actions with Religion, with an appearance of fidelity, and observation of the Commands of Justice. Shall this age be partaker of the sight of such men, as either in Religious habits, or pretending austerity of life, rob and devoure mens estates? it will be so, *Saturnus fert mala cum tarditate*; *Hermes Aphoris.* 90. *Saturn* produceth his influence slowly, and he makes the Jovialist, or the indifferent Clergie-man, a very worme-eaten Priest; give *Saturn* money and let the Parish-Clerk preach: *hoc sufficit*.

But

But I proceed, *Neque enim sufficit, vel satis est artifici scire, bonum fore aut malum, nisi proprietas cognoscatur, quale sit futurum, bonum illud an malum*: *Proclus in Ptol.* 71. *fol.* An Artist is not satisfied, in knowing whether the thing signified by a Conjunction be good or bad, unlesse he know the propriety or quality, *viz.* what manner of thing shall be good or evill: In our Scheame *Saturn* and *Jupiter* have in a manner the whole or the greatest Prerogative: *Cum planeta simul duo dominantur, erit judicium ex amborum significatione mixtum, cum autem dominus ipse alteri assimilatur, præcipuam quandam vim obtinebit*: *Cardanus, Seg.* 4. *Apho.* 21. When two Planets Rule, the judgement shall be mixed, and taken from them both; but when the Lord of the figure is joyned with him, or to either, he shall obtain principall Dominion: Actions signified by *Saturn* and *Jupiter*, shall give us the most eminent direction in our judgement; I say, then *Saturn* for his part according to *Escuidus, fol.* 13. *Significatio Saturni est ad res inceptibiles, ut sunt sectæ vices, regna, & quodcunque fieret in temporibus prolixis*: *Saturn* hath signification to some matters already begun to Sects, Mutations in the course of this world, Kingdomes, and what ever may require long time ere it be finished nor is this *Aphorisme* vaine, or shall posterity finde it erroniously alleadged; for my whole speech is in *Aphorismes*. *Saturn* prenoteth much decay in tillage and husbandry, much losse to those that deale in Minerals, and so in Coalemines, Tin, or Lead; for its probable, either the banks shall fall in, or water over-flow the works; and drown out the work-men; destruction (*in fructibus ex terra nascentibus*) to fruits produced or growing out of the earth, *sive in rebus quæ ex abditis terræ eruuntur*, or hinderance in such commodities, as are got out of the bowels of the earth; many curious buildings shall be levelled, and made as low as the earth: a generall tribulation amongst all men: the prisons full of people; hundreds of people undone by unlucky creditors: the inheritances of very many unjustly and irregularly wrested from them: extream perplexities afflicting the minds of most men many desirous but few shall be able to preserve a competency to subsist with; *In terra erit caritas fructuum, & penuria, & vastitas maximè necessariorum ad victum; Bestiarum, boum, equorum, sive ovium penuriam efficit: & eas quæ reliquæ sunt morbis affligit, adeò ut contagium ad homines perveniat, qui iis utuntur. In mari communiter naufragia, & sævas tempestates, difficiles cursus, penuriam & interitum piscium. In hominum corporibus morbos diuturnos, tabem & consumptionem, humorum perturbationem, fluxus, quartanas febres, exilia, inopias,*

 angu-

angustias, luctus, pavores, interritus, maximè senum efficit: Aeris turbationes, densas nubes, caligines, copiosas nives non utiles, sed damnosas, eruccas & locustas, damnum hominibus per diluvia & imbres, seu per grandines, eò usq; ut homines fame & similibus malis pereant, Ptol. in 2° Quadripart. fol. 99. There shall be scarcity of graine, penury, and great wast, or want of those things are most necessary for our food and living; it makes a dearth or scarcity of beasts, Oxen, Horses, and sheep; and so contaminates the remainder left behinde alive, that it breeds contagion in those that eate or use them. In the Sea commonly shipwracks and cruell stormes succeede; hard passages or evill voyages for the Merchant, scarce competent fish for our use; for a destruction of fish is intended. It pollutes the body of man with dayly diseases, consumptions, dry coughes, molestation of the humours, fluxes, quartane agues; banishment either voluntary or inforced, poverty, perplexities, mournings, feares, burialls, of old men especially: Troubled ayres, thick clouds, darkenesse, plentifull snowes, nothing profitable, but extream obnoxious: it breeds canker-wormes and butter-flyes to devour the tender buds, unseasonable showers hindring mens proper seasons, with haile, and men endangered thereby to perish with famine or want of bread.

A cold season followes, unseasonable mists and fogs, many apparitions in the ayre, the colour of the Elements changed, the skies many times varying from their former hue; sights of armed men, people in the night extreamly frighted with these like visions; if any faith be in the writings of the Ancients; when these or the like appear, or are more frequent than ordinary, *viz.* these strange alterations in the ayre, or in the heavens, in what part of the heavens these do rise, or where they first appear, or over what part of heaven they continue longest, let those expect vengeance is at hand: for whether nature being troubled, or the Aerie spirits presiding that quarter of heaven, are molested, and by this visible, but mute kinde of presage, declare to man what is approaching, I leave to be discussed by the more secret Theologers, that have yet a glimps of the more secret learning; but meddle not with it my selfe, though I am also *filius Artis.*

Vapores accensi per aerem currentes, sivè in forma Cometæ, sive in aliis formis, infirmitates calidæ acutæq; naturæ designant, prælia, & dissensiones regnorum: Currentes verò hinc indè per omnes partes, malum universale demonstrant, si in una magis quàm in alia, in illa magis erit significatum, sed si omnes igneitates in una parte discurrerint, in ipsa erit extremitas omnium malorum, simul & fames: Signa quæ videntur in

Cælo,

Celo, vel in Luna, que apparuerint extra motum & cursum nature, sed alio modo, ut ita dicam, ignoto velut cruces vel rotunditates circulares, vel sicut columne vel alie forme, si horam considerabis, in qua hec apparuerint, comprehendes, certificabisq; te in significatione harum, quamvis quod ee nunquam eveniant sine magna mutatione regnorum, illius climatis in quo apparuerint; Rigel. 87. Aphoris.

Kindled vapours streaming through the ayre, whether in form of a Comet, or otherwise, points out hot diseases of an acute quality, as also wars and the dissentions of Kingdomes: But running here and there and through all parts, they demonstrate an universall evill: if the appearance be more in one quarter of heaven than another, in that especially shall the extremity of the signification be manifest, and not long after that, famine. Signes which are seen in heaven, or in the Moon, which appear beyond the course of nature; but, as I may so say, appear after an universall manner, as Crosses, or circular rotundities, or pillars, or of any other form, if you consider the time of their first visibility, you may divine what they intend, yet be sure they never in vaine appear, without great alteration of that Kingdome where they so first happen to be seen.

Since 1628. to this present year, we have had in *England* our share of these unnaturall sights in the ayre. I have observed many my self; if after the writing hereof we have any more of these unusuall astonishments in the Elements, see the rules above written be rightly applyed: and let not the *French, Irish, Danish, Scots*, or *Hollander*, or any other Nation of *Europe*, forget these observations. We had one strange circular appearance about the 26. of *March* last 1645. at what time *Saturn* entred into *Aries*, which might verifie that 33. *Aphoris.* of *Hermes*, *Saturnus quidem transeunte ab uno signo in aliud, fiunt in Celo Diachohontes; quod Arabes vocant Assub, vel quedam alia signa ignea*: When *Saturn* passeth out of one signe into another, there are in the heavens strange fiery Meteors, or burning flames in the skies, which the *Arabians* call *Assub*; usually upon this his transit there are extraordinary gapings or the like, in the Firmament. These notions come to my memory occasionally, some perhaps will make good use of them, others smile, because they can conceive no naturall reason for them. I onely say, *Res multe sunt, que non videntur ratione naturali esse, ut tamen experientia multorum seculorum eas verissimos effectus habere comprobavit*: There are many matters performed, which seeme not at all to be done by naturall reason, and yet the experience of many ages have approved them to be most true.

The signification of Jupiter *in this present Conjunction.*

FRom Nature we derive naturall effects and judgements, and therefore in order I come to handle the matters wherein *Jupiter* may have a signification: for it being a *Conjunction*, one Planet cannot, though never so well dignified, have all the power of disposing the effects and events to himself, but must have familiarity with others, though the quality of the events, shall most manifestly appear by such men, and in such things as he is principall dominator of.

Jupiter naturally signifieth, matters Politicall, Ecclesiasticall affairs, or Church Government, Cannons, or Presbyteriall Ordinances, Corporations of Towns and Cities, Subjects Priviledges; Courts of Justice, Obedience to Princes, Justice of Kings to Subjects; Lawes, Statutes, Ordinances, Decrees: *Johannes Anglicus Distinct. 2. Cap. 1. Et relata est significatio Jovis super observationes legis atq; decretorumq; similia:* The signification of *Jupiter* hath relation to the observation of Laws, to Decrees, and such like. Of Persons he lookes principally upon Clergy-men, because the *Conjunction* it self is in the house of *Jupiter*, and in the degrees of Ecclesiasticall men, upon such as are great, but extreamly corrupted by the presence of *Saturn*: who represents covetousnesse or superstition: In a word, this intends Superstition in Religion, and much discord in Religion, or in such things as concern the Ecclesiasticall party: Bishops, Abbots, Popes, Munks, Fryors, Protestant Ministers, Preachers, Lawyers, Civilians, Judges, Country Gentlemen; are all concerned by this *Conjunction*, and if I had said, Nobility of the best rank and quality, I had spoke truth; for what concerns the Gentleman hath affinity to their fortunes; For of late most of them were no better. Being that *Jupiter* hath not equall Authority with *Saturn*, I say the quality of men before named, shall suffer most: The Divines suffer by reason of the Comets passage now through the house of Religion: The Gentleman, because *Jupiter* is afflicted, and is also Lord of the twelfth and first house; Which denotes they have done themselves most wrong, and are occasioners of their own sufferings; and therefore harme-watch, harme-catch.

I also observe this *Conjunction* is in the fifth house from the tenth: *Caveant Reges, principes & Magnates; ne nimium indulgeant filiis.* Let Kings, Princes, and great men beware how they too much cocker their children. *Caveant & Caveant ab insurrectione, & perfidia filiorum*

rum & rogautorum: Let the persons named, again and again take heed, their own children and Kinsmen prove not Vipers, and raise Insurrection. *Filius ante diem*. Jack would be a Gentleman before his Father dyeth. To as many as these words shall arive, let them observe, and preserve the sense (*inter secreta cordis*) amongst their greatest secrecies; what I say to Kings, I say to Nobility, Gentry, &c.

All former Lawes confirmed during the revolution of 40. years now last past, by this pernitious *Conjunction* and evill Influence of *Saturn*, and weaknesse of the rest of the Significatours, that would assist, but cannot, or will not, shall be in danger of subversion and utter ruine.

Many Common-wealths and Townes Corporate shall either totally be undone and impoverished, and scarce have a face of government, or else absolutely lose both Town and government at once.

Men must not expect these accidents to happen so soon, as the words are out of my mouth; there's a time for all things: its long ere this *Conjunction* leave working, the Comet is yet in force, what remaines when the Comet hath done, this Conjunction shall prosecute, what the Conjunction leaves imperfect, the Eclipse 1654. in *Leone*, will be sure to determine; at, or neer which time if we have no new blazing Star, as the Precursor of some eminent person,

What Champion may with such a man compare?
Or who, thinke I, shall be against him set?
Who is so bold? or what is he that dare
Defend his force, in such encounter met?

I much wonder: but this is out of my Text.

Those Lawes, those Constitutions, Courts of Justice, Commonwealths, Kingdomes, Monarchies, Titles in honour, or earthly families, that either had beginning 1603. or since, or much about that time increased their Authority over the poore Client, Tennant, or afflicted Complainant; these men, these Officers, these Landlords, these cruell Courts, during the effects of this *Conjunction* shall finde small cause to rejoyce, and lesser cause to insult, then ever they dreamed of: The providence of Almighty God doth so order the affaires of this troublesome age, by guiding the Celestiall influences according to his immutable Decree, that all excesse in tyranny, government, command, or exercise of illegall commands, must yeeld to justice, to a troubled and disturbed kinde of Justice. All imperiousnesse in rule, all strict and hard Lawes incroached upon the Subject by tyrannous Commanders, must either have a period or disturbance.

Those censures Canonicall, or Injunctions Civill, of too strict performance, shall either now be abolished, or alleviated, so as they shall no more be a burthen; either to the weak Christian or modern Protestant. If fire be not converted into water, or if there be not a contradiction in celestiall constellations at this present to precedent ones, or if this *Conjunction* be not dissimilar to the last, then perhaps I may speak false, but if in Art I finde the truth of what I write, and such a conversion or transversion of every place in the Zodiack to the last, and last but one *Conjunction*; I may then Mathematically conclude, here are strange and wonderfull things to be performed, totally contradictory to the actions of the two last precedent *Conjunctions*. And certainly, as the two Planets which in effect are the subject of my discourse, are the two waightiest; and represent great actions, so the actions intended hereby, will in the full measure of time break out to be of as much concernment as I write. *Cum superioribus nunquam judicia de rebus parvis facies; cumq; inferioribus de rebus magnis, vilescunt tamen superiores per dispositionem inferiorum, uti magnificentur & amplificentur virtutes eorum inferiores per superiorum dispositionem, Rigel. 59. & 40. Aphoris.* Judge not of small matters by the superiour Planets, nor of great actions by the inferiour: the superiours are vilified by the disposition of the inferiours, but the vertues of the inferiour Planets are augmented and amplified by the disposall of the superiours. By what I have said, I perceive, Princes will do no good of the matter, if during some succeeding yeares they intend any enlargement of Prerogative: the time is past, and Fryer *Bacons* brasse head hath lost its opportunity of speaking.

As *Mars* is the next in Order, so is he the next in dignity, for hee hath three, and is Lord of *medii cœli*, and hath exaltation in the Ascendent, therefore his judgement must not be pretermitted, hee being also Lord of the Comet in 1618. and having, or ruling the Triplicity where the Conjunction is, as also a tearm, whereby hee is made capable of copartnership in judgement. I say, hee must not with silence be passed over, for he is Angular at the *Sunne* his ingresse into *Aries*, presently after the Conjunction, hee was also in the tenth House, in the preventiall new Moon, and postventionall full Moon before this Conjunction. *Conjunctio duorum superiorum in signo aquatico, significat multitudinem pluviarum & pestilentias. Escuidus, fol. 17.* The Conjunction of the two superiours, in a Watry signe, intimates many showers, and a great pestilence. So hee in generall tearms. But to go on in an Astrologicall discoursive way: As the

two

two superiors, who make up, or give plentifull matter for present discourse, are in a bycorporeall, double bodied, or common signe, so is also *Mars*, of whom I am now to speak in *Geminis* near *oculus Tauri*: *Significatio principalis hujus Conjunctionis pertinget ad homines, Reges, Principes & Nobiles.* The principall signification of this Conjunction, hath relation to Kings, Princes, (not Utopian) and to Noble-men. *Haly* gives the reason, why the Conjunction being in a bycorporeall signe, should have such signification of men. *Quia sicut signa bycorporea significant, sive participant de natura fixorum & mobilium, ita homo habet participationem cum aliis substantiis omnibus: unde dicitur, microcosmus, id est, minor mundus*; Because as double-bodied signes, do participate of the nature of fixed, and moveable signes, so a man hath participation with all other substances, whereupon he is called, a little World, or a *Microcosme*.

Princes are subject to the Lawes of Nature, (*unius ejusdemque naturæ sumus omnes*, saith *Caius Marius*) and were it lawfull to deale as freely with them, as other men, certainly many most grievous calamities might have been prevented by a judicious prescience, either what might naturally, or contingently have happened to their private, and so particular fates, or as they are involved in a more generall way, by the Republique, unto their Subjects in generall: I do as much scorne to flatter them, as any calling whatsoever, and therefore I say: Let all the *European* Kings, and Princes that are this day living, carefully mannage the government God hath committed to them; for without doubt, this present Coniunction, and the precedent Comet, and some Constellations immediatly succeeding, will engage them, both in forraigne and domestique broiles and wars.

In Conjunctione superiorum in aqueis signis, bella magna exoriuntur propter Scorpium, quæ tamen in pacem non internecionem plerunque rediguntur propter Cancerum, & Pisces. Cardanus seg. 5, Aphoris. 48. The Coniunction of the superiours in watery signes, shew great warres will arise, because of *Scorpio*, yet notwithstanding they end in peace, or are brought to a peaceable conclusion, because *Cancer* is *Jupiters* exaltation, and *Pisces* his House.

Et relata est significatio Martis ad bella, & ad guerras, & ad victorias, & consimilia, quæ sunt quasi fines rerum, & fines quæ significant dissolutionem earum: nam bene non accidunt, nisi per observationem legis, vel earum mutationem, sectarum vel regnorum. Escuidus. diff. 2. cap. 1. *Mars* hath signification of strife, and wars, battells, victories, and the like, which may seem to be the ends of matters, of such

determi-

determination at concludes undoubtedly; for warres arise not, where Lawes are maintained, but where there is mutation of them, and new sects arise, &c.

This gives gentle caveats to all incroaching Rulers; Its good they be wise in time. Can all the rules of Astrology so faile me, that I shall in this deliver a false Position? There's none but God, by a divine providentiall hand, can prevent the destruction of many thousand families in *Europe*. This is a hard Chapter; hee that reads it, let him amend one, and then he need fear the lesse. The effects of the Coniunction shall not easily passe away. *Cum fuerint fortes significatores, & planetæ dominatores fortes fuerint, diutius durabit effectus. Anglicus fol.* 17.

When the significators are strong, and the Planets well dignified that rule, the effects shall continue the longer. But let us see what the Ancients speak, when *Mars* hath any signification; I am sure in our Conjunction he hath, and therefore men must participate, and Martiall designes have a principall signification. You may beleeve *Ptolomey, lib.* 2. *Quadrip. Mars ciet bella, seditiones intestinas, captivitates, excidia urbium, populi tumultus, principum iras, & propter eam causam subitas neces; propterea & febres tertianas, sanguinis eruptiones, morbos acutos, violentos interritus, juvenum violentias, injurias, incendia, homicidia, rapinas, latrocinia. In aere vero æstus, ventos calidos, pestiferos, & tabificos, fulminum jaculationes, turbines, siccitates, in mari subita naufragia, propter flatus turbulentos, & fulmina, & similes causas, &c. Mars* having dominion in the Conjunction, tells you of wars, intestine seditions, imprisonments, the besieging of Towns and Cities, Popular tumults, wrath of Princes, and therefore sudden beheadings, or making away with the parties, violent diseases, eruption of blood, the unusuall and sudden violent death of young men; violence, injuries, burning of Houses and Towns, murthers, rapines, high-way-robberies; In the ayre, there are stirred up poysonous windes, dispersion of thunder-bolts, hailestones, droughts, sudden shipwracks, by reason of extraordinary tempests.

By this it appears, that mens actions, guided by such an influence, or participating with it, are inclined to do and commit such, or actions of such like nature.

Men represented by *Mars* in *Geminis* generally, are handicraftsmen, Tradesmen, Merchants, Schollers, Apothecaries, Physicians, Chirurgions, Cannonneers, Musketteers, Highway-theeves, Brokers, and Scriveners. Particularly, in our Scheame he signifieth, Generals of

Armies,

Armies, Kings, Princes, Colonels, Serjant-Majors, Captaines, Men of Authority, Commanders of Towns, and Forts, men given to blood and slaughter, Scoutes, Quartermasters, Drummers, Trumpeters of war, &c. So that I perceive, the kindes, or qualties of the events, shall appear in the things specified, and shall be performed by men accordingly qualified.

The effects which we shall assuredly feele, and of which we shall in time bee sensible, are excellently set down by *Pontanus* in *Urania. Lib.* 1°.

Magnum opus: & jam signa Dei fulgentia terrent
Armorumque haurit strepitus, clangorque tubarum.
Ipse Deus, rapidis insistens pronus habenis,
Tela manu quatit insultans, acerque cruento
Ore tonat, pellunt agili temone jugales
Exanguis metus, atque tremor; tum ferreus ora
Terror, sanguineusque pavor, quatit ante flagellum.

God is now doing a great work, his glistring signes affright us: We hear the noise of weapons, and the sound of trumpets; God himself inclines to punish us with a sharpe bridle. God shakes darts with his hand over us, and thunders with his angry voyce. Pale fear, and trembling drives away men equally yoaked in the same condition of misery; hard hearted threatning, sanguine dread gives warning before the lash. All this works nothing with some: Yet in these kindes specified by mee, and by such men as are Saturnine, Joviall, Martiall, &c. shall the great work, by God intended to be done after this Conjunction, bee performed. And of this I am confident, and now come to the parts of the World materially signified, wherein the events shall most manifestly appear.

Kingdoms, and Countreys, wherein the effects of the Conjunction *shall have most predominancy.*

All Authors agree not in the distribution of the severall Countreys of the earth, to such or such a Planet. or Signe. The *Arabians* divided the severall habitable parts of the earth into Climates, and so according to the severall Latitudes of each Countrey were used to judge of the events, depending on these Conjunctions, &c. *Ptolemey* in some measure refined their error, and out of the whole earth, known to him in those dayes, formed four Quadrangles, out of *Europe, Asia,* and *Affrick*, as if the earth were four-square. The East part he allotted to *Saturnus*, the West to *Mars*, the South to *Venus,*

nus, the North to *Jupiter*; the *Sun*, *Venus*, and *Mercury*, he omitted. In every Quadrant he put severall Triangles, or made in every Quadrant severall Trygons: *Aries*, *Leo*, and *Sagittarius*, hee attributed to *Saturn*, *Jupiter*, and *Mars*, and to *Europe*: *Taurus*, *Virgo*, and *Capricornus*, hee gave to *Saturn*, and *Venus*, and to the South of *Asia*: the third Triplicity, containing *Gemini*, *Libra*, and *Aquarius*, hee assigned to *Saturn*, and *Jupiter*, and the North of *Asia*, where *Scythia*, *Arsacet*, and *Cataica* are: *Cancer*, *Scorpio*, and *Pisces* hee allotted to *Mars*, and *Venus*, and to *Affrique*; and then again hee made many divisions, and partitions of every Trygon, *viz.* into the East, West, &c.

Sir *Christopher Heydon* did not allow of these his distinctions, and *Campanella* speaking hereof, *Patet, Ptolomæum curtum esse in his assignandis judiciis.* *Ptolomey* is too curt, or short in assigning his judgements in this nature. I intend neither to desert *Ptolomey*, or altogether to follow him. I conceive it most rationall, first to consider the signe, wherein the Conjunction is. 2. The Angles of the figure. 3. The signes afflicted, by the presence of any of the Infortunes. 4. Those places of heaven, the Conjunction it self casteth either a Quadrate, or opposite Aspect unto. 5. The Lords of those signes, and quarters of heaven they are in. And 6. Whether they are strong, or weak.

The signe it self is *Pisces*, a Northerly signe, and double bodied, for it represents two fishes; the Conjunction is in 25. degrees of the signe, not farre from entring *Aries*, an Easterly signe, Equinoctiall and fiery; so that hence, one may conceive, Religion, and breach of Lawes and Priviledges, or questions about such things, &c. The signe is Northerne, yet past the middle the Conjunction is: from *London* full North; and North-East shall many of the actions intended by this Conjunction be performed. Absolutely the signe points out the North, and North-East part of *Europe* from *London*. There's no Planet in any Angle, but *Mars* Lord of *Scorpio*, viz. the tenth, and *Jupiter* of the Ascendent, *Mercury* of the seventh, and *Venus* of the fourth: they all point out the North part of *Europe*, with some small Westerne limitation. The signes afflicted, by presence, of infortunes, are *Pisces*, *Gemini*, and *Aries*: the places of heaven with Quadrat, or Opposition are *Virgo*, the opposite signe to the Conjunction, *Sagittarius* with perfect Quadrature, and also *Gemini*; the Lords of those signes are *Jupiter*, and *Mercury*, both in succedent Houses, the one afflicted by *Saturn*, the other within the limits of combustion.

The

The preventionall new Moon, before this Conjunction, points out *Italy*, and *Ireland*; not much better then deſtruction to that Kingdom: Peace with a qualification to *Italy*, after ſome broyles, but with much ado, and that but for a while. The Conjunction deſigneth *Spain*, and the Northeaſt parts thereof, therein ſhall be much deſolation. famine, and many tumults, uproars, &c.

The City of *London* in *England*, by the unlucky poſition of *Mars*, in her ſigne, being Cadent from *Aries*, and alſo *Mercury* his Diſpoſitor combuſt, and in detriment, ſhall indure many hard ſhocks, two plagues, extream dammage in her wealth, the loſſe of many valiant Citizens, and yet ſhall it bee with honour, and to her perpetuall renowne, becauſe that *Mars* is with *Oculus Tauri*, one of the moſt notable fixed Stars: Nor ſhall any man yet alive, ſee the dayes Mother *Shipton* ſpake of concerning *London*; yet in time all Cities muſt have end: I rather conceive, that about the year of our Lord God 168[illegible]. the City ſhall be in great danger, then come to a finall Cataſtrophe, during the revolution of that fifth Conjunction.

If *Cancer* bee the Aſcendent of *Scotland*, as ſome affirme it is, though *Henricus de Fenby* think otherwiſe, let us conſider the *Moon*, and we finde her in *Gemini*, in the twelfth from *Cancer*. This Conjunction will affoord much diſtraction, diſcontent, ſorrow, and penury to that Nation, ſo alſo to *Venice*, when ſhee leaſt thinks of it, and to *Conſtantinople*, and the City of *Rome* her ſelf, and the change of two Popes, if not more, before 1656. *Hungaria* is immediatly to feele the hand of warre, and not long after *Slavonia*, *Bulgaria*, *Moravia*, and *Dalmatia*; *Dalmatia* will laſt ſmart, but to moſt purpoſe. *Calabria* is now threatned; *Portugall* will bee invaded, but not reconquered. Some parts of *Normandy*, in *France*; *Paris*, and many very honourable and rich Cities in *France*; as *Lions*, *Tholous*, are all ſubject to the laſh, to popular tumults, inſurrections, the ſword, and peſtilence, &c. Many domeſtique broiles ſhall *France* endure, more troubleſome then a forraigne invaſion, though both may bee feared. Some Cities of *Zeland*, and Towns in *Holland* ſhall murmur, and intollerably ſuffer by ſhipwrack, and Piracies. *Denmark*, though * yet in Peace, by the effects of this Conjunction, and Cometary influence, 1644. or 1645. may expect a bitter potion of trouble, if the providence of Almighty God, give not an underſtanding, and preventionall knowledge in that State: If Art fail not, it ſhould be ſo. By that, and the *Scottiſh* actions, I conceive I am right.

* It was when I firſt wrote this.

I muſt write from my heart, what I conceive Aſtrologically to bee intended. There is *Aries* in the Scheame, afflicted with *Cauda Draconis.*

Jacet extremis in partibus orbis
Oceano cincta, & Pelagi resonantibus undis,
Gens Orco sata, gens Ditem commenta parentem
Caruleis quondam tellus habitata Britannis.

England these Verses meane; and so do I; It will be said,

Efferus has habitat sedes Deus: huic comes haret
Et bellum, bellique parens discordia, & ira,
Injustum, insidiaque, & pallida tabe cruenta.
Cedes, inque suum rabies armata cruorem.

Some angry God, for some years possesseth our habitations; his companions, warre, discord, and fury, the parents of warre, injustice, fraud, pale murther, with cruell Consumptions, and armed madnesse into his owne destruction.

Norway under the *Danish* Government, must be sensible of our judgment, for its subject to *Scorpio*, and both by the Comet and Conjunction must be the subject of trouble. *Flanders* I pitty thee: *Brabant* weep: *Catalonia* belonging to the Empire of *Spain* hath already suffered, and as I heare is still in Armes; be it in Armes now, or not in Armes, *Catalonia* must not yet be quiet from further molestation. *Germany*, both Comet and *Conjunction* point out; even she that is,

Dives aquis, dives nemorum viridantibus umbris
Sevarumq; parens facunda, altrixq; ferarum.

I would I might live to see an end or conclusion of thy intestine wars, I cannot yet give thee comfort: If *Scorpio* be the Ascendent of that most honourable house of *Austria*, (which I extremely honour) thou wilt in time want friends and support; this *Conjunction* and the Cometary influence, designe thee out a greater blow then yet thou hast had: but be comforted, thou shalt flourish many yeares: that Crosse shall humble thee and bring thee on thy knees; but then thou wilt perceive thine enemies that for many years have betrayed thee; thou wilt take vengeance on them; but for ever after live a free Prince, untill the measure of years alotted for continuation of thy house have Period. The first Eclipe in *Taurus* and with *Caput Algol*, shall molest thee, but some of the *minor Conjunctions* in *Taurus* undoe thee.

I wrote my mind a little before of *England*, the North-East quarter of the Kingdome, and Southwest especially are to be sensible, in an ill manner, of the effects of this *Conjunction*, but the Comet pointeth out the whole Kingdome. By the Map of *England*, any may almost point out the place (*consideratis considerandis*:) *Guido Bonatus, fol.* 157. *Si significata earum Conjunctionum cadunt ut pluries super ea quæ significantur per signum Ascendentis, vel per ejus dominum, & per signum Conjunctionis, si fuerit in Septentrionali parte, accident mutationes ibidem, &c.* If the signification of those *Conjunctions* do happen, as many times it doth, to take place from the signe ascending, or by the Lord thereof, and by the signe, in which the *Conjunction* is; if these be in the North, from thence expect the beginning of changes and Alteration. There are many other places, Cities, and Countries, which purposely I passe over without denomination; though I am perswaded, all or most of the Countries and Kingdomes, on this North side of the Equinoctiall Line, and most of all the famous Cities therein scituated, shall have vexation and annoyance at one time or other; let their Latitude be more or lesse: For as the Comet passed over the Æquator, and so by degrees had more and more Declination, though at first very little, yet left not his appearance, untill he came to have 60. degrees: by which meanes, one time or other, during its continuance, it was verticall to all Kingdomes and Countries in *Europe*, and so in due time its effects will manifest themselves. We have few Countries, habitable with rationall or sociable men, that exceed in their habitation the Latitude of 60. or 61. *deg.* and therefore it were needlesse, in our judgement, to exceede any Country beyond that proportion of Latitude: And yet without doubt, those Savages that live neer to 61. and somewhat more in Northern Latitude, shall sensibly perceive great alterations in their petty Common-wealths, 1646. 1647. So that if no Invader oppose, they will kill one another. For what the Comet in 1618. the *Conjunction* in 1623. the terrible Eclipse in 1639. the severall lesse *Conjunctions* of *Saturn* and *Mars*, and *Mars* and *Jupiter* do not performe; that shall have incouragement from this *Conjunction*, which comes in a preposterous order; and what this cannot perform, shall with a witnesse in 1654. 1655. and 1656. be accomplished by the formidable Eclipse of the Sun, and divers other configurations, then in force. But lest any one think I have deviated from *Ptolomie* and his followers, in this my partition, I shall alleadge *Proclus fol.* 61. *lib.* 2. *Considerandum est signum in quo contingit Conjunctio, & ejus triangulus & eo perveniens quadrans, nam in regionibus quadranti subjectis, eventum esse dicemus*: Let us consider the signe wherein the *Conjunction* is, and his Triangle, and the Quadrant or quarter of heaven belonging thereto, we pronounce the event to shew its self in those Regions belonging to that Quarter of the world: I have, for satisfaction of some friends, declared my mind herein, but with this caution, that my arguments are not demonstrative, or can be made so: I acknowledge my Prognosticks to be onely grounded upon conjecturall probabilitie, and are not subject to the senses, or Geometricall demonstration; this I speak to avoid carping.

A Probable conjecture of the Authors, concerning the space of time, in which the effects of this Conjunction shall shew themselves; and when the world may expect a period, and England *better dayes.*

IF the presidents of former *Conjunctions* may either helpe our judgment, or get credit with the Antagonists of Astrologie; or if experience in matters naturall, may be beleeved; as amongst Soules rationall it should: I shall make it appear, that not any one of these *Conjunctions*, hath ever hapned in our quietest times, without some extraordinary or almost miraculous accident, and passages memorable, signified precisely by the *Conjunction* precedent, or eminent at hand: But not alwayes at the moment of its *Conjunction*, or in that year, or in some years subsequent: this was in nature preposterous, who irregularly doth nothing; we must consider in the first place, what every *Conjunction* principally is made the fore-runner of: secondly, in what proportion of time the events may shew themselves: thirdly, when any Eclipse, or *minor Conjunction*, or Annuall revolution doth put that act or accident forward into the world; do not we know that, the Physition giving a medicine to his patient, expecteth not that it shall immediately operate, some houres he alloweth for the medicines operation. God is our Physitian, the heavens his storehouse or shop; the Planets his Instrumentall medicines, and druggs; their motion his time he gives in operation. If Physick work not, as the learned Doctor conceiveth it ought; (*aliquid latet*) there is an obstruction he little thought of: If I faile in my Prognostick, God perhaps reserves the honour for some more worthy man, and so blinds my senses, or permits not me to see so much truth, as I should.

Non semper eodem modo eveniunt, sed alias plus grassantur, alias minus. The effects chance not alwayes after one manner, but sometimes assailes us more forcibly at one time, than another: *Impedimenta quæ ventura*

ventura sunt, in annis Alynthia evenient; cum pervenerit annus mundi ad corpora malorum, unicuiq; signo da annum. Almansor proposit. 82. The Impediments which are to happen or chance in the world, will appear in the years of profection (for the *Arabians* call *Alinthia profectio*) when the year of the world comes to the bodies of the infortunes, give to every signe one yeer. The meaning of *Almansor* is thus; that if the profectionall sign in any year, be the signe and degree, wherein at the time of one of the lesser or greater *Conjunctions*, an infortune was: the evill intended by that Planet in the *Conjunction*, or perhaps an Eclipse, shall apparently shew its selfe, according to its fortitude or debility, and also relation, being had to the figure of the world; which is the ingresse of the *Sun* into *Aries*.

I finde much difference in my Authors concerning the time when, and the time how long the effects shall continue. *Vide ubi ceciderit locus Alkirem minoris ab ascendente Anni in quo fuerit illa Conjunctio: & secundum quantitatem quam fuerit inter illum & ascendens ex signis; erunt anni usque ad majus quicquam in illa Conjunctione fuerit:* this is the 58. *Aphoris.* of *Ptolomey*: by *Alkirem* he meanes *Conjunction.*

Haly expounds it thus: *Cumque sciveris illud ascendens Anni: & signum Conjunctionis: aspice quid fuerit inter illa loca ex signis & gradibus, & pone omne signum annum; & gradus partes anni secundum proportionem suam.* See where the place of the greater or lesser *Conjunction* falleth from the Ascendent of the year wherein it is; according to the number of signes betwixt that and the Ascendent, the years shall be betwixt that and the great action, the *Conjunction* intends: or thus, as *Haly* in his Comment, When thou knowest the Ascendent of the year and signe of the *Conjunction*, consider the number of signes and degrees betwixt them, and give to every sign one year, and divide the parts of degrees accordingly.

Trapezuntius will have this *Aphorisme* understood of Profections in Nativities, and illustrates it by his own Nativity: In Nativities we have the directions of the 5. hylegiacall places which better directeth to the fatall or happy year, far more certainly then Profections do: for if Profection be admitted to do any thing without a particular direction; then every twelfth year the same actions must happen; but they do not so; therefore I hold *Trapezuntius* not right in this his exposition, nor indeed in many other. *Pontanus* following the steps of *Trapezuntius*, is angry any one should think otherwayes: *Hoc Ptolomæi præceptum tempestate nostra non modo non servatur ut parum*

rum

rum intellectum, verò malè conversum ad Jovis Saturniq; conjunctionem refertur: quod ne somniari quidem Gracè ex verbis Ptolomei potest. In our age this precept of *Ptolomey* is not onely not kept, but ill understood; and worse than that, is converted to signifie the *Conjunction* of *Jupiter* and *Saturn*; which cannot so much as be dreamed of, out of the Greek words of *Ptolomey*. The two last mentioned Authors translate the *Aphorisme* thus: *Adverte Conjunctionis locum, in quo loco ab ascendente Anni est*; *viz.* Marke the place of the *Conjunction* in what place it is from the Ascendent of the year: when the Profection comes thither, the accident happens. Some would have this understood of the *Conjunction* preceding the ingresse of the *Sun* into *Aries, viz.* if the place of heaven, wherin the *Conjunction* before the ingresse into *Aries*, be considered, and then in what part of heaven, at the Ingresse, it happens, and observe the aspects then cast to that place, or when any lesser *Conjunction* is in that degree, or in aspect to it; that then, and in that moneth, &c. For my own part I conceive, it may with much limitation be so understood; but certainly its the more rationall way to understand and make use of the *Aphorisme* according to *Haly*; for its most probable that he, being an *Egyptian*, and living 400. yeares before *Trapezuntius*, had as exact a Greek coppy to follow, as those times could produce: and if he have translated it right, the Controversie is ended.

Johannes Anglicus in Tract. 1. *Cap.* 10. *fol.* 17. hath these words, which do absolutely satisfie me: *Aspice quantum est inter Conjunctionem minorem, & ascendens anni in quo est, & intellige hic per Conjunctionem minorem, Conjunctionem* Saturni & Jovis, *cum mutatur de uno signo ad aliud, scilicet in* 20. *Annis, & quot signa fuerint inter illa duo loca, ad tot annos erit major significatio, quam ipsa significat.*

See the difference betwixt the *Conjunction* and the ascendent of the yeer wherein it is; and understand by lesser *Conjunction*, that of *Saturn* and *Jupiter*, which they make every twenty years, out of one signe into another; so many Signes as are betwixt them, so many yeers shall the greatest signification of the *Conjunction* shew its self. We will make use of this Rule in our present *Conjunction*, but must not take the ingresse of the *Sun*, immediately succeeding the *Conjunction*; but I must take the ingresse, the preceding, *viz.* that of 1642. whose ascendent is 29. *degrees*, 36. *min.* in *Gemini*, or after, 2 *signes*, 29. *deg.* and 36. *min.* the *Conjunction* is after 10. *signes*, 25. *deg.* and 26. *min.* if we substract the place of the *Conjunction* from the ascendent of the years Revolution, there will remain, 3. *Signes*, 4. *deg.* and 10. *m.* which

which representſ three yeares, and neer two monethſ; ſo that 1643. 1644. 1645. and part of 1646. it is apparent that the effects of this Conjunction ſhall extreamly and moſt forcibly work.

But ſome may demaund this nicety, why I take not my meaſure of time from the aſcendent of the year ſucceeding the Conjunction: to this I anſwer: That the Conjunction it ſelf falleth not in that Revolution, but in the former; for the *Sun* his entrance into *Aries* is the time when we begin our Aſtrologicall Revolution, and before he come to the ſame point or beginning of *Aries* againe, we cannot ſay he hath performed his yearly Revolution: now the Conjunction being celebrated the 15. of *February*, you know preceded the ſubſequent ingreſſe almoſt 24. dayes, and therefore I could not make ſubduction in difference of degrees from the aſcendent of the year 1643. But becauſe experience will onely make manifeſt the Queſtion to future ages: I will alſo perform it the latter way, though I am ſatisfied in the former.

Aſcendens Revolutionis, Anni 1643. 4. deg. 29. m. Virgo.	*Sig.*	*deg.*	*m.*
Virgo, or after ———————————————	5.	4.	29.
The Conjunction is after ———————————	11.	25.	26.
I adde 12. *Signes*, to the years Revolution and then the difference is ———————	5.	9.	3.

By this reckoning: 1643. 1644. 1645. 1646. 1647. and half a yeer more almoſt, will be the ſpace of time wherein the effects may moſt vigorouſly operate.

Give me leave to adde my private conjecture, concerning the heate of this Conjunctions operation: I did conceive, becauſe we were involved in broyles before the being of this Conjunction, that wee might expect a ſmattering of comfort at what time *Jupiter* by direction, not Tranſit, might get into *Aries*, the Aſcendent of *England*; and perhaps this may prove no vaine conjecture; it doth alſo very neer jump with the meaſure of years above writ. We ſee in the Scheam *Jupiter* is in the Termes of the infortunes, it may be hoped when he arives to the firſt degree of *Aries*, the Aſcendent of *England*, wherein he hath a Terme and Triplicity, and meets with no impediments, he will aſſiſt the *Engliſh* either with forraigne or Domeſtique ayde: My way was thus; to take the Circle of Poſition of *Jupiter* in the Conjunction and ſo to perform the work.

Longitudo.	Jovis 25. *degrees*,	26. *Piſces.*	
Latitudo.	1.	6.	M. D.
Declinat.	2.	45.	*Merid. Sub. terra.*

O *Aſcend.*

Ascend: Recta. 356. *degrees,* 11. *minutes.*
Distantia ab. J. Cœli. 34. *degrees.* 21. *minutes.*
Circulus positionis. 33.
Ascensio obliqua. Jovis *sine Latitud.* 356. *deg.* 59. *min.*
Cum Latitudine. 358. *deg.* 5. *min.*
Distantia Jovis *a primo puncto Arietis, Cum Latitud.*—1. *deg.* 55. *m.*
Sine Lat. ——3.—1.

By this conjecture of mine, which is not altogether discrepant from *Escudius*, I say, that 1643. and 1644. we shall have very great action, nor shall it determine, or much cease, untill after 1645. And so it may be hoped by this order of direction, that in the year, 1645. towards the latter end thereof, we shall have great likelihood of being in a better condition then now we are in. About this time or not far from hence the Comet seemes to transmit the war to more remote Countries and habitations: That we should have any established peace before that time, I scarce beleeve, (God grant it then) for *Saturnus* on the 25. of *March* 1643. entred *Aries* the Ascendent of *England*, and therein he continueth untill the 21. of *May* 1645. at what time he enters *Taurus*, where having made progresse almost five moneths, he again, the 26. of *Octob.* 1645. comes tumbling by Retrogradation into *Aries*, (as if then he would bring in a Forraigner with a vengeance.) But on *Munday* the ninth of *February* following, he leaves *Aries* and again enters *Taurus*, (beware *Ireland*) no more then visiting our English Ascendent in almost thirty years: In *Anno* 1646. *June* 19, *Saturn* and *Jupiter* come to a *Sextile* Aspect; *Saturn* in 15. *Taurus*, *Jupiter* in 15. *Cancer*: *Aspice Ascensionem Planetæ, & gradum exaltationis, gradum quoque sui casus; nam hæc sunt quæ significant homines, & eorum opera: Almansor. proposit.* 129. Behold the Ascension of a Planet and the degree of his exaltation and fall; for these signifie both the men and their works: *Jupiter* in the Conjunction now, being Lord of the Ascendent and of the signe the Conjunction is in, being then 1646. got into *Cancer* his exaltation, and in *Sextile* to *Saturn* in *Taurus*, the signe of the fourth house in the *Conjunction*, and at or neer that time, all the Planets except *Mercury* saluting each other with one benevolent aspect or other: those do most undoubtedly declare, that the miseries of the afflicted English do draw neer to a Period. And yet things may not be perfectly setled, or there may not be a visible face of safety untill, 1647. Let none understand me, as if I thought that about these times we should have so firme a peace or such a durable happinesse as many of us have seen formerly:

formerly: no, it will be a great comfort if then we sensibly feele some melioration of fortune to our State in generall: All the time that *Saturn* passeth through *Aries*, *viz.* about 1643. to 1645. I expect nothing but either destruction, molestation, war, famine, plague, forraigne Invasion, or the like, to the English; one mischiefe happening in the neck of another; all being thought concluded this day, the day following produceth new matter; and in such a condition shall we be in for some yeares, according to the course of heavens: I am doubtfull that this year 1643. *Saturn* will afflict us in the City of *London* with the plague, strange, consumptions, giddinesse in the head, and a kinde of stupid Lethargie; neither known or thought of by *Galen* or *Hypocrates.*

Towards *September* 1644. if not before, *Saturn* will be malicious to the English in afflicting another kinde of disease, dulnesse, and stupidnesse all over the the body; some shall be visited with the Plague or consumption of the Lights, and dry Coughs; and an exact Phrensie to purpose, making prophets.

In the year 1645. *Saturn* and his Angel *Orifiel* will be more mischievous (if *Sol* and *Michael* his *secundeian* Intelligencer prevent it not) for not long after he is to take his leave of *Aries* and *England*, and so he will with a witnesse, if the plague in men, and scarcity of provision for men, and a generall misfortune, be any terrour or affliction. These are like to happen, God not preventing.

It was observed by the learned *Cambden*, that *Saturn* cannot passe through a signe of the fiery Triplicity, but he will afflict the City of *London* with a Plague; A Plague to the City is a curse to the whole Kingdome: I have in my time seen some experience hereof: did not *Saturn* in 1625. passe through *Leo*? Did he not in 1636. passe through *Sagittarius*? the position of *Jupiter* and *Venus* in the sixth house 1644. may mitigate his fury somewhat; but 1645. I fear he will maliciously oppresse the City of *London*, if not the whole Kingdome, or most of our great Towns, either with a Plague, which is most probable, or with some generall calamity as bad, &c. For then in that years Revolution, *Mars* and *Sol* are in *Quadrate* Aspect, out of *Cardinall* signes: the *Dragons Taile* is in the Ascendent (I fear the poor Commonalty) the *Moon* neer the degree Ascending at the lesser *Conjunction* in 1643. and in the 12. house, the people will be full of sorrow; *Saturn* in the 12. of *Aries* his fall, and in the third house; now Treacherous Kinsman, Act thy part: Wo to some Eastern Countries, *Jupiter* is not much elongated from the *Pleiades*, the Nobles play fast

 and

and loose, and pay for it: the *Moon* separates from a Trine of *Saturn*, and goes to a squar of *Sol*; Kings of *Europe* offend not your people, provoke them not too much: the almost degree of the Comets appearance, now culminating, shews now, as if all the whole world were up in Armes, and all Nations mad or drunk with the fury of the Comets last Salutation, and the influence of the *Conjunction*, and co-operating Eclipses and *minor Conjunctions*. Indeed in 1646. *Jupiter* in the *figura mundi*, is in the Ascendent, but *Mercury* Lord of the Ascendent with *Mars* in *Piscibus*; matters are not yet right and perfectly setled, yet better then formerly. Some Prince either fled or Captivated. 1647. *Saturn* in 15. *Taurus*, and in the *medium Celi* of the worlds figure, one Monarchy begins to totter; and so by degrees God brings his purpose to perfection: but these judgements will be displeasing: for Princes love not to hear of such matters; I will return to my intended task; and do remember that of *Cardane*, which in some sence materially concerns this matter. *Card. Seg.3. Apho.85. Planeta quilibet virtutem suam ad actum perducit per Luminaria, non quod Luminaria talia significent.* Every Planet brings to passe his vertue by the Luminaries, not that the Luminaries signifie such things: if this be so, why shall not the *Sun* being in the same signe our *Conjunction* is in, give us light at what time God will openly manifest the secrets of his decrees by this *Conjunction*; if we chance to direct him to the bodies of *Saturn* and *Jupiter*. I conceive if I take the Circle of position of the *Sun*, and under the Elevation of that Pole, both the oblique Ascension of *Sol*, *Saturn*, and *Jupiter*; I shall discover the year, or very neer, when the effects shall break out, and be most visible, or when the great and principall matter of the whole *Conjunction*, shall be most in force. For I am doubtfull, because both the lights are under the earth, it will be long ere this *Conjunction* accomplish his effects, or declare what it would have to any purpose, Let no one think that because we are in *England* at the time of the Conjunctions appearance, in Armes one against another; or because we have many new and Novell opinions, and speak of Reformation of doctrine and discipline, that this is all shall happen, No: its not all: Or that these quarrells shall soon be composed, and Religion established: Let us go on, I confesse the influence of the *Conjunction* doth operate already, though but obscurely; for it is at present impedited by the Comets Influence, which being above the course of nature, must needs hinder naturall progressions, untill its turn is served, and that its not yet ended, there's one English man of my mind, and

he

be very learned, though he professe himself no friend to Astrologie. *Nuntius Propheticus, 35. fol. Natura mea semper hactenus a predictionibus eventuum ex astris ab horruit*: My nature (quoth he) hath hitherto abhorred any prediction of events from the Stars: and yet see how he goeth on, in the next lines: *Fateor super-calestia maxime in hac sub-calestia agere*: I confesse the heavenly bodies have much to do upon our sub-celestiall. *Fateor etiam coitum superiorum erronum malorum Iliade ut plurimum Comitari, & consequenter multum energia & portenti habere*; I confesse the congresse of the superiour erraticalls are lightly accompanied with an Iliad of mischiefe; and so consequently to have signification of some eminent matters and materiall operation: but the conclusion, he thinks, kills us all; with *Ipse dixit: Sed id, quicquid est extra humanam scientiam, atq; dijudicationem, positum cum Tychone Brahe in re non dissimili arbitror*: But if the Astrologer can give any judgement, or if these Conjunctions signifie any thing; 'tis above humane knowledge and judgement, and in such like a matter I conceive *Tycho* was of the same opinion. What this Schollers intention was to acquaint us with the star in 1572. learnedly explained by *Tycho*, or of the Comets before 1618. of *Keplers* Astrologicall prediction in generall; and of *Sybilla Tiburtina* her Prophesie, and mother *Shiptons*, and *Alstedius* his conjecture of the *Conjunction* in 1643: and yet abhors predictions, I know not: sure I am none of these can be predicted without Astrologie, and for him to mention these predictions, and directly affirm, man hath no knowledge in the interpretation. Certainly it seems to me, *Nuntius* writ that Tract to shew he could write Latine, but either could not, or would not interpret the meaning of them; without which it were better we know them not, or that he had not collected them. But *Nuntius fol.* 22. and *I*, agree very well: *Sane opinor significata Cometa, 1618. Licet vates non sum nondum expirasse, hoc est, ut luculentius agam universas mutationes, qua per hoc insolens & portentosum ostensum innuebantur, nec dum terminari.* Though no Prophet, yet he judged the universall mutations, intended by that Comet, were not yet determined. But let us see when the *Sun* comes to the body of *Saturn* and *Jupiter*, for more full manifestation of the grand action of this *Conjunction*.

Longitudo Solis 7. 34. *Pisces.*	}	*Circulus Positionis.*	40. 0.
Declinat. M. sub terra: 9. 0.	}	*Asc. ob. Sol. ad eandem: Ele.*	346. 21.
Ascentio Recta. 339. 16.	}	*Asc. ob Jovis cum Lat.*	358. 30.
Distantia ab I. Celi. 50. 33.	}	Differentia ———	12. *deg.* 9. *m.*

The Oblique Ascension of *Jupiter*, is the same, some minutes excepted of *Saturn*: If I adde 12. years to 1642. it produceth 1654 but added to 1643. it maketh 1653. Which years if they prove not admirable, I am much mistaken. If there were any Prince borne about the year 1618. or 1623. that is naturally of heroicall disposition, he may perhaps shew himself near the *Alpes* about that time, and perform wonders with small help, I am confident, the greatest Action signified by this Conjunction, shall then, and in those years appear, to the terrour of many thousands. The very action I cannot divine, but I verily conceive, that it shall most concern the Pope and Clergy of *Rome*, who though hee shall not be absolutely then destroyed, yet shall he be so shaken, so tossed, so curbed, so forsaken, as his power after that will daily sink and decline, untill the full measure of his time is accomplished, after which hee shall never againe have either strength or being. Certainly, it may be conjectured, that about those years, God will miraculously raise up a potent Prince in *Italy*, or near to *Italy*, for that work onely, that shall little care for Bulls, or Papall curses, and one that shall either subdue *Rome*, or break the strength of the Popes authority in *Italy*. But shall *Italy* containe him? It cannot; like a whirlewinde he runs through, oo:ooo. (but a Northern star extinguisheth that light, &c.) Where hee assists as a friend, he conquers like an enemy, &c. But because the *Moon* is the Luminary of the time, I will see in what space of degrees shee will get above the earth, and put them into years; perhaps when she gets to the Cusps of the seventh House, a discovery of some grand actions may be.

Longitudo Lunæ.	15.2. *Gemini.*	*Descensio ob. cum Lat.*	109. 2.
Latitud.	4. 40. *Mer.*	*Descensio sine Lat.*	101. 20.
Declinat. Bor.	18. 1.	*Descensio Cuspis* 7.	116. 10.
Ascensio Rect.	74. 13.	*Dist.. Lunæ ab angulo* 7. *cum Lat.* 7. *grad.* 8. *min. sine Lat.* 14°. 50. *min.*	
Dist. ab 7. *Cœli*	44. 42.		
Elevatio Poli.	48.		

If I adde 7. years to 1642. it cuts out 1649. but if I adde 7. to 1643. it points out the year 1650. But assuming the distance of the *Moon*, without Latitude, from the Cuspe of the seveth House, they fall to make almost 15. years, which points out the year 1657. and 1658. Surely the explication of this Conjunctionall influence upon *Europe*, will be difficult to finde out, or of more concernment then at present we imagine. The swift motion of the Planets, shew a celerity in action, the sublimity of the two grand Planets being princi-

pall

pall Agents, shew the greatnesse, durability, or Magnitude of the action. *Ea nimirum seditiones quæ a Saturno & Jove portenduntur sunt durabiliores.* The stirrings, proceeding from *Saturn* and *Jupiter*, are more durable.

That the principall matter intended shall not presently break out, I do judge, because both the lights, and all the Planets are under the earth. *Latet plane res, quum stella eam significans aut sub terra est, aut in alieno loco Soli conjungitur; contra patet quum edepressione in altitudinem tollitur, proprioque in loco collocatur. Ptol, Aphoris. 26.* The matter is obscured, when the Planet signifying it, is either under the earth, or joyned to the *Sunne* in an obscure House: on the other side, all is manifest, when a Planet is brought out of his depression to his Altitude, and posited in his proper Sphear, or Element.

If wee observe the Conjunction in 1603. we shall finde it above the earth, though obscured in the twelfth House; yet the two Luminaries in Angles; the *Moon* in perfect Opposition to the *Sun* and *Venus.* Part of the action, signified by that Conjunction, broke out immediatly: As King *James* his accesse to the *English* Crown rather preceded; but other matters not so soon, but lay cunningly smothered, and yet to this day are: Let the Jesuite tell you what. Look upon that 1623. The *Moon* is ascending, and the *Sun* descending, and yet in reception, as if both King and people were deluded, but yet the *Moon* getting first above the earth, discovered part of the secrets intended by that Conjunction. The *Moon* is in this Conjunction going to a *Quadrat* of the *Sun.* If not fairly, the people by foul means will discover the secrets of Princes; By foulnesse, I mean warre; for *Moon* and *Sun* are in square, and yet there's such jugling, to this day all is not yet discovered; but it will be shortly, &c,

The wars we now grone under, and the infinite pressures wee suffer, by his Majesties aversnesse from his Parliament, and City of *London*; the desertion of those many Lords, and untrusty Members of the House of Commons, do all make way, and prepare matter for their owne, and posterities confusion in the first place; and next, for the utter desolation of this Kingdom, and his Majesties Posterity: And I know there's a Family, or Faction of Christendom smiles, and laughes at the folly of the *English*, sith wee do our selves what they would, but never could, without these dishonourable breaches in the Lords, and the too too obstinate Commoners, absent at this present from *Westminster*. It grieves me to see a people so misled, and yet know not by whom; For of the Cabinet Counsell they are not, nor his Majesty himself, &c. Well; Let them bee advised in time; *Post est occasio calva*: Let not specious and luke-warme pretences delude them any longer; let not them indeavour to raise a people that hate the name of Gentleman. Let the undeserving Bishop, and Clergy-man suffer; they onely have stirred these tumults, with the assistance of the Jesuite; but I forbear, &c. *Non argumentis, aut ambagibus in judicando uti debemus, aut adulationibus*: Wee must not in these manner of judgements use arguments, trifles, or flatteries, but speak truth, &c.

For my own part I conceive, that for three years and a half, or thereabouts, from the beginning of the Conjunction, wee shall have sharp and quick action, afterwards perhaps, some seeming quietnesse; About 1650. or 1649. a whispering of some greater matter, or some new matter, not formerly divulged agitated, or first receives impression: matters after for two or three years, may seeme composed; In 1654. 1655. or 1656. all things are as apparent as the Sunshine, and then, either hee, shee, they, or something, declare what hath for some years been clofited in the breasts of a few: That is most certaine, *Operationes Planetarum nunquam cessant, donec contraria, a planeta aut fixa stella, aut signi parte contrariæ qualitatis impediantur vel in Solis radios incidant.* Planets never cease to work, untill contradicted by some Planet of contrary nature, or fixed starre, or signe, or happen upon the Sun-beams. If this be so, it makes me more confident, that when the Sunne comes to the bodies of *Saturn* and *Jupiter*, things will happen as by me Predicted; and that in the interim, more or lesse, the effects of this Conjunction will *Annually* cause some alteration in humane affairs, and stir up mens mindes, and fit matter to receiue that judgement, which God in his providence hath from eternity decreed, and which will about that time crave the execution of his preordained Ordinances: and if that wee beleeve *Almansor, Proposit.* 30. *Cum planetæ ponderosi fuerint occidentales a sole, dabunt probitatem circa finem vitæ*: Weighty or ponderous Planets, being Occidentall of the Sunne, give goodnesse in the latter part of our life. Why may not this be applied to our Conjunction? and we after (*tot tantosque labores*) enjoy a most blessed time, peace, quietnesse, and all earthly blessings, which we formerly have enjoyed.

I have run somewhat an extravagant way, for determining the time of the events of this Conjunction, having no certain limitation, more then conjecturall, from the Ancients, in deciding the controversie; Yet it will not be amisse, if we try the rule of *Hermes*, prescribed in

Aphoris.

Aphoris. 100. *Terminatur finis eventuum omnis inceptionis, omniumque dubitabilium ipsius per hos significatores, videlicet per 4. locum, & dominum ejus, & per planetam, si forte fuerit in eodem. Item per Luminare cujus erit authoritas, & dominum ejus, & per planetam cui luminare ipsum conjungitur & dominum ejus:* The end of events of every inception, aad of every doubtfull matter, is determined by these significators, *viz.* by the Cuspe of the fourth House, his Lord, and the Planet therein, If any be; also by the Luminary of the time, and his Lord, and by the Planet to whom that light is conjoyned, and by the Lord thereof, &c. *Venus* is here Lady of the fourth House, the *Moon* is the light of the time, the Conjunction being Nocturnall, she is as it were separated from a Quadrature of *Mercury*, and applies to a *Trine* of *Venus*: In degrees, the difference betwixt their comming to Aspect, are 7. *grad*, and 44. *minutes*: but if under the Elevation of the Lunar Pole of Position, we take their distance by Oblique descension, we shall find them 9. *grad.* and 24, *minutes*, which added to 1643. and allowing one year for each degree, it pointeth 1652. and almost one half year, before the events be fully concluded. The Retrogradation of *Venus* may happily shew the many probabilities of determining sooner; but as things many times are near to an end, and yet are not finished, *Multa cadunt inter calicem supremaque labra*: So doubtlesse, one inconveniency or other, may for many years, when things are near conclusion, break off, and hinder our happinesse, untill the exact measure of time be fulfilled: for you must observe, that the signe of the fourth House is fixed, as also that *Venus* is in a fixed signe, so that the signification of things hereby promised are prolonged and continued.

It will be questioned by some perhaps, why I give for each degree in distinction of time, one year? Besides that I my self hold it fittest, I have some encouragement from the learned *Almansor. Aporis.* 41. *Cum significator fuerit inter septimam & quartam, erunt anni.* When the significator is between the seventh and fourth House, in judgement of time, you shall giue years, &c. The *Moon* being in that quarter, and the light of the time. I think I have not done amisse. And that the *Moon* is to have great prerogative in determining the end of these events, *Rigel. Aphoris.* 84 *lib.* 2. confirmeth. *Finis rerum est periodus significatoris, & per quartum & dominium ejus, quando Luminare temporis cum ipso adjungitur.* The end of things, is the period of the significator, and by the fourth House, and his dominion, when the light of the time is joyned with the Lord of the fourth.

I have now almost done what I intended, but because *Origanus, fol.* 411. or rather *Cardane*, whose words they are, saith, *Non solum conjunctiones, verum etiam oppositiones & Quadrati radii superiorum planetarum magnas in mundo mutationes designant.* Not onely these Conjunctions, but their Oppositions and Quadrate Aspects designe great mutations; I have therefore inserted the progression of *Saturn* and *Jupiter*, in the severall Aspects they make each to other, before the year 1663. at what time they come to their third Conjunction in the fiery Trygon.

The severall Aspects of Saturn *and* Jupiter *to each other, untill their next* Conjunction *in* 1663.

Yeeres of our Lord.	*Moneth, Day, and Time of the Day.*	*Sign, Degree, and Minute of Saturn.*	*Signe, Degree, and Minute, of Jupiter.*	*The Nature of the Aspects,*
1646	*Friday*, June 19. 1.15. P. M.	*Saturn* 15.7. *Taurus.*	*Jupiter*, 15.7. *Cancer.*	*Sextile.*
1647	*Thursday*, Septem. 30. 19.10. P. M.	*Saturn*, 1.44. *Gemini.* Retrogr.	*Jupiter*, 1.44. *Virgo.*	*Quadrate.*
1648	*Thursday*, August 10. 13.13. P. M.	*Saturn*, 15.6. *Gemini.*	*Jupiter*, 15.6. *Virgo.*	*Quadrate.*
1648	*Thursday*, January 18.	*Saturn*, 9.32 *Gemini.* Retrog.	*Jupiter*, 9.38. *Libra* Retrograde.	*Trine Platick.*
1650	*Saturday*, May 18. 9.12. P. M.	*Saturn*, 0.40. *Cancer.*	*Jupiter*, 0.40. *Scorpio.* Retrog.	*Partill Trine.*
1650	*Wednesday*, Octob. 9. 7.12. P. M.	*Saturn*, 14.53. *Cancer.*	*Jupiter*, 14.53. *Scorpio.*	*Trine.*
1652	*Sunday*, February 27. 00.30. P. M.	*Saturn*, 6.22. *Leo*, Retrograde.	*Jupiter*, 6.22. *Aquarius.*	*Opposition.* 1.
1653	*Sunday*, July 10. 3.23. P. M.	*Saturn*, 13.43. *Leo.*	*Jupiter*, 13,43. *Aquarius.* Retrog.	*Opposition*, 2.

The

The Aspects of Saturn *and* Jupiter *after their two Oppositions by* Argoll *his Ephemerides.*

1656	*Thursday*, the eighth of *May*.	*Saturn*, Stationary 16. 33. *Virgo*.	*Jupiter*, 16. 33. *Taurus*.	*Trine*. 1
1656	*Saturday*, the first of *November*.	*Saturn*, 2. 40. *Libra*.	*Jupiter*, 2. 40. *Gemini*, Retrog.	*Trine*. 2.
1657	*Saturday*, the fifteenth of *August*.	*Saturn*, 4. 43. *Libra*.	*Jupiter*, 4. 43. *Cancer*.	1. *Quadrate*.
1657	*Thursday*, the first of *October*.	*Saturn*, 10. 14. *Libra*.	*Jupiter*, 10. 14. *Cancer* going R.	2. *Quadrate*.
1658	*Tuesday*, the seventeenth of *May*.	*Saturn*, 12. 3. *Libra*, Retrog.	*Jupiter*, 12. 3. *Cancer*.	3. *Quadrate*.
1659	*Munday*, the 22. of *August*.	*Saturn*, 27. 22. *Libra*.	*Jupiter*, 27. 22. *Leo*.	1. *Sextile*.
1659	*Sunday*, the 22. of *January*.	*Saturn*, 12. 15. *Scorpio*.	*Jupiter*, 12. 15. *Virgo*, Retrog.	2. *Sextile*.
1660	*Thursday*, the 31. of *May*.	*Saturn*, 6. 30. *Scorpio*.	*Jupiter*, 6. 30. *Virgo*.	3. *Sextile*.

A short Astrologicall judgement upon the precedent Aspects.

WEre it not for the malicious Quadrature of *Mars* to *Saturn*: *Aprill* 30. 1645. (both the infortunes at that time in their falls) *Saturn* being in 27. 32. *Arietis*, beholding the Ascendent of the last Conjunction with Trine Aspect: we might I say expect a mitigation of war, penury, plundring, misfortune, and other destructive miseries, and sicknesses then afflicting us, and approaching to disturb us more fiercely; but that malignant Aspect, preventing the pious intentions of the honest Protestantine party, seems to keep on foot preceding mischiefes, and by the conniving of a distempered and dissembling Religious faction, our happinesse is impedited. Men of desperate fortunes, have unlucky designes; Let *Mars* and *Saturn* command, *viz*. the needy Souldier and superstitious Sectary; Englishman look for an end of our wars at Doomsday. Oh I cannot endure

 these

these whining raschals, that pretend Conscience and Religion, and yet neither fear God, honour their King, or are in charity, or ever will be with an offended Neighbour: But let these dregs of irreligious villaines passe; the onely destruction of our flourishing *London* and Common-wealth; the onely incendiaries of every Common-wealth, let me leave them, I say, to the mercy of an enraged people, when their hypocricy is discovered, &c. and the measure of their iniquity at the height, &c. But how long shall we suffer them.

The first *Sextile* of *Saturn* and *Jupiter* is the 19. *June* 1646. it may be judged some better attonment amongst us; some Treaties or forraign Embassadours may arive to intercede, and compose our unluckie differences: for *Saturn* then is in 15. *Taurus*, neer the Cuspe of the fifth in the Conjunction; and *Jupiter* in 15 *Cancer*, in Trine to the signe culminating, viz. *Scorpio*: If God give a blessing; and the presence of *Mars* in 19. *Taurus*, lately in *Conjunction* with *Saturn*, cause not some disturbance by *Ireland*, or the Popish *Irish* faction; much good may then be expected: Now, the true meaning and doing Protestant, Divine, and Gentleman, begin to weede out the Apostate counterfeits, who disperse to severall parts of the world, their purses well filled with the spoil of a desolate Nation: many remain amongst us, and swear outward conformity; but we cannot lade the Sea dry, &c. or ever dive into the depth of these Anabaptisticall and Independent, Seditious, intentions, &c. These are the onely *Achans* have molested us since 1642.

Upon the first Quadrature of *Saturn* and *Jupiter*, *Sept.* 30. 1647. *Saturn* then ariving to the place of *Mars* in the Conjunction, and *Jupiter* to a square of *Saturn* by Transit; the peregrination of *Jupiter* in that signe not hindring by a double debility in signe and house, *viz.* if there were then no underhand dealing, juggling, shirking, and dissembling fellows in request; we might hope well, and that with some trouble we should sensibly taste the fruits of peace, or have a glimpse of it; but whether the hypocritically Religious Saints, or the disturbed Trade of an impoverished people produce nothing; or above all this the much lamented and untimely death of a gallant, and not to be paralel'd Generall, or brave field Officer, put us in confusion, I know not; here's much time spent to no purpose; but it being not the first time, fowl actions smooth over deceitfull pretensions; I leave all to God: Let the Sun shine upon the Author this year, & *omnia bene.*

's, and

most

most Nations either engaged; or having had their bellies full of war famine, plague, murrain of cattle, and civill discord; *Saturn* at length comes the 10. of *August* 1648. to a second Quadrature of *Jupiter*: Now cunning *Saturn* being Transited to the very degree of the *Moon* in the *Conjunction*; the people have now enough seen their own folly, they sturdily resist an incroaching Clergie, and Gentry: the *Londoners* are not the last in this action, their impoverishment and sufferings are without example. Well, tyranny in Religion first broke the neck of an insulting *Episcopacy*: if now too much austerity and a little Coveousnesse and partiality produce an uproar, and work confusion; let some silly Asses thank themselves: *Merlinus Anglicus* is not of the Faction. Yet in *January* 1649. there being a Platick Trine betwixt *Saturn* and *Jupiter*, he being neer the place of the *Dragons head* in the *Conjunction*, who was then in the 9. house, properly signifying Religion; we have strong confidence of being quite cured of our distempers: both significators are Retrograde; nothing but dissimulation; fair words butter no Parsnips; both parties play fast and loose: The Comet now seemes to have performed its effects, we may lament that it operated so long; it leaves us, and we begin to smile: but Monarchy is not in such great request as formerly, nor by reason of a Pestilence amongst them, shall our Neighbour Enemies rejoyce; Provision may be dear: and my mother *London* had neede in time to look out, for she will have many poor; and very many sicknesses.

But behold, 1650. in *May*, *Saturn* in 00. 37. of *Cancer*, a Cardinall signe; and *Jupiter* in 00. 37. *Scorpio*, signes of long Ascensions, do promise us a setled beginning of much happinesse, if we over-do not: its not good to be over-wise: this Trine is neer the degree culminating in the *Conjunction*, as if Kings and Authority should recuperate a little, (by what meanes I urge not) I dislike nothing in this *Trine*, but that the Commonalty entrust some Potent Nobleman or else some grave Councellour, that will play the knave with them; and with many figured Protestations (if those will serve) deceive them, he appeares like a Wolf in sheeps cloathing; and being the Puppy of an old Fox, he knows how to betray and cozen the Country by Petit degrees: and now either time or very shame compells us to unite a little in points of Religion, &c. This is but conjecturall concerning the Religious. About the 9. of *October*, 1650. *Saturn* and *Jupiter* come to a perfect *Trine*, *Saturn* in 14. 53. *Cancer*: *Jupiter* in 14. 53. *Scorpio*. Ere this year go about, plain dealing is more used:

 and

and things reconciled handsomely, mens purses pay for former mistakes, the heavens shine cleer: and if the *London* Merchant escape Pyracy at Sea, he may prove a rich man.

About *February* 1652. *Saturn* and *Jupiter* make their first opposition, *Saturn* in 6. 22. *Leo*: *Jupiter* in *Aquarius*: this their opposition is in partill *Conjunction* with the degree of the second and eighth house of their last *Conjunction*. A curious eye may search further; Woe, to a great family of Europe, that was, is now, but shall be no more: its not old, its not ancient; like an untimely birth its cut off, and shall never again flourish, either in branch or root, &c. Lord God! Shall the number of fifty cut off more then five? or shall lesse then 90. be alotted for 4. Shall the Virgin be barren, and the Lyon have no issue? Shall lesse than 36. end in two? Shall the second end in a Cipher? Shall 7. come to be one, and then none, &c. doth *Italy* now begin to murmur, and *Rome* to tremble: In *Europe* we begin to shoot neer *Rome*; we misse our mark a little, we make breaches, but enter not. How ever this opposition of *Saturn* and *Jupiter* is in direct termes averse to the *Conjunction* in 1623. Old men dye of Consumptions, and every year the *Londoner* fears the Plague.

About *July* 1653. the degree of the seventh house in the *Conjunction* of 1623. is the place of *Saturn* in this second disastrous opposition: here's Transversion of figure in the heavens, so is all unity and friendship amongst the *Italian* Princes, quite dissolved, *Tom Jesuite* will have it so: what hath been obscured since 1623. now plainly appeares by a large *manifesto* to all the world: The European Princes perceive by whom and whose meanes the troubles of this present age were fomented and raised, and what Prince would have been *Dominus fac totum*: most men are wise, when its too late: the Retrogradation of *Jupiter* in this opposition makes me mindfull to perswade every one to bear a little, another war, or a new combustion may undo us: if the all dissembling Pharesee trouble us not at home, we may do pretty well: and the world alse, &c. But in 1654. when some wise *Italians* are in consultation how to conclude of peace, war, like a thunderbolt, suddenly breaks out; and the Pope thinking to benefit the Church by encroachment, in seising on the Dutchy of of a deceased Prince, or estate of a defunct fat Cardinall, indangers hereby his Papacy, and stirs up such a flame as about 1655. 1656. or neer these times, almost confounds his Primacy and consumes his Patrimony: these years seeme to be the first of his down lying, wherein his Fatherly authority begins to be slighted under his nose. In 1656.

Saturn

Saturn and *Jupiter* come to two Trine Aspects; *Ireland* begins again to be populated, after a large time of devastation; the yeer spends it self in frequent Embassages amongst the Inhabitants of *Europe*; nor do I see any reason why the Scepter of the *Ottoman* family should not now either be extinguished, or a family arising and setting up for its selfe, that will share *Greece* and some of his Dominions with him.

In the year 1657. and moneths of *August* and *October*; *Saturn* and *Jupiter* come to two Quadrate Aspects; *Saturn* in *Libra*, and *Jupiter* in *Cancer*, and to another Quadrature in the same Signes the next year 1658. the Signes are the Exaltations of these weighty Planets; very great matters are now in agitation all over *Europe*; the Noble *Austrian* family is much herein concerned: the *States* of *Holland* appear more splendid. The *Scottish* Nation have a great hand in these two years Actions; One new Pope, and he no fool, a very gentleman. More muttering these two years about Religion, mens fancies not yet setled, as if the Divines of times preceding, and now in *esse* were dolts, and knew nothing; hot disputes, cold conclusions, with difficulty some things are for a time soldred, but not perfectly; moveable signes fix nothing: Sores ill healed break out again to worse ends: A *German* Prince pricks up his eares, he may advance. We *English* are pretty quiet, and in a good posture. If the *Hollander* encroach too much, we shall be angry, and retort, and remember former matters, slumbring, but not buried in sleep. We shall now begin to ballance, or one for us, or we for all: forget not.

In the years 1659. and 1660. *Saturn* and *Jupiter* make three *Sextile Aspects* out of signes of long Ascensions; Some strict League more firm then any formerly, betwixt the Pope and Emperour of *Germany*, who yet stands up: these superiour Noble Planets in their first *Sextile* do both with *Partill Aspect*, behold the degree ascending of their last *Conjunction*; this their friendly Salutation comforts us in *England*, every man now possesses his own Vineyard; our young youths grow up to mans estate, and our old men live their full years; our Nobles and Gentlemen roote again: our Yeomanry many years disconsolated, now take pleasure in their Husbandry; the Merchant sends out ships and hath prosperous returns; the Mechanick hath quick trading, here's almost a new world, new laws, some new Lords: now my Country of *England* shall shed no more teares, but rejoyce with, and in the many blessings God affords her annually.

Deinde vidi Cœlum novum & terram novam: primum enim cœlum & prima terra abierat; & mare non amplius exstabat: Et absterserus est

est Deus omnem lacbrymam ab oculis eorum; & mors amplius non extabit: neque luctus neq; clamor; neq; labor exstabit amplius; quia præcedentia abierunt, Revel. 21. *And I saw a new heaven, and a new earth, for the first heaven and the first earth were passed away, and there was no more Sea*: After which time God will wipe away all teares from the eyes of his people; there shall be no more death, neither sorrow or crying; neither any more paine, for the first things are passed away. *Finis*.

The Eclipses both of the Sun, and Moon, untill 1663. *and some lesser* Conjunctions *of the other Planets.*

	Eclipses and *Conjunctions*, the *Signes*, and *Degrees*.	*Moneth* and *Day*.	*Time* of the *Day*.	*Visible* or not.
Anno Dom. 1644.	*Solis*. 18. 56. ♓.	*Feb.* 27.	6. 12. P. M.	Not in *England*, but some parts of *Russia*.
	☉. 9. 5. ♍.	*Aug.* 21.	17. P. M.	Kings and Queens are mortall.
Conjunct.	☉ ♄. 10. 52. ♈.	*March* 20.	Scotland the Comet.	Many changes of fortune.
	☉ ♃. 8. ♉.	*April.* 17.		No peace appears this year.
	♄ ♂. 19. ♈.	*May* 31.		Its a ticklish one, quick action.
	♃ ♂. 29. ♉.	*July* 26.		Horrible treasons and treachery.
1645.	Ecl. ☽ 22. 40. ♌.	*January* 31.	7. P. M.	Visible in *Tartaria*, *Persia*, *China*, *Magellanica*.
	☽. 15. 15. ♒.	*July* 28.	1. 17. P. M.	I fear the Plague generally.
	☉. 8. 18. ♓.	*Feb.* 15.	20. 34. P. M.	Visible to the *English*; unluckie and fatall to some great Prince, whose life is in danger, if not quite cut off: Gods will be done.
	☉. 28. 28. ♌	*Aug.* 11.	00. P. M.	
Conjunct.	☉ ♄. 24. ♈.	*April* 3.		Dost thou come? welcome.
	♄ ♀. 26. 48. ♈.	*April* 24.		States of *Holland*, if *Flanders* revolt to you, remember me: bee wise, and not precise: yet take heed.
	♃ ☉. 14. ♊.	*May* 24.		
	♃ ♀. 16. ♊.	*June* 3.		

♂ ♀. 10. ♎

Year	Aspect	Date	Time	Remarks
	♂ ♀ 20. ♎.	Septem. 22.	–	
1646	☉ ♂. 8. ♐.	Novem. 19.	18. P. M.	Totally conspicuous to us.
	Eclipse ☽. 11. ♌.	January 20.	5. 5. P. M.	These are not visible in England. Scarce in Europe.
	☽s. 4. 20. ♒.	July 17.	11. 40. P. M.	
	☉s. 27. 12. ♑.	January 6.	6. 15. P. M.	*Denmark:* what said *Ticho Brahe?*
	☉s 15. 14. ♋.	July 2.	11. 1. P. M.	
	☉s. 15. 41. ♑.	Decem. 26.		*Arise, O Lord, and help.*
	♄ ♀. 1. 27. ♉.	Feb. 24.		Scarcity of bread and provision.
	♄ ☉. 7. 40. ♉.	Aprill 17.		
	☉ ♀. 8. 20. ♉.	18.		*Scotland* a little disturbed.
	♄ ♀. 3. ♉.	19.		The Salvage *Irish* run into boggs: famine there.
	♄ ♂. 14. ♉.	June 12.		*Swethland* and *Poland* totter; the Sun shines
	☉ ♃. 17. 21. ♋.	29.		not ever in one place.
	♃ ♂. 8. 24. ♌.	Novemb. 3.		
	☉ ☿. 5. 40. ♐.	17.	9 40. P. M.	No Eclipses visible.
1647.	☽s. 1. ♌.	January 10.	0. 40. A. M.	
	☉s. 10. ♋.	June 22.	12. 40. P. M.	Our great cattle grow scarce and few in number: the Murraine
	☉s. 4. 16. ♑.	Decemb. 15		offends us.
	♃ ♂. 4. ♌.	January 12.		Forged matters come to nothing. A Lawyer
	♃ ♂. 28. ♋.	March 23.		clapt up.
	☉ ♄. 21. ♉.	May 2.		Sectaries in some Countries not yet quiet.
	☉ ♃. 19. 20. ♌	August 2.		Wo is me, a very great man comes to untimely end:
	♂ ♀. 16. ♐.	Novem. 10.		a rot of sheep and men: Is any Nobleman beheaded? What if many be?
1648.	☽s. 15. 4. ♐.	May 26.	1648.	let Justice take place.
	☽s. [illegible] 44. ♊.	Novem. 19.	00. 11. P. M.	Not visible.

	☉ſ. 0.1. ♋.	*June* 10.	18.40. P.M.	Conſpicuous to us.
	☉ſ. 23.9. ♐.	*Decemb.* 3.	21.33. P.M.	Totall Eclipſe, but not viſible.
	☉ ♂.8. ♒.	*Jan.* 18.	12.40. P.M.	Not to be ſeen here.
	☉ ♄. 5. ♊.	*May* 15.		*Spain* hath much dammage at Sea.
	♄ ☿. 8. ♊.	*June* 4.		*Londoner*, adventure not too much to ſea.
	♀. 9.	12.		
	♄ ♂. 11. ♊.	27.		Some plots are acting, beware of fire, and treaſon in *London*. *Brabant* mutinies. Its a good morſell.
	☉ ♃. 20. ♍.	*Septemb*, 1.		
	♃ ♀. 20. ♍.	2.		
1649	*A terrible year by reaſon of two Eclipſes of the Moon, and one of the Sun.*			
	☽e. 5. ♐.	*May* 15.	14.40. P.M.	Altogether ſeen in *Europe*.
	☉ſ. 13. ♏.	*Octob.* 25.	2. P.M.	Viſible.
	☽ſ. 27. ♉.	*Novemb.* 8.	18.40. P.M.	Not ſeen here in *England*.
	♄ ♀. 14. ♊.	*Aprill* 7.		Poor *Spain* loſeth more men and Ships.
	☉ ♄. 20. ♊.	*May* 31.		An accurſed Incendiary woman dyeth.
	♃ ♂. 3. ♎.	*July* 2.		The *Catalonians* ſtir. *Hollanders* loſe oppertunities: *Germany* ſwels. *France* is unquiet.
	♃ ☉. 20. ♎.	*Octob.* 2.		
1650	☉ſ. 10. ♉.	*Aprill* 20.	5.20. P.M.	
	☉ſ. 1. ♏.	*Octob.* 14.	16.48. P.*M.*	
	☽e. 24. ♏.	*May* 5.	8.00. P.M.	Theſe two laſt conſpicuous.
	☽e. 16. ♉.	*Octob.* 28.	19.20. P.*M.*	Is *Ireland* in any danger? Is *Auſtria* over-run? An unlucky marriage.
	☽ ♂. 21. ♈.	*March* 31.		
	☉ ♀. 10. ♉.	*April* 19.		Does any quarrell with their friends?
	♄ ☉. 4. ♋.	*June* 15.		Beleeve me ſome do ſtoutly: A new Sect of Monſters are hatching.

♄ ♂. 9. ♋.

	♄ ♂ 9. ♋	July 18.		
	☉ ♃ 20. ♏	Novemb. 1.		
1651.	☉ɪ 29. 44. ♈	April 9.	18. 4. P. M.	Neither seen in England.
	☉ɪ 20. 57. ♒	Octob. 4.	1. 50. P. M.	Doth the Sea make irruption into Holland or Zeeland? Dost smile?
	☉ ♄ 18. ♋	June 30.		
	♂ ♃ 5. ♐	Septemb. 13		What's done in Scotland? A tempestuous time at Michaelmas: many shipwracks in the North of England.
	☉ ♃ 20. 20. ♐	Decemb. 3.		
1652.	☽ɪ 5. 16. ♎	March 14.	16. P. M.	The three first visible in our Horizon.
	☉ɪ 19. 16. ♈	28.	21. 30. P. M.	
	☽ɪ 25. 15. ♓	Septemb. 7.	6. 22. P. M.	Strange apparitions and unusuall sights in the South East parts.
	☉ɪ 9. 54. ♎	22.	4. 0. P. M.	This not to be seen with us.
	♂ ♀ 8. 30. ♈	Februa. 24.	England	A year full of Embassages.
	☉ ♂ 17. ♊	May 27.	be thou	A preparative in the heavens for a great plague: The Florentines make tumults: Italy is fearfull: wars in Bohemia: uproars in Rome.
	♄ ☉ 2. 20. ♌	July 15.		
	♄ ♂ 5. 30. ♌	Aug. 9.	Content.	
1653.	☉ɪ 9. 44. ♓	Feb. 17.	5. 8. P. M.	Scotland beware a famine and some stirs. Not apparent to us.
	☽ɪ 24. 8. ♍	March 3.	15. 50. P. M.	Visible to us.
	☉ɪ 0. 1. ♍	Aug. 12.	13. P. M.	Not to be perceived here.
	☽ɪ 14. 57. ♓	28.	22. 45. P. M.	Nor this. Divided Counsels, Sects and Heresies disturb every Commonwealth of Europe: we have our share: A magnificent Cardinall poisoned: Spain loseth at the West Indies. Every Country suffers by shipwrack: Pirates good store: An earthquak threatens some parts neer Italy: fire and dissention threatens Constantinople and the
	♃ ☉ 25. ♑	Jan. 4.		
	♃ ♀ 4. ♒	March 15.		
	☉ ☿ 1. ♌	July 13.		
	♀ ☿ 11.	19.		
	♄ ☿ 15.	21.		
	♄ ♀ 16.	22.		

♄ ☉ 16. ♌

♄ ☉ 16. ♌ July 29.
♃ ♂ 12. ♒ Novem. 18
☍ ♄ & Decem. 10.
♂ 26. ♒ ♌ 7.
♃ ♀ 18. ♒ Decem. 16.

1654. *No contemptible Year.*
Rome *fears her down-fall.*

☉ 28. 59. ♒ Feb. 7. 18. 15. P. M
☽ 13. 2. ♍ 20. 18. 27. P. M.
☞ ☉ 19. 34. ♌. Aug. 2. 22. 8. P. M. It endures 2. 27.
☽ 4. 32. ♓ 17. 11. P. M.
☍ ♃ ♄ 25. ♌ ♒ Jan. 17.
☍ ☉ ♄ 24. ♌ Feb. 1.
☉ ♃ 29. ♒ 8.
☉ ♂ 29. ♋ June 19.
☉ ♄ ♍. 0. Aug. 13.

1655. ☉ 17. 50. ♒ Jan. 27. 0. 40. P. M.
☉ 9. ♌ July 24.
☽ 24. ♌. Aug. 6.
☉ ♀ 22. ♒ Jan. 31.
♃ ♀ 4. ♈ March 6.
☉ ♄ 6. ♈ 16.
☉ ♄. 14. ♍ Aug. 27.

Italy, remember me.

1656. The End Proves our Actions.
☽ 20. 28. ♋. Jan. 1. 8. 40. P. M.
☉ 6. 26. ♒ Jan. 26. 2. 24. P. M.

great Turk: commotion about a new Emperour.

The *English* do pretty wel. *Holland* lately escaped a scouring: Its news to see a Forraigne Army invade *Spain* it self.

I was, I am still, *London*, not sick but fearfull: bear this storm patiently, which is at hand: then no more: the Plague is probably like to afflict thee; some dangerous fires if not carefully prevented.

Visible every where, all over *Europe*, let *Italy* pay the Porter.

Why not a *Comet*: strange Meteors. A Virgin Monarchy hath been; is no more: I was a Prince, thou seest me now: a branch is lopt off from me: It grows no more: I am dying: some new progeny ariseth to a Kingdome: or some new *Alexander* is born, or appeares in the East, and doth great acts: I trow not here: *Mars* enters *Virgo*, and leaves *Leo* his *quondam Aphelium.* This visible, or may be no other.

The Chrim *Tartar* moves towards *Turkie* or his confines. The *Sweds* agree not. *Savoy* quarrels: finds an enemy without looking for. *England* rejoyceth, but not in plentifull crops of corn: An Earthquake affrights the *Turks* in *Greece*. We are unhappy of all Nations in our Clergie: An Angel knows not what they would have Scripture.

Conspicuous to the *English*.
This also: but not the rest.

☽ 14. 44. ♈.

	☽ ε 14. 44. ♑	June 26.	1. 4. P.M.	What's to be done: The *French* Nation bewaile her dead.
	☉ ε 29. 30. ♋	July 11.	11. P.M.	A terrible yeere in *Italy*: poison, up-roars, wars, fright the Pope.
	☽ ε 10. 38. ♑	Decem. 21.	00. 00.	
	♃ ☉ 13. ♉	April 21.		Strange news from the *East Indies*, but who erects a Monarchy, or comes neer it in the *West Indies*. Much is promised, little performed. An earthquak, famin.
	☉ ♂ 3. ♍	Aug. 15.		
	☉ ♄ 26. ♍	Sept. 8.		
1657.	☉ ε 20. 43. ♊	June 1.	11. 10. P.M.	Not apparant.
	☽ ε 4. ♑	June 15.	8. 48. P.M.	Visible.
	☉ ε 12. 49. ♐	Novem. 26	19. 49. P.M.	Not.
	☽ ε 00. ♋	Decem. 10.	7. P.M.	Conspicuous.
	♃ ♀ 5. 13. ♊	March 30		The Heavens promise faire to *English* men.
	☉ ♃ 19. ♊	May 28.		To the *Londoners* and to *Ireland*.
	☉ ♄ 9. ♎	Septemb. 21		*Germany* and *Austria* not yet quiet: *Spain* looseth by tempest. The State of *Venice* loseth at Sea.
	♄ ♀ 14. ♎	Novemb. 4.		
1658.	☉ ε 10. ♊	May 21.	15. P.M.	No one Visible.
	☽ ε 24. ♐	June 4	22. P.M.	*Rome, Rome*: where's thy wit cunning Jesuite?
	☽ ε 18. ♉	Octob. 30.		
	☉ ε 3. ♐	Decemb. 4.		The *French* would; but must not make a Pope.
	♃ ♂ 9. ♋	May 1.		*Londoner*, trade not much Eastward: November produceth ill weather.
	♃ ♀ 18. ♋	June 13		
	☉ ♃ 23. ♋	July 5.		*Russia* now is not the same.
	☉ ♂ 9. ♎	Septemb. 21		
	☉ ♄ 22. ♎	Octob. 4.		Some great one deposed, he may be a King: or in danger of losing a Kingdome.
	♄ ♀ 23. ♎	11.		None of these much Visible.
	♂ ☿ 26. ♎	16.	7. P.M.	

1659.	☽ e 15. ♏	*April* 26.	16. P.M.	Sturdy actions in *Germany*, &c.
	☉ ſ 29. 30. ♉	*May* 10.	15. P.M.	*Ireland* hath no minde to be quiet: do, and thou darest.
	☽ e 6. 33. ♉	*Octob.* 19.	2. 40. P.M.	
	☉ ſ 22. ♐	*Novemb.* 4.		Now behold: who shewes himself?
	☉ ♃ 24. ♌	*Aug.* 6.		Hee's no fixed star, but a Planet.
	♃ ♀ 29.	30.		The West is threatned: the North-East is not quiet:
	☉ ♄ 4. ♏	*Octob.* 16.		The *Swede* is not Emperour of *Germany*: A new
	♄ ♀ 4. ♏	22.		Pope, if you will.
1660.	Foure Eclipses not Visible, or worth mentioning.			All the Merchants in *Europe* lament their losses.
	♃ ♂ 16. ♍	*July* 27.		Now the Nobility and Gentry begin to wrack their Tenants.
	☉ ♃ 25. ♍	*Sept.* 7.		
	☉ ♄ 16. ♏	*Octob.* 26.		Some jangling with the Clergie: A new found Doctrine deludes many:
	☉ ♂ 20. ♏	30.		beware of *Cancer*.
	♄ ♀ 21. ♏	*Decemb.* 15		A bonny *Scot* acts his part.
1661.	☉ ſ 10 ♈	*March* 20.	10. 40. P.M. not Visible.	Fevers, Plurisies, and ill markets; heavie Taxes makes *London* male-content.
	☽ e 25. ♎	*April* 4.	3.40. nor this	
	☉ ſ 0. 41. ♎	*Septemb.* 13	02. 10. P.M.	Visible with us.
	☽ e 15. 5. ♈	27.		*Austria* is in good hope.
	♂ ♀ 16. ♒	*Feb.* 26.		The *Hollanders* smile, perhaps alter the frame of
	♃ ♀ 18. ♎	*Septemb.* 9.		their Common-wealth: Newes, Newes, all men
	♃ ☉ 25. ♎	*Octob.* 6.		are glad; for what? a great Navie perisheth by tempest.
	♄ ♀ 23. ♏	7.		
	♄ ☉ 27. ♏	*Novemb.* 8.		Be meek and humble, God rules all.
	☍ ☉ ♂ 20. ♑ ♋.	*Decem.* 29.		Ah pious Prince dost thou dye.
1662.	00. 00.		00. 00.	
	☍ ☉ ♄ 2. ♊ ♐	*May* 12.		Old men of *Spain* dye apace.

	♃ ♂ 19. ♏	*Octob.* 12.		Behold a miracle: who is converted?
	♄ ♂ 7. ♐	*Novemb.* 4.		Why so many imprisoned for their Consciences?
	☉ ♃ 25. ♏	6.		
	♃ ♀ 29. ♏	26.		*Venice*, thou stately City, detain no *English* goods:
	♄ ♀ 10. ♐	*Decemb.* 4.		A Queen suspected of too little honesty: is she questioned? yes in private.
	☉ ♂ 13. ♑	22.		
	♂ ♀ 14. ♑	23.		
1663	☽ ☍ 3. 40. ♍	*Feb.* 11.	15. 21. P M.	Visible.
	☉ ☌ 19. ♓	27.	5. 50. P. M.	Not.
	☽ ☍ 25. 32. ♒	*Aug.* 8.	7. 45. P. M.	Visible.
	☉ ☌ 18. 42. ♍	21	7. 18. P. M.	Not. *Europe* disturbed with Embassadours.
	☉ ♀ 26. ♒	*Feb.* 4.		*Portingall* in danger.
	☉ ☿ 7. ♊	*May* 17.		*Normandy* Rebels, if too much opressed.
	☍ ☉ 14. ♊	*June* 22.		
	♄ ♐			FINIS.

THe third Conjunction of *Saturn* and *Jupiter* in the fiery Triplicity, is this year 1663. the 9 *October* 14. *houres* 37. *min.* P. M. *Saturn* and *Jupiter* in 13. *degrees* 31. *minutes*, 39. *seconds* of *Sagitarius*: *Mars* 9. *deg.* 20. *min. Leo*: *Sol* 26. *deg.* 34. *min. Libra*. *Venus* 6. *deg.* 26 *min. Scorpio*. *Mercury* 20. *deg.* 21. *Scorpio*. *Luna* 11. *deg.* 13. *min. Gemini*. The *Dragons head*, 27. *deg.* 10. *min. Leo*. the *M. Cœli* 6. *deg.* 0. *Gemini*. The Ascendant for the Meridian of *London*, 11. *deg.* 47. *Virgo*: who pleaseth may erect the Scheam of heaven, &c.

A Gen-

A Gentleman, born in the year 1585. sent me the time of his birth, with some accidents to verifie it, and required my judgement; whereupon, having rectified it, and brought the Ascendent to its perfect degree, I sent him the subsequent Discourse.

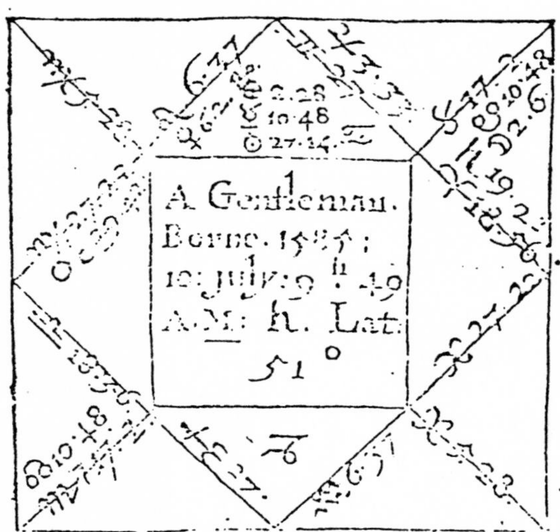

My first intention is to give a Mathematicall briefe judgement, upon the twelve houses of heaven, which generally represent the whole state, and life of every man, his fortune, honour, preferment, &c.

Next I will see if according to precedent directions, this Native have had sutable and proper accidents, such as may naturally be derived, in an artificiall way, from those directions, or whether in measure of time, they jump with my limitation, yea, or not: In both these wayes I will bee short, holding it fittest to bestow most time upon the remainder of years, this Native may happily live, according to the naturall course of heaven, &c.

First House. Person, Stature, Condition.

For this Natives corporature, it should be mean, or hee of a middle stature, because the latter degrees of a signe Ascend, yet having the Lord of the Ascendent in Cancer, and Sol, and Mars, in friendly Sextill, in should bee decent, well composed, not vitiated with any blemish; It denoats a ruddy, and pleasant countenance, lovely, and gracefull, nor are the conditions repugnant to the feature signified by the platick Sextill of Mercury, and Luna, be very witty, and be docile, of good invention, facetious, affable, humane, and complementall, somewhat given to jest, by reason of the square of Venus, and Luna, he should be hospitable, a great womans friend, though to his own cost: He should by his own merit and industry rise to preferment; for Gemini, and Virgo, are both the houses of Mercury, the one signe culminating the other ascending: he should love a sedentary life, books and study, and to be free from the cares of this world: a fixed friend himself, though he finde failings in many; but to say truth, he knows how to apply himself for his own benefit, in a rationall discreet way, he can be angry, and hee will to purpose, for it were strange, if Mars in the East Angle, should not make him passionate, conceited, and of aspiring high conception, &c.

Second

Second House. Riches: Worldly estate.

His wealth and estate in this world should be very great; the quality of his birth considered, for Spica Virginis on the very Cusp of the second House, promiseth a bountifull fortune, and that it shall be fixed, and indure to this Natives death; for Venus, Lady of the second house, is in a fixed signe, and Jupiter a generall significator of substance, is with Oculus Tauri, a regall fixed Star, nor is it the least testimony of an ample estate of the goods of this world, that the Natives part of fortune is in Cancer, in the tenth house, and in partill sextill Aspect with the Moon in Taurus, her exaltation: yet to judge nothing but all honey, were to flatter the Native, do not I see Saturn with his malicious opposition afflicting the cuspe of the second out of the eighth, & this plainly intimates that the Native shall have his estate impeached, wasted, and lessened, by meanes of the deceased, viz. either by probates of their Wils, or setling their decayed Estates, or of, or concerning some such engagements, as his dying friends may entrust him with; it bids him beware of medling with Morgages of lands, tenements, &c. The fortunes notwithstanding being more prevalent then the malignants, here's no cause for the Native to despair of a considerable subsistence during his whole life, &c.

Third House. Kindred, &c.

It imports much Kindred, but they not so powerfull, or able to live as the Native, for the significator of them being Mars, is disposed by the Lord of the Ascendant: It sayes the Native shall bee advantagious unto them, regulate them according to his discretion, and will, and wholly order their affairs. Many short journeys he may undertake, both by water and by land, signified by Scorpio in the third, and Mars in Virgo: the Dragons-head somewhat neer the Cuspe, promiseth much pleasure in them, but most towards the South, or East quarter from his birth.

Fourth House. Father, Lands, &c. and Inheritances, &c.

The father of this Native is signified, partly by Jupiter and Sol, the geniture being Diurnall: and hee should have been of good condition, but not provident of the things of this world; for seeing Saturn Lord of the fifth, or substance of the father is in the eighth House, peregrine and feeble, I do conjecture the freedom of the fathers heart was such, he left the sonne no patrimony to be proud of; but Saturn in Aries denoats no such bounty, its Sol in Cancer, and Jupiter in Geminis, argue largenesse of heart.

Fifth House. Children.

It were folly to treat of children, sith the Native was never married, yet do not I find him defective in the acts of Venus, but sufficiently potent; I cannot but think, Venus in the eleventh House, in Quadrate to the Moon, might have afforded him Gentlewomen, not unhandsome, to have wrought an experiment upon, yet Saturn in the eighth, few would have lived, &c.

Sixth House. - Diseases, &c.

A fortune being Lord of the sixth, and he in the ninth, with a fixed Star, of somewhat an impetuous nature, in Sextill with Venus; It imports our Native to have but few sicknesses, and those easily cured by medicine, the diseases may be the wind collick, stone in the raines, fluxes, paine many times in the reines of the back, without any gravell appearing, surfets, and casually violent fevers, the posture of Mars in the Ascendant, may cause much headach accidentally, &c.

Seventh House. Women, &c.

Which properly hath signification of women, wives, law-suits, partners in any profession, &c.

I will endeavour by the Rules of Art, to give reasons why this Native hath not, or is likely to marry hereafter, &c.

Ptolomey, Leovitius, and all the Learned say, If Venus and Luna bee in barren signes, the Native will hardly marry.

Venus is here in Leo Retrograde, one argument of not marriage. The Moon is in Taurus, afflicted by Cauda Draconis in the eighth house of heaven; these two Planets so constituted, Conjugium negant, aut a conjugio animo alienore reddunt: They deny marriage either at all, or incline men to be more averse from it. The posture of Mars also in a barren signe, being partly Lord of the seventh, or having much dominion there, may be some occasion of a single life. Neither is lesse consideration to bee had to Jupiter, who is Lord of part of the seventh house, and he is in a barren signe: so that by the testimonies both of Venus, Luna, and Jupiter, the proper significators of marriage, a single life was designed for him; yet Luna neer the Dragons tail, hee cannot have avoided some false aspersions by womens means.

Ninth House. Travell, long journeys.

Which designeth whether the Native shall travell, yea or not, and with what successe, herein we consider especially Mercury, the Moon, and Venus, these Planets do denoat some excursions of this Native into forraigne parts, and if the successe bee required from the tenth house, which is the substance obtained by travell, I conceive he obtained what hee occasionally sought for, without any let or disturbance, he may have travelled Southward by Sea, from the place he was born in, the Countreys subject to Taurus, but especially Gemini, would have suited best with the good Angell of this native &c.

Tenth House. Preferment, estimation, &c.

What amongst Nobility is called honour, amongst people that exercise a trade, is termed reputation, estimation, credit, and the like, &c. Having the Sun, Mercury, and part of fortune in the tenth, and the Moon Dispositrix of the Sun, in her exaltation, I cannot but pronounce, that this Native shall exceed in fame and repute, and in the goods of fortune most of his Ancestors: he shall have high esteem amongst the best sort of people wheresoever he shal live, and according to the degree of his birth, live in a glorious, and illustri-

ous

ous way. The profession the native hath formerly used, may be descried from Mercury, and Luna, who signifie a profession wherein a voluble tongue may be exercised, and for the kindes of it, in such things as are delightfull to women, &c. I forbear particulars, because my friend is living, &c.

Eleventh House. Friends, and friendship.

It may signifie that our Native shall have the acquaintance, and friendship of many persons of good quality; both Courtiers and Citizens; those signified by Venus, may prove reall but unable, those by the Sunne mutable. those by the Moon, she being in Square to the Cuspe of the eleventh, and especially women, unprofitable, burthensome, and never satisfied. I should have mentioned both the Hyleg, and Alcochoden, and have spoken of death, captivity, &c. But I forbear these till I judge the directions.

The Authors judgement upon many directions, since the Natives birth to this year, 1641.

IN the fifth year of his Age, the Ascendant comming to the body of Mars, might cause the Measels, or Small pox, some windinesse in the bowels, impediting his health for a time, but the other directions at the same time, being under the termes of the benevolent, caused a restoring to former health. The year following, about July 1591. the Sun comming to the Square of the Moon, might import some impeachment to the eyes, and some cold rheumes to descend into them, whereby the Native might for a time bee distempered; It also pointeth out some infirmnesse to the mother, if she were then living, which I conceive she was.

He had the measels, &c. but remembers not the year.

The year following, viz. 1592. our Native should have enjoyed a healthfull time, and be kept close to School, as is signified by the Sunne to a Sextill of Jupiter, and all the Hylegiacall places to good directions.

This he saith is true.

In the year of our Lord 1596. the occourse of the Moon to the Dragons tail in a bestiall signe, might intimate some sudden accident should have hurt the Native, either on the head, arms, neck, or shoulders, or some four footed beast by violence, have indangered the members abovesaid, or else by the fall of some rusticall, and bestiall materiall, but the Sextill of Mercury happening in the same degree and minute the direction falls in, Mercury being Lord of the Ascendant, some Mechanicall man should have lessened this accident, and annihilated the aforesaid malevolent radiation.

He really confesseth, a Cart-wheel had like to have fallen upon him, but that a Wheelwright standing by prevented it.

About the 16. year of his age, the Medium Cœli comming to the body of Mercury, and some other directions to the termes of Saturn, its probable the Native came to London to be a servant, and to indeavour for preferment in his profession, Mercury being Promittor denoat it might be good and profitable.

This is really true, as himselfe tells me.

 During

During the time of service, much cannot bee expected, saving that about the year 1605. the Ascendant meeting with the square Aspect of Mercury, might declare some difficulty in his Accompts, and some frowardnesse in his Master, and immediately after a journey beyond the Seas.

He then travelled into France, &c. Nor was the rest false.

About, or in the 26. of his age, the Mid-heaven comming to the Square of Saturn, declare a turbulent and unquiet year, and years unto the Native, by the aspersions of some malevolent vulgar people: years of much affliction and discontent, years of much expence of substance unexpectedly, some detriment in his profession, by such as he dealt, or negotiated with.

This proved too true, but in what nature I forbear, &c.

About the 27. year, the Sun directed to the Trine of Saturn, might cause a reconciliation of former differences, and great expressions of love from an aged Citizen, or a rich widow: and now the part fortune, comming to the body of the Sunne, might cause the City to take notice of his Trading, and manner of living; It begot very good acquaintance, much increase in wealth, and prosperity in all worldly affairs, nor do I see any contradiction to this happinesse, unlesse some fall from a Horse, about June 1611. might indanger his safety, &c.

I remember not what answer was given to this.

From the year 1611. to the 36. of his age, he should live in great happinesse, have the proffer of many fair Gentlewomen, delight in horses, and horsemanship, in Musicke, History, and all delightfull studies, hee should have plentifull trading, feast, and be feasted, live jovially and merrily.

This was so.

But in 1620. the Ascendant comming to the Opposition of Saturn, both Promittor, and Direction being Malignant, it might cause some Melancholie humours to abound, much ventosity all over the body, a great weaknesse in the back, backsliding in estate, by some morgage, or meanes of ill servants, much troubled to get in Debts, many Law suits, much labour to get in the goods of some deceased party, or creditors: It denoats ill digestion, a weak stomack. This year was enough to undo many a man by losses, and other casualties incident to such a Direction.

He confesseth both the sicknesse in the parts of the body named, and the rest of the Accidents to have fallen out exactly.

In the year 1625. the Moon comming to a Sextill of Jupiter, a principall significator of Preferment; It might incline the Native to aspire to some better preferment, then at present he had; it should give him some notable Office in the Common-wealth, to the Natives credit, but no increment of wealth; for although this Aspect is very good, yet was it not of sufficient fortitude, to effect what immediatly succeeded; it produces our Native, or should so do, some familiarity with a person of honour, and intimates familiarity with a learned Lawyer; it denoats divers motions for a wife, &c.

These are acknowledged.

In

In July 1626. being compleat 41. yeares of age, the Sunne was directed to a Trine of the Moon, and Medium Coeli to a Sextill of Iupiter, near the Cuspe of the 11. house. Now he had a good Office.

By this accident I rectified the whole Nativity.

From the time of his accesse to Office, till this present 1641. some memorable accidents must have happened, which purposely I passe over.

I conceive the Medium Coeli to the body of Venus 1628. and Currant 43. of his age, might intimate some affaies to a young Gentlewoman, and might offer opportunity of marriage.

This was true.

When the Ascendant 1636. and 52. of his age came into Scorpio, and therein to an opposition of the Moon: It should designe some infirmnesse in those members represented by Scorpio.

This was so, a virulent effluxion of matter issuing *Ex partibus prædictis*.

But in November, the Moon comming to the termes of Venus, by benefit of medicine he was cured.

He was subject to Surfets that year upon small occasion.

In the 54. year of his age, Part Fortune comming to the termes of Mars in the last degrees of Leo, and Pisces being the Ascendant in the profectionall figure, some slimie flegmatique humours were stirred up, and caused some obstructions in the small guts, and much pain in those parts, but Iupiter being then in a benevolent place, all things by benefit of medicine came to a good conclusion.

This was also true, &c.

I now passe to the remainder of years yet unexpired.

1644. passeth without any Annuall directions, wherefore the Action of this year must participate in the nature of what preceded in 1642. and 1643.

1645. Part Fortune comes to the termes of Mercury, whereby its intimated, the Native will be solicitous to procure in moneys, either formerly lent, or to acquire some more to adde to his former Bank: But forasmuch as Mercury is Lord of the 12. house, as well as of the first, it points out some cunning fellow or other indebted unto the Native, will delay payment of what is justly due. Mercury represents Secretaries, Lean men.

The Clymactericall year beginning 1647. 9. July, 21. houres P. M. Year 63.

THe 20 of Virgo is ascending in the Revolution, and Mars in 21. degrees of the signe.

This year being many times fatall, requireth consideration of all the five Hylegiacall places, of the Revolution, yearly Profection, auspitious, and unfortunate Transites, and whatsoever the Artist can do for happy direction of the Native, and better prevention of Casualties depending upon that year.

Medium Coeli and the Sunne come both to the termes of Mars, here's probability

bability of distemper in the body, principally occasioned by choler and vexation of the spirits about some kinsman, whereby the humours are depraved, and so in July, upon, or near the day of birth, the distemper may be at its height: the Native shall do well, if in April 1647. he feel any symptoms of such like disease, or have any craziness to oppress, let him take advice of the learned Physician, and have such medicine prescribed, as may lessen choler, and melancholly; and he may conveniently take his physick the 19. and 20. April 1647. The bowels or small guts seem to be burdened with vicious excrescencies, &c. He will have some fits of the stone, and passions of the wind chollick, gripings in the bowels, &c.

But because Mercury, Lord of the Ascendant in the Revolution, is going to Conjunction of Jupiter, and is in the very degree of Venus at the birth, I doubt not, but the Native by means of such a Physician as is represented by Jupiter, will diminish the force of the influence, and so evade any sickness of long continuance, which is also foreseen by the position of the Moon in Pisces, a bycorporeall and common signe: The Native is desired very little to credit Ecclesiasticall men with matter of money; nor will it be healthfull to travell into the South-west of England this year.

The Native is premonished to be carefull of himself, these following dayes, 1647.

15. August, The Ascendant by profection comes to the body of Mars, beware of anger, of watery places, bee not stirring too early in the morning, least foggy mists cause stopping, and venemous ayres to get into the body.

14. October, Come not on Horseback, or amongst Cattle, avoid stables, out-houses, deal not in any old house-hold stuffe: the Moon then comes to the Dragons tail.

27. October, The Sunne comes to the body of Venus; the Native may be cheerfull and fear not, nay his heart will be merry. Some society with a good Gentlewoman, &c. or entertained at a good Ladies House.

17. March, Part Fortune comes to a Trine of the Moon; some woman payes in money formerly borrowed; some small present from a loving neighbour.

2. Aprill, 1648. The Ascendant comes to opposition of Saturn: The native for two or three dayes falls into vain fears, that an old acquaintance lately dead, is died so poor hee shall lose by him: time makes it appear there was no cause, for if the generall infelicity of England at that time hinder not, the native regains his money with advantage: For I finde after the 15. August, Jupiter is Divisor of the remainder of the year, and that Venus hath dominion of the Alfridary, both which considered, induce mee to judge that the native shall happily evade any infirmnesse, or casualty depending on this Climactericall year, and also overcome any difficulty incident unto him upon any directions.

The

The 64. year, beginning July, 1648.

Wherein the Ascendent comes to the Dragons-head, and to a Trine of Mercury, 3. Febr. 1648. and to the termes of Mercury May 1649.

The first Aspect is equivalent to a Fortune, both put together, in effect, tell the native so much; That like a man escaped out of some small danger, herejoyceth, and solaceth himself at a Kinsman or friends house; though now in years, here's probability of a journey beyond Seas; or into the remote parts of this Kingdom: the native will be much imployed in taking accounts, perusing reckonings, reconciling many disagreeing neighbours, and friends; he may be carefull in setling some estate upon a Kinsman, and shall more then many years before be conversant with Lawyers, Clerks, Secretaries of Estate: the Aspects denoat, not onely, an extraordinary acquisition of substance, and money, but some publike imployment from the States, or from that person, or those persons of greatest quality, where he shall then reside, unexpectedly some new, beneficiall and materiall preferment. It's probably like to be a year of great action unto the native; wherein notwithstanding he is advised to be very carefull.

Because in the 65. year, and 1649. September 24. Part of Fortune comming to the Square of Iupiter, some Gentleman, or Statist of quality will disturb him in his proceedings, or question his actions. The adversary is more words then matter; its for a Debt, owing that this mans malice appears so great: yet things seem to be reconciled by an honest Divine; and so the native again followes his imployment, which yet continue,

In December 1649. the Moone comming to the termes of Mars, stirre up some cholerick matter, and causeth a little weaknesse in the eyes, for a day or two, after which, the remainder of the year passeth without more then common accidents. Some years have no directions.

1652.

Being entred the sixty and eighth year of age, Part of Fortune comes to the termes of Venus, which intimates little more then a healthfull constitution, and some small increase of a temporall estate, a continuance of former imployments.

The 70. year of Age, which begins 10. July 1654. *ending* July 1655.

The Moon now comes to the degree culminating; to a man active and desirous of preferment, this direction would perform it. It intimates health, estimation, respect, and what not unto the native, that his age, or place are capable of in a very high measure: Aged Ladies and Gentlewomen visit the native. The man in the highest authority neer his habitation, will much respect him. Some new preferment, or removall for better.

In November 1654. the Sun commeth to his own Sextill, shewing a chearfull old man, and that nature by art doth much comfort life, with convenient Cordialls. In Aprill 1655. the Sun comes to the degree ascending at birth, which reconciles some stubborne adversary, and now as the Sunne becomes

becomes more powerfull, and more near to our northern Clime, so the native becomes more lively, and passeth his time with greater tranquillity of minde, enjoying in a plentifull manner all those contentments the world afforteth to a private man; which is the more increased by the comming of the Medium Cœli to the Trine of the Moon. The native shall finde this year somewhat formidable to the City of London, by reason of a great plague, and shall also hear wonders out of Italy, the Pope beginning to be ruined: there will also in divers Countries of Europe break out suddenly such actions, as shall astonish the living, &c. I have considered the Revolution of this year, which onely gives the native caution, to avoid crude and raw fruits.

71, Year of age, beginning 10. July 1655. *ending* July 1656.

The Sunne in December 1655. comes to the termes of Saturn, who at the birth being ill posited, may stirre up some clownish fellows to contest with the native, it provokes the native to waspishnesse, care, and melancholly, some slight infirmnesse is sensibly perceived, hee cannot bee always young: The native takes cold, and is therefore vexed with a cough all the winter, and abundance of spittle, reume descends into the right eye: but the spring approaching, and the profectionall Figure being benevolent, the Sunne, and Mercury divolved to the place of the Moon, and Venus to the place of Iupiter, and the Dragons head to the signe Horoscopating, the native is admonished to change his ayre, by benefit whereof he grows lively, and lusty according to the measure of his age.

72. Year, from July 1656. *to* July 1657.

The Part Fortune meets with the Sextill of Mercury, the day of his birth, going on the 72. year of age; It promiseth some Annuall increase of his revenues, and getting in of former lent moneys, it invites to a purchase, moderate health is foreseen; it provokes to devotion more then formerly, it invites to a setling of estate: The profectionall Figure presents Mercury in his own house, Venus in Cancer, the Moon in Aries: Hee is afflicted at the death of a friend; the times vex the native, hee is doubtfull how to provide for one; he fears in vain; let him serve God, the place God puts him in at beginning of the year will be secure.

73. Year, and probably, like to be the last year of the Natives life,
from July 1657. *to* July 1658.

The profectionall Figure of this year being the same of the birth, the Native must return to the place from which he came, viz. to the earth. Not, that the Profections absolutely do signifie such a thing, but the concurring of two interficient Directions in one and the same year, and almost moneth, make me confident of the great danger the native will be in this year.

In September 1657. the Moon comes to the Square of Mars; the same Moneth the medium Cœli to a Square of Iupiter; in November the Sunne being Hyleg, and the temporall light at the birth meets with the body of Mars, who

who is Promittor to both Significators. At the fall of the leafe, the native becomes ill, and is oppressed with the wind chollik, but striving to be rid of that, and his Medicines not operating to purpose, it puts the native into a Fever, of which, about the 5. of December 1657. according to naturall causes, he ought to die. I positively conclude not his death, for thats onely in the hands of God.

For the measure of time in Directions I have followed the rule of Naibod, who allows for one degree of the Aequator one year and 5, dayes, and 8. hours, and for every minute six dayes and 4. hours: This measure of time Maginus prefers before that of his own in his Primum mobile, fol. 52. The Ancients did give for every degree one year, and for every minute six dayes: let every one use that measure of time he finds most truth in; I do verily beleeve Naibods to be most exact. The Learned in Art, must pardon mee for performing this Nativity so slenderly, I have made it plain of purpose, and omitted all termes of Art, and the Directions; which would have been troublesome, had they been inserted by the Printer, for our Nation seldome Print any thing of Astrology: I remember not any thing of this Subject printed since Dariot 1598. Such as it is, receive, either with love, or disdaine, thou that art ignorant: for I value thee not.

S The

The Urine of John Pym *Esquire; a member of the House of Parliament, brought to me, without his knowledge or consent; and my judgement required whether he would live or dye.*

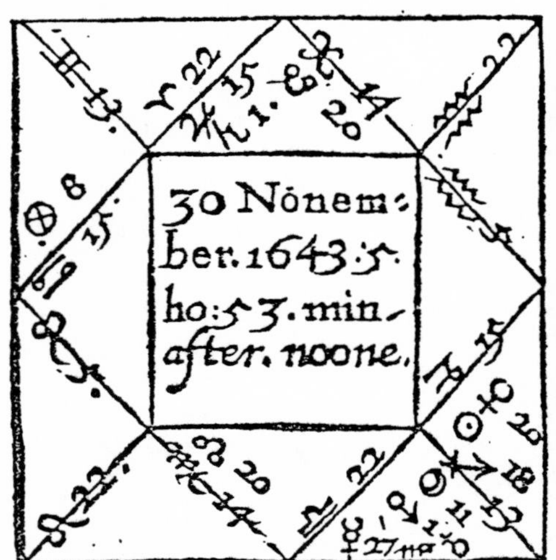

Astrologers know, Cancer is here the Ascendant of the figure, and signifies the brest, upper part of the belly, cold stomack, &c. because no Planet afflicted that sign, but Jupiter Lord of the 6. house, with his Quartile Sinister. I judged the brest and stomack were not so much at present afflicted, as formerly they had been: yet I said there appeared small or little digestion: I had then recourse to the sixth house, in which were the Moon, Sol, and Venus; the Moon lately seperated from a Conjunction of Mars and Cor Scorpii. Ile not say he was poisoned, perhaps it was some former surfet, &c. finding the Moon Lady of the Ascendant, to be the temporall light in Sagittarius, and Sol also both subterranean, and posited in the sixth. I collected what part or member they signified in that signe, and found they denoted the heart, the back, bowels, and belly; seeing therefore foure Planets, as it were, in the sixth house, and its descending signe, and it of the fiery Triplicity, I judged the principall cause of the disease to be a drinesse or stoppage in the belly, guts, or bowels; which was also confirmed by Jupiter in Ariete, a fiery and dry signe: the Lord of the Ascendant going to combustion in that house, which naturally signifieth diseases, I judged he could not live: the Moon applyed to a Trine of Jupiter, and he then stationary, I judged the disease was so setled, he should not be cured, yet because of Jupiter his frustration partly by combustion of the Moon: I said he would not dye that day, or the next; but would live untill the eighth of December, at what time the Moon came to Conjunction of Saturn, Lord of the 8. house: and my Reason was, because Luna wanted 7. degrees of the Conjunction of Sol, it should signifie 7. dayes, but finding the Moon the 7. day, came to no interficient Planet, I said it would be 8. dayes: and so it was, as I have been informed: the figure speaks him a right good man, honest and vertuous, and not as some scandalize him. Many I know would think he should have lived, because Sol and Venus are in the 6. house; indeed I have found many times, when the Sun was in the 6. the party hath recovered beyond expectation, and when all men despaired; for the Sun being Fons vitalis potentiæ, is most part a significator of good to the sicke: but in this figure, the Moon being Lady of the Ascendant, and going to Combustion of the Sun, which is the worst of mis-

misfortunes in sicknesses, and in the proper house of infirmitie, must needs cut off life. Si dominus ascendentis, aut Luna sint combusti a Sole, ipsi dant certum testimonium mortis, Ganivetus, fol. 191: he goeth further and saith. Si unus ipsorum tantum sit combustus, &c. and fol. 196. Si Luna sit prope Solem, signum est mortis, quanto propinquior & in combustione, tanto pejor. viz. If either the Lord of the Ascendant or Moon are Combust, its a signe of death.

The Tryall of a Law Suit.

The Moon in Cancer is for the Querent, being Lady of the Ascendant: Saturn, Lord of the seventh is for the Adversary.

Jupiter Lord of the 10. house is significator of the Judge, with whom Mars hath participation, because placed in the 10.

The Question is easily judged, for according to the strength of the significators the judgement is determined: If the Lord of the Ascendant be stronger than the Lord of 7. the Querent shall overcome, and so the contrary.

Of this opinion is Guido Bonatus, fol. 273. Ille cujus significator est fortior, debebit obtinere; fortior erit qui est in angulo maxime in aliqua suarum domorum, viz. He whose significator is most strong, ought to obtain the better, and he is best dignified that is in an Angle, and in any of his own houses: Seeing in this figure the Moon to be in her own house and in the Ascendant, in Trine to Mars in the 10. and in Sextile dexter with the Sun, Lord of the second, and part of fortune with the dragons head: I judged the Querent should overcome his enemy, and so he did; Cauda draconis in the 10th. I said that the judge at the tryall would be angry, and so he was, for the adversaries witnesses knew not what to swear, you see the quesited his significator Peregrine, and in his fall; yet in accidentall dignities, prettily fortified, but wanting essentiall, it nothing availeth; whereas the Moon is essentially strong, increasing in light, number and motion. The Querent was a sanguine complexion Gentleman, of a generous Martiall disposition, big-bon'd, strong, and very discreete. The defendant was lean and thin bodied, hollow cheekes, sad brown haire, bending forward, malitious, wilfull, and neither better or worse than a true Saturnine man. If two go to fight, or make war, the question is thus resolved for the most part; but you are to consider in war, the second house, and the Planets therein, signifie the friends and assistance the Querent shall have on his side;

the 8th house, and the Planets therein posited, shew the same for the enemy: Now if it happen that the Lord of the 2d is Peregrine, weak or unfortunate: so shall the friends of the querent be, viz. men that promise much, but not able to performe any thing: if the Lord of the second, out of the 6. 8. or 12th Aspect the Lord of the Ascendent with square or Opposition, the Querent shall have no ayde come to him, though he be promised some; and moreover it may be doubted, he or they that promise assistance, will betray the Querent, and yet seeme to be willing to help him, but will in fine do nothing: and this is more certain, if the Lord of the second have any benigne Aspect to, or with the Lord of the 7th, they then wish better to the Enemy then the Querent.

And this, to the everlasting dishonour of some in the world, was in August 1644. verified: when the noble Essex was worsted, in not having timely assistance, which I foresaw by the houre of his going out, being exactly taken for me: he that could never be beaten by an Army or Armies of men, was foiled by plaine treachery, under pretence of I know not what parsimony: if men forbear to speak of this, the stones of every street will be transformed into Cryers, and cry aloud for vengeance against the perfidious.

Goods Stolen, Who was Theefe?

This Question is resolved, when the goods are certainely known to be stolen, by the Peregrine Planet in the Ascendant, midheaven seaventh or second; I could never finde any truth in a Peregrine Planet in the 4th. if none be in the houses aforesaid, take the Lord of the seventh. &c.

Mars in this Scheam being cut of all dignities, posited in the 10th house and very near the Cuspe thereof; I said, it was such a one as is signified by Mars, viz. A fellow of middle Stature, strong and wel set, broad large shoulders, a wrangling swearing fellow, of some earthly sordid Occupation, that did frequently do drudgeries in the house, of a darke flaxen curling haire, a sun-burnt Complexion, and some materiall cut or gash neer the left eye. I described Iupiter a more elderly man, to be also mistrusted, but in my judgement acquitted him: I said further, because both the Moon and Venus applyed to Mars, the fellow had two sweet-hearts at that time; and that the man signified by Iupiter, was a very friend of the theefes, &c. Upon my words the party applyed himself to such a man

man as I described, and he well knew, and had part of his goods again: For Venus in the second house promiseth part, but not all, because Mercury Lord of the second was Retrograde.

Unlesse for a very friend, I hate these questions: the which usually bring scandall to the Artist: few men beleeving the person of the theefe can be described by any lawfull Art, as also many times the party is mistaken, one man being accused for another, and so much mischief comes thereon: for if the Artist describe a person any thing neere to the shape of the party they mistrust, they build confidently on the judgement, let us do what wee can to contradict them. I have known the judicious to have benefited themselves very much by our judgement, and to have recovered beyond expectation, &c. And so on the contrary.

A Gentlewoman desired to know if she should have an aged man; yea, or, no.

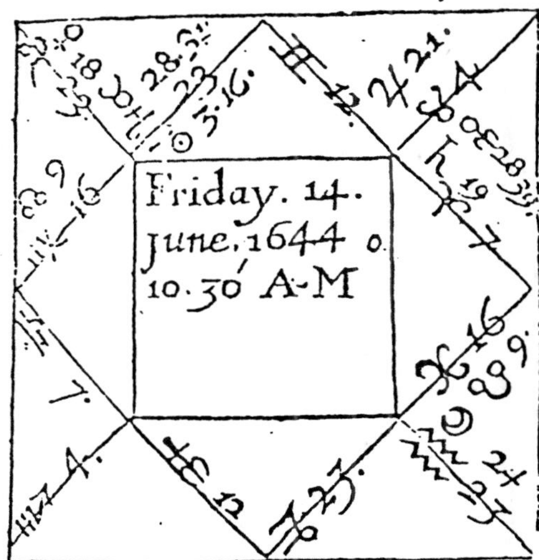

The Querent hath Mercury onely for her significatrix. Jupiter is for the aged man and party quesited after. Considering Mercury had lately seperated from a Sextile of Jupiter, and the Moon by a Quadrate, I judged there had lately been some treaty about it, (which was confessed:) and that the old man did much importune it, because Jupiter receives Mercury in his exaltation, and casteth a friendly Trine to the degree Ascending; this was so: seeing the Moon carried the light from Jupiter to Mars, and Mercury was going to a Quartile of Mars; I judged the maids affection was alienated from the old man, and that she desired such a man as Mars, viz. a Captaine or Souldier, &c. and that she should be crossed therein, by reason both Mars and the Moon were in unfortunate houses: nor had Mercury or Luna any dignities where Mars was, or in the signe, and degree where himself was: all this was acknowledged with teares; because I found Saturn and Mars in the eighth, and that Mars was the impediting Planet; I bad the maide require a Joynture of the old man, and see what it would do which at next meeting she did, but then it appeared he could not make any, there being an incumbrance upon his Land, as Saturn with Mars; in his second house of substance doth excellently signifie: after this they broke off all termes of marriage, directly as I told her.

The Querent was of a meane stature, strait bodied, of a lovely brown complexion and haire, round visaged, well spoken, modest and judicious. The Quesited I judged to be a man fleshy and full bodied, oval visaged, stout, brown colour, dark sad hair, his stature tending to tallnesse, a man worldly and covetous, for Jupiter *being in* Taurus *the Emblem of* Labour, *doth insinuate so much: it was so confessed.*

To the Astrologers of EUROPE.

GENTLEMEN,

I *Thought to have concealed my private Notions, in hope, that, amongst so many learned men of other Countreys, some of you would have published your endeavours upon this Conjunction, $164\frac{2}{3}$: But seeing it's a full yeer since the Conjunction, and no mans Labour or Learning hath appeared unto me, upon that Subject; I my self have adventured and presumed, to put forth This, long since written; a rude piece of Stuff, a meer Chaos and mixture of Confusion: And yet, how mean soever it be, it may stir up some more able hand to second it, and to polish my ragged Inventions;* Res facilis addere inventis. *Were I now to perform it again, I could do it twice so well: perhaps I will,* Si venia dabitur.

There's a time for all things. Some may guesse I have done little: Dulce Bellum inexpertis: *Others will storm and rage at me, because*

Terribiles toti mundo divinitùs iras
Postremi Secli venturas tempore pando.

Let them say what they will, I care not: I say to all,

Sola est causa mali cunctis dementia habendi.

Had not this madnesse of encroaching possessed the Europeán *Demi-gods, we had to this day been quiet in most Countreys of* Europe; *whereas now*

Infœlix vita adveniet, tempusq; cruentum. *To* England *what shall I say?* Eheu: immanis regio, gens barbara valde.

After a while, I fear, nay at present

Tibia multiferi non turbat pectora cantu.

No mirth or melodie: the heavens deceive us not, when they say,

Splendentemq; Cometam
Appellant homines Stellam mala significantem,
Imminet ut multum Bellum, vastatio, strages.

Our times of perill are before our eyes, and approaching,

Nam sic in fatis fixum vertentibus Annis.

I write to you that are versed in heavenly Constellations, and desire you would peruse the Books of the Ancient, and not slight our Modern Writers, you shall observe abundant verity in Astrologie; you, I mean, that are the sons of Art: Never did the world afford more matter to work upon: the heavenly Bodies do as plainly discover the times succeeding, as if they were in present view.

Quicunque conditionem Cœlestis harmoniæ notam haberet; tam præterita quam futura cognosceret. *The Key of our Art,* de futuris contingentibus in mundo, *is, I confesse, involved in many Riddles, so that very few obtain it.*

Quis mihi dabitur ex millibus unus, qui hanc harmoniam intelligat cœlestem: *Let us labour that every one may understand a little, and attain to the knowledge of this celestiall harmony. The ascent thereunto is by Nature, plain Nature; and the exact knowledge of the nature and property of every Planet, and intelligence:* Inferiora enim superioribus subjecta sunt, & sola similitudine, quæ substantia, accidente, potentia, virtute, numero, gradu ac proprietate constat, per applicationem unius ad aliud, &c.

He

He that reads Mixaldus *his* Harmoniam microcosmi cum macrocosmo, sive humani corporis cum Cœlo, *may perceive something more, and, as in a certain Scale, may ascend to greater matters. Nor shall I at any time attribute more to the heavenly Constellations then God hath given: I well know,* Astra nullum imperium habent in mentem, nec aliquod in nos dominium habent, qui Spiritu ambulamus, confitentes Dominum Jesum Christum omnia in sua potestatem habentem, &c. *They are* Designatrices temporum, *and of that mutation which is as well in man, as in this world, by the permission of the All-seeing providence of God. When God will crosse Nature, he works by Miracles; when he will not have man to understand his Ordinances, he clouds his understanding with doubts, fears and errours.* Ars longa, vita brevis. *Art is tedious, our life ends when we are but Smatterers in any learning. Indeed our intentions never fix, we would ascend to a higher measure of knowledge then God is willing we should: A fault* Adam *was guilty of.*

Persuasus conjuge, partem
Æternam oblitus sprevit clarissima jussi.

By which miserable fall and failing of Adam, *we have warning to be content with that measure of knowledge God imparts unto us in Nature, and by Nature, and not to invocate the Spirits to our assistance, or to use any unlawfull Course in our Predictions: For, certainly, he that understands the face of heaven, and frame of nature rightly, shall see abundance of matter, and all the negotiations of this later Age, concurring with the heavenly Constellations, and ordered according to the course of the heavens; and shall not need to tread in any illicite path of knowledge.*

I intended onely, at first, to have handled the Conjunction in $164\frac{2}{3}$: *But being engaged in the Action, I found I could make nothing of it, unlesse I ascended to former times. Doubtlesse, as this Conjunction is the last of the Watry Triplicity this Return, and is by divine providence, after fourty yeers continuance of the Fiery Trygon, permitted to make its Conjunction in a Watry Signe, and is invironed, as I may so say, betwixt that Conjunction of* Saturn *and* Jupiter *in* Leo, 1623; *and that in* Sagittarius, 1663. *The Effects hereof shall assuredly be more admirable, and more miraculous, then any that hath preceded these many yeers.*

The Cavils of some pragmatick Novices, and of seditious Sectaries, that have undone us, I neither care, nor fear: You cannot make it sink into their noddles that, there's twelve Houses, or seven Planets; or that there's any influence in the Stars, though God himself name the influence of the Pleiades, *and ask these fools, If they can restrain it: Let them passe,* Sic canibus catulos, &c. *Who knows not,* Accessu Solis vegitantur vires, velut resuscitatæ excussaque veterno; discessu ejusdem seu, destitutæ adminiculis necessarii præsidii elanguescunt: *Experience in every man tells us,* Sunt & sensus cogitationesq; acriores aut heb tiores uno magis quam alio tempore, non ex ulla causa obvia, aut nota; Sed ut vis illa ætheria in corporibus nostris a Cœlesti lumine incitatur, aut retunditur. *I ingenuously confesse, That I have, in some Considerations, omitted many curious judgements; so have many, before my time, purposely kept back much learning from the knowledge of the world:* Res mundi pulcherrimæ ob arrogantiam hominum ignorantur, dum nihil statuunt credere, nisi humana mens rationem illius perceperit; *which is impossible: Who gives the reason of the curing at a distance by the weapon Salve? What reason hath found out the vertue, and the cause of it, in the Load-stone? So long as time is, and men upon the face of the earth, there will be difference in Opinion: All men will not approve of all acts. How many hundred yeers was it, before Physick was admitted in the Romane Common-wealth? and yet who knows not the excellent benefit that man hath, by means of the learned Physitian? our lives, in many conditions, were miserable, without it, and the Physitian. But I hasten to a conclusion. For writing to you that understand Astrologie, I need no Apologie:* Rogamus itaque omnes cœlum aspicientes & colentes hæc studia, ut boni consulant & contra Scorpiones, & maledicos Mathematum hostes ac caluminatores defendant, & ut meam quoque existimationem tueantur etiam atque etiam rogo.

And

And my request to forraigne Astrologers is, Ut si qui Exempla genituratum colligerunt summorum principum atque Heroum & singularium casuum in Francia, Hispania & Germania, aut vicinis Regnis, nec non aliis versantur, geneseos ad nos; vel tempora saltem transmittant: *And I will returne in exchange thereof such as have come to my hands, either of our own Nation, or any other. I have in most places delivered my minde Astrologically, some few excepted, yet no judgement but extracted radically from the Art, my words are in length, and not for every word a letter, as* Sibilla Delphica *dealt with* Romulus, *who desiring to know the fate of* Rome, *had no answere of the* Sibill, *then these* 14. *letters, wrote in the barke of trees:* R. R. R. T. S. D. D. R. R. R. F. F. F. F. 437. *yeares after this Prophecy,* Sibilla Erithra *came to* Rome, *who did so interpret and expound them, as if she and none other had composed them; in this manner.* Romulo, Regnante, Roma, Triumphans, Sibilla, Delphica, Dixit, Regnum, Romæ, Ruet, Ferro, Flamma, Fame, Frigore: *The Prediction proved exactly true; as any that read the* Romane *historie will finde out. I could have delivered some truths in the like nature, had I so desired, perhaps now and then I may.*

The last thing in which I crave your gentle acceptance, is the measure of time concerning the determination of the effects of this Conjunction, *accuse me not, untill you finde it erroneous, which if you do, let my errour teach you to measure the time aright; I have not done it with confidence that events will answere my proportion alotted. I have endeavoured divers wayes, time and the successe will either confirme or disprove it, and by this meanes finde out one certain measure, the thing I onely aymed at. Remember we are men, no one man knoweth all things, no not in any Science.* Illa Deus in Magnete proposuit oculis mortalium spectanda: qualia aliis in rebus subtiliori mentis indagini, & sedulitati experiendi majori, invenienda reliquit: *words as true as truth it selfe: let us modestly seek, and we shall finde that proportion God hath appointed for us, whether in knowledge of this, or any other Science; and let all men know:* Duplices sunt stellarum omnium radii: alii sensibiles sive luminosi, alii secretioris influentiæ: hi omnia quæ in hoc mundo continentur penetrant: illi ne adeo penetrant, quodam modo impediri possunt: *If understood I wright enough, not apprehended I write too much.*

Three Flower-de-luces neer Somerset house in the *Strand.* Octob. 16. 1644.

WILLIAM LILLY

ERRATA.

PAge 1. line 12. read *Taurus*, p. 3. l. 34. r. 2942. p. 7. l. 3. *Anglicus.* p. 12. In that figure and 11. house put. ♀. 0. 14. and ☽. 7. 52. p. 17. l. 25. r. *Opposition.* p. 19. l. 27. read parts, p. 22. In the 2d. figure, r. by the *Rudolphine*, p. 23. l. 29. r. *Medes.* p. 24. l. 10. r. matter, p. 29. l. 5. r *Secundeian*, p. 31. l. 5. r. *Conjunctions*, p. 32. l. 28. r. signes, p. 36. l. 1. r. *mortem*, l. 12. r. *alter*, l. 26. *naturæ*, p. 41. l. 22. r. or otherwaies, p. 48. l. 36. r. that Aphorisme, p. 52. l. 13. r. *proveniet*, p. 65. l. 10. *Proclus*, p. 66. l. 16. *infirmitatum*, p. 76. l. 1. r. weare, p. 90. l. 8. r. *Catayja*, p. 94. l. 18. r. imminent, p. 115. l. *ult*, for *Constantine*, r. *Constantinople.*

FINIS.

Printed in the United Kingdom
by Lightning Source UK Ltd.
109707UKS00001B/125